Advance Praise for *Leadership Is Half the Story*

"This book practically glows with energy and vision! In highly accessible, entertaining portions Sam and Marc Hurwitz have presented us with a forward-thinking, prescient guide to success in business in today's unpredictable market. Build agile, innovative, efficient teams in your organization today for greater success tomorrow!"

Marshall Goldsmith, top-ranked executive coach; Thinkers 50 Top Ten Global Business Thinker; author or editor of 34 books including the global best sellers *MOJO* and *What Got You Here Won't Get You There*

"Samantha and Marc Hurwitz have made leadership whole. Teams need great leaders as well as great followers."

Razor Suleman, Founder and Chief Achiever, Achievers, Inc.

"In this timely and refreshingly quirky book, 'Team Hurwitz' models great leadership and followership to powerful effect. There is plenty to excite the imagination and to experiment with in our quest to create the generative partnerships that we desire, and know we are capable of, but can rarely sustain in an increasingly contingent workplace."

Brad Jackson, Head of School of Government, Victoria University of Wellington, New Zealand

"In this remarkable book, Samantha and Marc Hurwitz radically challenge the conventional wisdom on leadership. Leaders aren't more important than followers, they say. To innovate fast, leaders and followers must be equal partners – together creating co-flow. *Leadership Is Half the Story* is essential reading for anyone who wants to know how companies, organizations, and governments can adapt, innovate, and thrive in a rapidly changing and increasingly complex world."

Thomas Homer-Dixon, Chair of Global Systems, Balsillie School of International Affairs; author, *The Ingenuity Gap* and *The Upside of Down*

"Marc and Samantha Hurwitz are making the next important development in leadership and followership studies – weaving the behaviors of the leader and follower roles into a collaborative relationship that drives effective teams and organizations. This integrative approach will be of great interest to performance at both ends of the leader-follower dynamic."

Ira Chaleff, author, *The Courageous Follower*

"This book is wise and entertaining. It blends research, theory, and fascinating stories from practice that can help us all to become better leaders – and followers. It is a book to read, and then read again."

Dennis Tourish, Professor of Leadership and Organisation Studies, Royal Holloway, University of London; author, *The Dark Side of Transformational Leadership*

"Wow! I have never come across a book on organizational truths that combines such deep knowledge of and respect for empirical evidence, and the capacity to explain it well, with absolutely practical, hands-on tools."

Linda J. Page, President and Founder, Adler Graduate Professional School, Toronto; co-author with David Rock, *Coaching with the Brain in Mind*

"By bringing the discipline of followership up to equal status with leadership, Marc and Sam introduce a new lens through which we can all re-evaluate ourselves and our performance. More than just a great read, this book is full of great tips and powerful inspirations for any business leader today. Practical, purposeful, and delivered with passion. Well done!"

Ken Whyte, President, Quarry Integrated Communications

"If you are committed to unleashing the performance of others, this book is a must read. Packed with insight, it has fundamentally shifted my approach to teaching leadership, career planning, and driving performance."

Andrew Martin, Vice President Human Resources, Joey Restaurant Group

"What a gift! This book fills a void that needed filling in the discussion about leadership. And it is done with solid research and practical application."

Barry Johnson, author, *Polarity Management*

"*Leadership Is Half the Story* is anything but the usual self-help or how-to book. The reader has a choice to make in embracing the balanced principles of leadership and followership. If he or she does, we will see an emerging world of business leaders with a growing mastery in building and maintaining an altogether happier and more fulfilling workplace for everyone involved."

Bill McLean, Chief Operating Officer and Executive Coaching Practice Leader, Optimum Talent Inc.

"Samantha and Marc Hurwitz truly understand the essence of happy and productive organizations. *Leadership Is Half the Story* is a very important book and an easy read, and it contributes to our knowledge in a kind of fresh, creative way that I have not experienced in similar publications the past number of years. The way that the authors unpack leadership-followership made so much sense and sets this book apart."

Kobus Neethling, President, South African Creativity Foundation; international-al best-selling author of more than 90 books

"Sam and Marc have a novel and magic recipe to help us chart our course as we transition from a green intern to the CEO."

James McAnanama, Senior Engineer, L-3 Wescam

"At last a balanced view! *Leadership Is Half the Story* is substantive but not stuffy, with wonderful use of examples from other disciplines and life experiences. Who knew that stickleback fish and *30 Rock* could appear in the same work?"

Dr. Liz Monroe-Cook, Clinical Psychologist and President, Monroe-Cook & Associates (Chicago)

"It is refreshing to see a book that draws on numerous practical examples to illustrate the mutuality of the leader/follower relationship in a business context, and the roles and responsibilities that lay the foundation for the types of fruitful partnerships that are critical to agile organizations."

Ian Hendry, Managing Partner, Karian & Associates; President, Strategic Capability Network

"I enjoyed and got personal benefit from this book! It would be a very good book to purchase for a mentee, or for a member of one's staff who is moving up to a leadership level. This is an excellent coaching tool to be used in any leadership development program."

Janet Pierce, Vice President Education, Certified General Accountants of Ontario

"Samantha and Marc have done an excellent job of weaving together their personal stories, the concepts of leadership and followership that underpin their work, and cases that illustrate how these concepts apply in the real world."

Robert W. Jacobs, author, *Real Time Strategic Change*

"*Leadership Is Half the Story* is a breath of fresh air. In this very readable book, Samantha and Marc Hurwitz introduce dozens of innovative and useful insights about the dynamics of effective leadership and followership. But it delivers much more than just theory. It offers practical tips, exercises, and methods for implementing more productive, more creative, and more rewarding collaboration skills. I've read hundreds of business books. Most are rehashes. This is a game-changer."

Tim Hurson, author of the global best seller *Think Better* and co-author *Never Be Closing*

LEADERSHIP
IS HALF THE STORY

**A FRESH LOOK AT FOLLOWERSHIP,
LEADERSHIP, AND COLLABORATION**

MARC HURWITZ AND **SAMANTHA HURWITZ**

UNIVERSITY OF TORONTO PRESS
Toronto Buffalo London

© University of Toronto Press 2015
Rotman-UTP Publishing
Toronto Buffalo London
www.utppublishing.com
Printed in the U.S.A

ISBN 978-1-4426-5013-8

Printed on acid-free, 100% post-consumer recycled paper with
vegetable-based inks.

Library and Archives Canada Cataloguing in Publication

Hurwitz, Marc, author
Leadership is half the story : a fresh look at followership, leadership,
and collaboration / Marc Hurwitz and Samantha Hurwitz.

Includes bibliographical references and index.
ISBN 978-1-4426-5013-8 (bound)

1. Leadership.   2. Followership.   3. Teams in the workplace –
Management.   4. Organizational effectiveness.   I. Hurwitz, Samantha,
author.   II. Title.

HD57.7.H87 2015   658.4   C2014-907221-X

University of Toronto Press acknowledges the financial assistance to its
publishing program of the Canada Council for the Arts and the Ontario
Arts Council, an agency of the Government of Ontario.

 Canada Council   Conseil des Arts
for the Arts   du Canada

 ONTARIO ARTS COUNCIL
CONSEIL DES ARTS DE L'ONTARIO
an Ontario government agency
un organisme du gouvernement de l'Ontario

University of Toronto Press acknowledges the financial support of the
Government of Canada through the Canada Book Fund for its publishing
activities.

To our fathers,

Dr. Harry Hurwitz, or, as many people call him even outside the immediate family, Uncle Harry. A man of many talents and an active philosopher still blogging into his ninth decade, he has been an unabashed supporter of our many ideas, changes, digressions, and versions of the book, all of which he read and commented on over the two years it has taken to write. With his generous support, it is a richer book than we could have hoped for.

&

Andrew S. Kerr, who is most remembered for his kindness, patience, gentle humor, and steadfast encouragement of others to reach their full potential.

Contents

!fliPtips! Tools

Preface:
Our Stories and Why We Wrote This Book

This book is personal for us. Why? Because we sure could have used it 10 years ago! Back then a series of events convinced us to switch careers, work together, and embark on the research and field testing needed to write this book. We never dreamed it would take a decade to complete it. However, let's begin at the beginning, "Once upon a time ..."

Marc's Story (written by Sam)

 For me, it all started with Marc's big "aha." When Marc and I met, we were both executives and new peers at a financial institution going through a massive acquisition. We started having lunch together and quickly discovered we were kindred spirits. He confided in me what he had been experiencing in the year and a half before we met.

From Top Talent to ...

As a bit of background, Marc had been working at the head office of the firm for about seven years after running, then selling, a business he had established. Hard times and family duty led him to the corporate world for a secure paycheck. Marc's varied background and talents propelled him quickly into the executive ranks. He moved from information technology to human resources to actuarial to marketing, receiving three promotions in five years. Things were going swimmingly! He was getting top evaluations and, after a battery of assessments, was selected to be part of an elite top talent development program.

Then along came a new boss. Within a year of her arrival Marc's performance appraisals plummeted from "exceeds" to "average," and his job satisfaction nosedived. He was assigned increasingly lower-profile tasks, and his career progression ground to an abrupt halt.

Initially he reacted as many others do in these situations. He blamed his boss for being a lousy leader, he was upset that his talents and previous contributions were not being recognized, and he felt angry with the company for letting him down. Eventually Marc regained his objectivity and began to reconsider what had actually happened.

The Aha That Changed Everything

At this point in the telling, I can't help but picture the Grinch Who Stole Christmas digging his heels in the snow ...

> Marc kept puzzling and puzzling,
> "How *could* it be so?
> Had my performance dropped as far as my appraisals now showed?
> What changed from a year ago when I was considered Hi-Po?"[1]

> And he puzzled and he puzzled, till his puzzler was sore.
> Then Marc thought of something that he hadn't before!
> "Maybe leadership," he thought, "isn't all I must explore.
> Maybe it's a flip skill, followership, that's as important or more!"

When companies merge it is a given that, to attain the cost savings baked into the purchase price, a large chunk of the management team gets let go. As Marc looked around at his colleagues receiving the choice jobs compared to those being given transitional roles (the temporary assignments that ultimately lead to a package), he noticed many being passed over who had strong technical skills, strategic ability, common sense, and leadership. It suggested that the ones getting the go-forward roles must excel at a skill that wasn't obvious, something that no one was talking about or, perhaps, even knew about. After a lot of thought he figured out it was followership.

Most acquisitions fail because of people issues.[2]

Marc said this was as much a personal insight as anything. He realized that followership was something he hadn't been conscious of. In his early days at the company he ignored the dress code and delighted in introducing provocative ideas. Marc knew that he had been recruited for his creativity and smarts, but possibly his bosses had only tolerated the other behaviors. Maybe he got promoted in spite of his followership skills.

His last manager – the one who evaluated him poorly – had been the first who hadn't specifically selected Marc. She had inherited him. And in this case Marc's creative spark wasn't enough for her to over-look what she didn't like. Unfortunately, rather than give him action-able feedback, she offered him the choice of a package or a job with less scope under someone else.

In her defense, there is a significant chunk missing from our organ-izational and managerial vernacular about followership. There is no language for it, no universal understanding of its competencies and skills, and no guidance on coaching or mentoring it. When Marc did his MBA (paid for by the company), followership wasn't mentioned once in any of the 20 courses he took.

The lack of awareness and understanding of followership skills re-sults in many capable people losing their jobs or getting pushed aside. In fact, I was almost a victim of that same fate.

Sam's Story (written by Marc)

Shortly before I met her, Sam went through a period of big changes: her beloved parents had passed away within a year and a half of each other, and her marriage was ending in divorce. As if that wasn't tough enough, my company had just acquired the firm she had worked at for 14 years. The expectation was that most of the executives from Sam's firm wouldn't be kept around after the acquisition.

Sam had grown up at her company. She started there at age 24 as a financial analyst. As the company grew so, too, did the scope of Sam's responsibilities, and she had become controller within several years of being hired. The culture there was warm, friendly, customer focused, and every employee felt empowered like it truly was *their* company. The motto was, "If it makes sense for the customer, do it!" By contrast, the culture at my firm was all about tight financial control, process management, and squeezing expenses out of every dollar invested. Our motto was, "Be number one or two in every market we enter," although unofficially it was more like, "Be sure you make a 17% return on investment."

Sam's Fabulous Job Offer

During the acquisition the chief financial officer (CFO) of my business unit decided to keep Sam because of her leadership and technical skills. I remember hearing the CFO remark on how impressed she was with "how Sam had her house in order." The offer was extended to all of Sam's team, and I can't think of anyone else who was offered a similar deal.

Fast Forward a Few Months ...

When we first met, Sam had just been made controller of my business unit, responsible for revenues of over $6 billion per year. She was already hard at work on the integration – long hours and heavy lifting – and was successfully accomplishing the work. But she was also experiencing culture shock and partnership shock. Even though the technical requirements were the same as at her old job, the two companies had very different approaches to almost everything. Worst of all, Sam was not connecting with her boss. Her new boss constantly asked for updates, additional reports, more decision support, and everything came with a hard deadline.

We got to talking and I shared my insights about followership. We discussed how the role seemed to involve getting on the wavelength of your boss and understanding how to thrive in the organizational culture. After some introspection, Sam recognized that she'd been assuming what had worked well with her previous bosses and company would continue to work. In other words, she was doing *nothing differently* than before.

Six Months Later, a Total Difference!

Sam was determined to learn from my experience and insight. It was clear she needed to take a lot more initiative to build the partnership and get on her boss's wavelength. Sam tackled it with renewed purpose: asking lots of questions, trying new things, evaluating what was working and what wasn't. In the end, Sam changed how she updated her boss, how she presented information to make decisions, and how she engaged in meetings. Sam aligned with her boss's goals, priorities, and worry spots. Most important, she took full accountability for building the partnership. Interestingly, the more effort Sam put in, the more her boss reciprocated.

Within six months they were in a terrific groove, so much so that when Sam's boss got a significant new opportunity, she asked Sam to join her.

That was when we became committed to a new path: helping others thrive in their workplace and steer clear of the stumbling blocks we ran into. We believed we could do this by adding followership to the organizational lexicon, by bringing a depth of understanding of the skills involved in it, and by bringing clarity to workplace roles and expectations. Over the next many months we read everything we could in the scientific and business literature; we talked with academics, C-suite executives, HR leaders, consultants, and entrepreneurs; we conducted focus groups; and we held pilot sessions on followership development for select companies. The reaction was universal. People said, "You are on to something big ... quick write the book!"

And that's what we did, except that it took a decade to get it done. Not because we are particularly slow or lazy but because the more we dug into the topic, the more we uncovered. Unearthing the role of followership led us to fresh thinking about the role of leadership and how the two complement each other to achieve partnerships that are truly generative.

Sitting back now, we realize that our partnership has become generative and that we have benefited greatly from this material.

It is our dream, hope, ambition, and wish that this book, and the guidance in it, helps you, too.

Samantha Hurwitz and Marc Hurwitz
Toronto, Ontario, Canada
July 2014

Acknowledgments

This book – and all the work leading up to it – is about building and nurturing partnerships that are creative, engaging, and productive: in other words, generative. It didn't happen overnight. And it didn't happen without the partners who have contributed in many generative and generous ways. Thank you all!

Thank you to Kym Manlow, our graphic designer of many years, who patiently and consistently created the perfect images to elevate our work.

Thank you to those who critiqued, challenged, and cheered earlier models and earlier manuscripts: Tracey White, Heather Worosz, Don Loney, Elizabeth Munroe-Cook, Neil LaChapelle, James McAnanama, Yoel Kluk, Janet Pierce, Stephanie O'Connor, Chris Tchorzewski, Barry Johnson, Jake Jacobs, Kobus Neethling, Dennis Tourish, Ira Chaleff, Thomas Homer-Dixon, Bill McLean, Kevin O'Leary, Ian Hendry, Marc Hurwitz (not the author! a different Marc), Dale Wilcox, Sheri Keffer, Marshall Goldsmith, Joseph Fung, Greg Evans, Mike Collins, Geoff Malleck, Wendy and Gord Hague, Scott and Michelle Lennox, Stephen and Deb Young, Andrew Annett, Marleen Guttensohn, Cydney Aiken, Jane Anderson, Corinne and Jack Duffy, Kirk McIntyre, Mel Holmes, Austin Agho, Terry Palmer, Margaret Seidler, Cliff Kayser, Jim Moss, Jim and Barb Ridge, Matthew Simon, Hubert Saint-Onge, Rich Rees, Michel Neray, Elizabeth Higgins, Tom Beakbane, James Danckert, Darlene Gies, Kathleen Kresky, Anne Marie Gill, Bonnie Bender, Ruthanne Ward, Kathy McIlwham, Glen Drummond, and Deb Harmon-Gasteiger.

Thank you to our editor, Jennifer DiDomenico, who believed in the book from the start and helped guide its path.

Thank you to the people whose work, research, stories, and guidance found their way into this book, making it a far richer one. A special thanks, also, to the creativity, polarity thinking, and followership communities who have inspired us.

Lastly, we'd like to thank our wonderful tribe – our family and friends – who give us no end of love, joy, and encouragement: Harry, Hilde, Chris, Sebastian, Bethan, Dianne, Ian, Robin, Tim, Franca, our five children and their partners – Naomi, Sean, Maude, Ben, Lisa, Natalia, Gregory, and Jazmin – and the rest of the fabulous bunch.

SECTION I

Introduction

Why 21st-Century Workplaces Require a Radically Different Approach and ... a Radically Different Approach

> Greetings! I am pleased to see that we are different. May we together become greater than the sum of both of us.
>
> *– Mr. Spock, giving a traditional Vulcan greeting*

Two different trends characterize work in the 21st century: the increased use of teams as the primary way to get things done, and the amount of interpersonal change in the workplace. Let's examine each.

Work Is Done in Teams – From Flow to Co-Flow

Think about a time when you were working on something and were so productive, so creative, so into the task that you lost all track of time. That perfect state of absorption was named *flow* by the noted psychologist Mihaly Csikszentmihalyi (also famous for his difficult-to-pronounce name, which sounds like *Me-high-e Chick-sent-me-high-e*). Athletes call it being "in the zone" and musicians might say "in the groove." Regardless of the words you use, flow is characterized by a total immersion in the task, a profound sense of fulfillment, a heightened awareness of the things that contribute to higher performance, and, most significantly, the achievement of extraordinary results.

Now think about a time when you had your best-ever team experience. It could have been with a single partner, a work team, in a band, playing a sport, or just playing. As a group you lost track of time, you were immersed in the group experience, creative juices bubbled up as great idea after great idea bounced from person to person. The team was exceptionally productive, problems turned into solutions, and working together was effortless. You probably didn't want it to end. The Beatles had it often. Top teams in sports do, too. We call this heightened group state *co-flow*.

Flow is a product of the "Me Generation." Consider that in 1980 only 20% of work was done by teams.[1] This reality was personified by Gordon Gekko, the fictional 1980s corporate raider from the movie *Wall Street*, whose response to working with others was, "If you want a friend, get a dog." Celebrated leadership gurus such as Lee Iacocca, Jack Welch, and Donald Trump espoused personal drive and individual achievement as the pathway to success.

By 2010, 80% of work was team-based, up from only 20% in 1980.

By 2010, however, a whopping 80% of value was created by teams. We now live in the "We Generation." You need more than a dog to succeed today: you need to collaborate. And you need to do it better than ever before. Whether it is in business, government, or academia (where the average number of authors per paper has increased over five-fold in the last 100 years),[2] the complex challenges of the 21st century require multiple minds and contributions.

> Because of the explosion in team-based work, flow has given way to co-flow as the target state. And that requires learning a new set of skills.*

* You will notice, from time to time, that we have a "FliPquote" or "FliPtip." FLIP stands for Followership, Leadership, Innovation, and Partnerships: it's the core material of the book, it's what we do, it's what we value, and it's the name of our company, FliPskills. FliPquotes are

thoughts and specific turns of phrases we have introduced based on our observations and research. FliPtips are practical tools and ideas that you can implement immediately.

Continuous Relationship Building – Interpersonal Agility Is *the* Essential Workplace Competency

Usually when people talk about change it is in the context of the new technology we are asked to absorb, increasing demands for new products, globalization, market shifts, or the explosion of social media. While all of these pose challenges from time to time, it is the rapid pace of interpersonal or partnership change that is most disruptive to people and organizations.

In workplaces today we face a near-constant state of building and re-building relationships. Interpersonal change can be triggered by a new job, a new boss, a new owner, or a new team. If you think about your own work over the last year, how many new people have you worked with? How many people are you no longer working with? Building new relationships is the most difficult and disruptive type of change because it affects our sense of self. When our tribe gets stripped away – the loss of a trusted leader, a dedicated team, a supportive colleague, or a good friend – we lose our support network.

This happens more than you might think. For example, people stay with a company for an average of only 4.6 years.[3] Workopolis reports "Job hopping is the new normal" with 51% of people staying in their job for less than two years, a sharp increase from 2000 when 33% stayed less than two years, and an even more dramatic growth from 1990 when 16% did so.[4] Add to that the many times people get new bosses, new projects, or new team members, not to mention the occasional corporate restructuring or acquisition, and barely a week goes by without a significant disruption to an interpersonal relationship. You may have to learn new software every couple of years, or figure out how to tackle a new procedure from time to time, but you have to learn how to work with new people much more often, and people are far more complicated than any software.

Sometimes you get to choose your partners. We met a senior executive at a large global bank the other day who was thrilled because, for the first time in her 35-year career, she got to pick her entire team. Usually, however, relationships are imposed. It is like going to a dance competition and being told whom you have to dance with regardless of whether the two of you are compatible, dance the same style, or have any practice working together.

New partnerships are fraught with risk, and the speed of business doesn't give us the time to let relationships develop naturally. People who thrive in this environment are the ones who can adapt to a new boss, integrate into a new corporate culture, or hit the ground running with a new team. It is interpersonal agility that wins.

> It is the rapid pace of interpersonal change that is most disruptive to people and organizations.

Two Trends – One Solution

These two trends – the prevalence of teamwork and the demand for interpersonal agility – are tightly coupled. Since most work is done in teams today, and teams are constantly forming and reforming, interpersonal agility is a must to navigate effectively from team to team, boss to boss, project to project, and even company to company.

Fortunately, there is a way to collaborate better AND build interpersonal agility. All it takes is a radical rethink of leadership. And followership.

And a methodological approach.

Introducing the Generative Partnership® Model

What Do We Mean by the Term *Generative*?

We often get asked, "What do you mean by a 'generative' partnership?"

A common dictionary definition offers this for *generative*: "able to produce or create something."[5] Merriam-Webster offers a more aspirational definition: "Having the power or function of generating, originating, producing, or reproducing."[6]

We needed a descriptor for partnerships that went beyond the standard ideas of functional, or even synergistic. Several years ago we were invited to present our model at the Polarity Thinking Learning Community. Polarity Thinking is the brainchild of Dr. Barry Johnson and is defined as an expansive way of seeing the world in interdependent pairs (for more information, www.polaritypartnerships .com). Barry says, "Sometimes you have a problem to solve. Often you have polarities to leverage." Inspired by his work, we realized that focusing on followership to the exclusion of leadership would inevitably flip the scales out of balance the other way. It was only by seeing them as complementary states that we could achieve sustainable excellence in both. We finished our presentation to warm and generous applause. Cliff Kayser, a kind and giving colleague, offered his appreciation and a recommendation. He asked us, "How would you describe the relationship between the two of you? Would you describe it as 'functional?'" We responded with an emphatic "No! It's much, much more than that." He nodded knowingly, "What you are talking about, and what your model develops, is far greater than simply functional. You need a descriptor that's more powerful, aspirational, and accurate. May I offer the term *generative*?" Thank you, Cliff!

A partnership that is generative accomplishes much more than each individual partner could on his own, and not just a greater quantity of work but more depth, breadth, creativity, and innovation as well.

Now we contrast the different levels of partnerships using these simple formulas:

- A **dysfunctional partnership** is $1 + 1 = 0$.
  Working together is so difficult you are better off on your own.
- A **functional partnership** is $1 + 1 = 2$.
  Working together works okay. You get out what you put in.
- A **synergistic partnership** is $1 + 1 > 2$.
  Working together is efficient. You accomplish more together.
- An **innovative partnership** is $1 + 1 = NEW$.
  Working together is creative. Your skills blend well and enable new insights, new ideas, new products, new possibilities, and new opportunities.
- **Generative** in a **partnership** is $1 + 1 > 2 + NEW$.

Together you are both more productive AND more creative. It creates a state where the group members are exceeding their full potential as a team, what we earlier called co-flow.

What makes a partnership or team truly engaged, productive, and creative?

Research stresses this: everyone on the team is equally important in getting the job done AND is viewed and treated that way. Essentially, followership must be an equal partner to leadership.

It sounds simple. But it only works when the roles of leadership and followership are acknowledged, understood, and optimized.

The Generative Partnership® Model

The model comprises five guiding principles, five skill pairings, and an array of associated behaviors.

The **guiding principles** are at the core of every partnership, team, and organization. They provide a framework on which the skills are built.

The **skills** come in matched pairs. The followership skill in each pairing is on the left-hand side of the circle. The complementary leadership skill is diagonally opposite on the right-hand side. For example, Decision Advocating is the complement to Decision Framing and, if you want great decision making, you need both.

The five skill pairings involve a multitude of associated **behaviors.** The behaviors could be considered best practice, but are better considered adaptive and adaptable. For example, whenever a situation changes, followership and leadership behaviors should be adapted to the situation. That's interpersonal agility.

The five areas of followership skill:

1. DECISION ADVOCATING: Adding value to decision making when it's not your decision to make.
2. PEAK PERFORMING: Taking initiative for your own engagement, development, and on-the-job performance.
3. ORGANIZATIONAL AGILITY: Aligning and thriving within the broader organization.

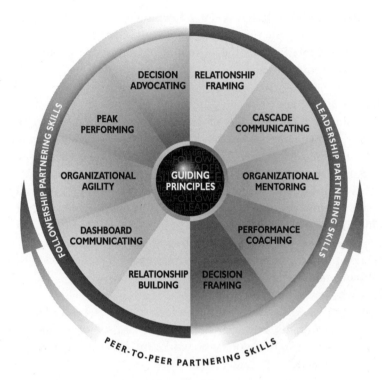

Figure 1.1 The Generative Partnership® Model

4. DASHBOARD COMMUNICATING: Keeping your partner well informed and stimulating the right leadership action.
5. RELATIONSHIP BUILDING: Developing rapport, trust, and an understanding of how to work best with leadership.

The five areas of leadership skill:

1. DECISION FRAMING: Creating an environment and process that optimizes collaboration and decision quality.
2. PERFORMANCE COACHING: Ensuring an environment of purpose, progress, and positivity.
3. ORGANIZATIONAL MENTORING: Helping to guide others on how best to navigate and operate organizationally.

4. CASCADE COMMUNICATING: Keeping team members informed and stimulating the right followership initiative.
5. RELATIONSHIP FRAMING: Creating a comfortable, professional, equitable environment for each team member.

Who This Book Is For

Leadership is something we all do, not just those with a formal role or title. Followership is something we all do, not just frontline staff. In practical terms, everyone has a leadership AND a followership role in an organization.

This is an empowering message because it opens up leadership to everyone while normalizing followership. It also enables us to have frank and useful discussions about both roles, and to coach and develop both roles in ourselves, our teams, and our organizations. This holistic approach, in turn, taps into more potential and builds better, healthier, and happier workplaces.

So, who is this book for?

This book is for leaders, future leaders, followers, future followers, coaches, consultants, HR and OD professionals, senior managers, entrepreneurs ... frankly anyone who works anywhere in an organization or helps others do so.

How the Book Is Organized

Chapters 2 and 3 – The next two chapters contain a brief but radical rethink of the roles of followership and leadership respectively.

Chapters 4 through 8 – Each of the five guiding principles are unpacked along with tools and tips you can use straightaway because, like you, we appreciate guidance that is practical and actionable.

Chapters 9 through 13 – The five skill pairings are unpacked – decision partnering skills, relationship partnering skills, organizational agility partnering skills, communication partnering skills, and performance partnering skills. Each chapter offers a fresh take on the skill along with adaptive behaviors, tips, and tools.

Chapter 14 – The final chapter puts the full Generative Partnership® model together for use in diagnosing individual, team, and organizational problems, as well as illustrating how to apply it to these situations.

How the Book Can Be Used

- For personal development, team development, and organizational development.
- For honing collaborating skills in yourself, your team and organization, or people you advise.
- For building and nurturing all sorts of partnerships – with your leader, your team members, your peers, your clients, your project mates, your committee members, your strategic alliances, and likely other partnerships that we haven't thought of yet.

All the material has been used, tested, and refined to improve mentoring programs, enhance leadership development, and build engagement in organizations. It has been used for personal coaching, organizational consulting, professional development, team building, and numerous organizational development engagements. It has been used with many organizations, from small startups to not-for-profits to global corporations.

While all the stories in the book are real, we have changed some names and organizational details to protect identities.

CHAPTER 2

A Fresh Look at the F-Word: Followership

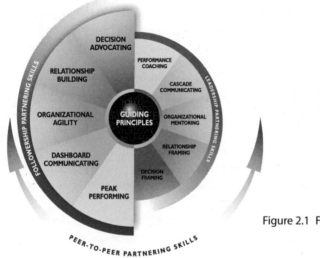

Figure 2.1 Followership skills

Have you seen the *30 Rock* episode where Jack Donaghy (brilliantly played by Alec Baldwin) presents Liz Lemon (equally brilliantly played by Tina Fey) with a Followship Award? If you haven't seen the show, it's a popular workplace comedy with Jack as the suave, egotistical, condescending, conservative network boss and Liz as his awkward, nerdy, feminist head writer.

The scene has Jack barging into Liz's team meeting, smiling, and announcing that she has been awarded the prestigious G. E. Followship Award. Liz is indignant, exclaiming that she isn't a follower. One of Liz's staff, Pete, pipes up that Liz doesn't even like people so how could she be the winner of a fellowship award?

It is at this point that Jack mentions the award comes with a prize of ten thousand dollars, at which point Liz quickly grabs the award from Jack's hand and says, "I accept this proudly on behalf of followers everywhere!"

This segment is telling: being a follower has a bad rap, no one really knows what followership is, followership is valuable to an organization, and so on. Interestingly, the fictional Jack Donaghy and his fictional company recognize that partnerships require followership, and they reward for it. After all, you get the behaviors you reward. However, in real life followership is mostly underacknowledged, underrated, and underdeveloped. It's more than the elephant in the room: it's the invisible elephant in the room. The word is often missing from organizational vernacular except, perhaps, as an "f-word" (followership, that is).

Followership is in urgent need of a rethink.

From Followersheep to Wolf Pack

Make yourselves sheep and the wolves will eat you.

– Benjamin Franklin

Have you heard the derogatory term "followersheep"?

Sheep have such a strong instinct to follow that if one jumped off a cliff, the rest of the flock likely would, too. It sounds absurd but it happens. That strong instinct to blindly follow wherever the leader goes makes for a lousy partnership. It is this followersheep behavior that leads to the precipice and beyond. It takes an exceptionally strong leader to be successful with a team of wooly grass-eaters.

Picture, instead, a wolf pack: a tightly bonded group that mobilizes to support and reinforce each other's efforts. No wolf is the leader all the time, not even the alpha dog. This fluidity of roles requires alertness, active involvement, and a commitment to take on whatever tasks support the mission of the pack. That's why wolves are at the top of their food chain.

Augustine Agho, dean of the School of Health and Rehabilitation Sciences at Indiana University, asked over 300 C-suite executives what they thought of followership.[1] You might expect a negative reaction to the f-word from this elite group, but the actual results were overwhelmingly positive. Here is what they said:

1. Followership has organizational value.
   - 98.6% say that effective followership improves work unit performance.
   - 99% say that effective followership affects work output quality.
2. Followership has personal value.
   - Agho didn't study this but we have. Followership is actually one of the most important determinants of career success.
3. Followership is a distinct skill.
   - 96.1% say that effective followership is more than simply doing what one is told to do. (It is not about being sheep!)
4. Followership requires development.
   - 95.7% say people don't know how to follow.
   - 92.7% say that leadership and followership are interrelated roles.

In other words, there was nearly unanimous agreement that followership is valuable, not well understood, and inextricably connected to leadership.

Let's dig deeper into each of these four facets of followership.

Followership Has Organizational Value

Imagine you had a secret formula that could improve each of sales, production, quality, revenue per employee, and customer satisfaction by 17% to 43%. What would it be worth to you? What would it mean for your organization? How much would you be willing to invest in that opportunity?

Two researchers from Indiana University, Philip Podsakoff and Scott MacKenzie, examined the impact of followership behaviors on performance across a variety of teams and industries such as insurance agency sales units, paper mill work crews, pharmaceutical sales teams, and restaurant staff.[2] In every case they found that positive followership behaviors significantly impacted every performance metric measured, including a decrease in customer complaints. This suggests considerable untapped organizational potential given the lack of attention the f-word has received to date.

Followership is linked to improvements of 17% to 43% on many key performance metrics.

Emotional Intelligence and Followership

You have likely heard about *emotional intelligence*. It is the ability to understand and manage one's own emotions as well as those of others, purposefully and to good effect. You might expect that teams with higher average emotional intelligence outperform teams with lower emotional intelligence.[3] That much is true. But is it because of leadership or followership emotional intelligence?

Troy Rieck, who was a masters-level student at the University of Guelph at the time of his study, set out to show that it is the leader's emotional intelligence that makes partnerships more successful.[4] Teams in his experiment had to build a tower out of colored blocks according to architectural drawings. The team – a pair of students – was given only five minutes to build the tower. One student was assigned the builder role (follower) and the other the coach role (leader). The task was made especially difficult because of a twist – the coach was allowed to give only verbal instructions to the builder, who had to build the tower blindfolded!

As you might guess, the emotional intelligence of the team did predict results. Teams with higher overall emotional intelligence were more likely to complete the task and, when they did, they built it faster than teams with lower emotional intelligence. But, surprisingly, performance depended only on the emotional intelligence of the follower! None of the outcomes Rieck measured showed a positive effect due to the emotional intelligence of the leader.[5]

Follower, not leader, emotional intelligence is the more important factor in team performance.

Now this was just one task and one situation, although others have reported similar results.[6] We aren't suggesting that leadership doesn't matter because it does.[7] But follower emotional intelligence is important, too, and in some circumstances it can be the primary determinant of success.[8]

Followership Builds Leadership

> Everyone is always learning and developing. Instead of feeling frustrated by your leader's lack of leadership experience, ask yourself how can I help them develop or grow those skills?
> — *Tracey White, director of Organization and Leadership Innovation,*
> *University of Waterloo*

There is a TED talk by Derek Sivers on how to start a movement. He shows a video of a young man dancing by himself surrounded by onlookers. Eventually another person gets up and boldly joins in. As Sivers says, "It was really the first follower that transformed the lone nut into a leader."

That's what strong followership does: it strengthens leadership. Sometimes it even creates leaders.[9] Having just one enthusiastic follower was the difference maker that enabled others to feel comfortable getting up to dance. The single follower became a crowd of followers, which turned into a movement that got everyone up on their feet. While the leader was important, he would never have started a movement without that first courageous follower.

Capable followership can also act as a counterbalance to poor or even disastrous leadership.[10] In his book, *Outliers: The Story of Success*, Malcolm Gladwell recounts the story of Korean Air flight 801 that crashed during the approach to Guam airport on August 6, 1997. Gladwell suggests that the copilot was not forceful enough in his opinion to sway the tired captain from a disastrous mistake, one that cost 228 lives. In other words, it is followership and not followersheep that makes a cockpit team stronger.

At times, the wolf pack has a responsibility to monitor and correct errors made by leadership. Spectacular corporate failures – Enron, WorldCom, Bre-X, Arthur Andersen, and the like – highlight the need for followers to take a stand. Books such as Ira Chaleff's *The Courageous Follower*, Robert Kelley's *The Power of Followership*, and Barbara Kellerman's *Followership* profile the activist role that followers can and must take at times.

Followership Has Personal Value

How do you define success at work? Is it getting the next promotion, not getting fired, developing a stronger team, being more productive, helping customers, winning an award, leaving a legacy, creating something daring and groundbreaking, or finding more happiness in your day?

For the fictional hero of the Shepherd Mead best seller and, later, hit Broadway musical *How to Succeed in Business Without Really Trying*, success meant becoming chairman of the board at World Wide Wicket. *How to Succeed* is a tongue-in-cheek romp through 1952 corporate America. In the story, J. Pierrepont Finch ascends the corporate ladder from lowly window washer to chairman of the board in record time. Contrary to the title Finch tries really hard to rise to the top and, mostly through followership advice he finds in a book, succeeds. Even though the show is a satire of corporate life, much of the guidance is still relevant today. For example, in one scene our hero makes a personal connection with a senior executive by learning (and singing) the executive's college song. Of course none of this is couched in terms of followership nor are we about to suggest you take up singing! But one aspect of expert followership is finding out your boss's preferences, something J. Pierrepont took to comic extremes.

Larry Bossidy, former CEO of Honeywell and COO of GE Capital, noted that followership is vital as a signal of future potential. He says, "I'll favor someone who exhibits the behaviors I expect over someone who doesn't, even if the latter's numbers are slightly better, because I know the former has the potential to contribute more to the organization over time" (Bossidy, 2007, p. 58). As Bossidy recognized, excellent followers get more done.

Excellent followers also get more latitude to act, are more satisfied with their career, win more promotions, have faster career progression, and get better performance appraisals.[11] While those with strong followership skills are granted all sorts of extra perks, those with poor followership skills are far more likely to get fired.[12] It is the number one reason middle managers are let go and accounts for a substantial percentage of senior managers who lose their jobs.[13]

Strong followers are given more freedom to take initiative. They also get more promotions, bigger bonuses, and experience greater job satisfaction.

Followership is the invisible criterion used to make all sorts of key organizational decisions about people. For example, in his *New York Times* best seller *Good to Great*, Jim Collins says, "[A leader's] first [job is to get] the right people on the bus (and the wrong people off the bus)" (2001, p. 41).

What should leaders look for in handing out bus tickets? As Coyne and Coyne (2007) point out in their *Harvard Business Review* article "Surviving your new CEO," what a new leader looks for in her direct reports are behaviors that have little to do with traditional performance measures such as technical proficiency or leadership. Their advice is distilled into seven followership actions:

1. Show your goodwill.
2. Leave your baggage at the door.
3. Study the CEO's working style.
4. Understand the CEO's agenda.
5. Present a realistic and honest game plan.
6. Be on your "A" game.
7. Offer objective options.

Collins further suggests that the right people aren't chosen for their technical skills but, rather, on being "self-motivated by the inner drive to produce" (p. 42) and having the right "character attributes" (p. 51). Getting a bus ticket, then, is about followership.

Consider Ramesh, the CEO of a former Bell subsidiary at the leading edge of communications technology. He has an interesting history, being one of the few HR executives to claim the top spot in a non-HR organization. When he took over as CEO, Ramesh had a talk with each of his former peers. He explained to us that they were all good people – he'd worked with each of them for years – but he had to know who was going to commit to making the partnership work. Before Ramesh was hired the company had gone through two leaders with very different styles in a very short time, and he needed people who were ready to build a new partnership based on the change in roles and direction. That's how Ramesh handed out his tickets to ride.

Many people encounter a challenging boss or have a poor result at some point in their career. The agility to get back on track is what counts; it is what separates the successful from the failed. A few important behaviors for getting back on track include clarifying goals, having organizational acumen and agility, being receptive to performance coaching, and obtaining/providing feedback.[14] In other words, it takes followership.

The reality is that followership behaviors are used to evaluate and promote, and to decide whom to retain after an acquisition and whom to choose for high-profile assignments. Understanding this, and giving everyone the knowledge of what is expected, greatly improves morale and engagement.[15]

Followership as You Move Up the Organizational Ladder

All things being equal, your people skills (or lack thereof) become more pronounced the higher up you go.
– *Marshall Goldsmith, author, executive coach, leadership guru*

As you move up the organizational ladder, leadership becomes increasingly important. What's interesting, though, is that followership does, too. About 30% of management performance is followership related,[16] an amount considerably higher than for frontline employees.[17]

There is a lot less forgiveness for poor followership at the middle-manager level because much more of the job is about building partnerships, setting an example, and working in the larger organizational context. Being technically strong is no longer enough to shine. At senior management levels followership becomes the *primary* consideration. In our experience senior executives have the highest levels of followership skill and the greatest conceptual understanding of it, and are most likely to acknowledge followership behaviors.[18] That's no accident.

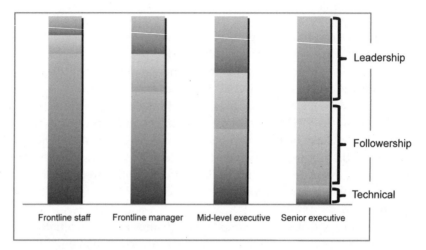

Figure 2.2 Percentage of time spent on leadership, followership and other work

---

***30% of management performance can be attributed to
followership skills.***

Followership Is a Distinct Skill

Dancing Backwards, in High Heels
Recall the famous line from a 1982 Frank and Ernest cartoon, "Sure Fred
Astaire was great, but don't forget that Ginger Rogers did everything
he did, backwards ... and in high heels." Why is this line so memorable
and quotable? Because following is harder than it looks.

Where this quip gets it wrong is that Ginger Rogers didn't do everything Fred Astaire did. Not even backwards. In the exquisite dance se-
quences from *Swing Time*, considered one of the classic dance films of all
time, Fred and Ginger only dance the same steps some of the time and,
even then, Ginger did it backwards in high heels! At other times they are
partnering but with different, *complementary*, moves. And at other times
they are performing solos. Ginger wasn't Fred, and Fred wasn't Ginger.

The essence of followership is having a distinct set of skills that are complementary to those of the leader. Likewise, the essence of leadership is having a distinct set of skills that are complementary to those of the followers. Having all leaders or all followers at the same time doesn't work, as we will see with guppies and stickleback in Chapter 4.

Excellent leadership AND excellent followership are needed to optimize a partnership. Having a strong leader push a weak partner around the dance floor is barely dancing. Having a strong follower pull a weak leader around is, at best, mediocre. It is the combination of technical mastery and skillful leader/follower partnership skills that creates a winning team. Followership and leadership are distinct skills. Unless both partners are proficient at their respective roles the final result is diminished.

Wearing a Halo

Forbes magazine published an article in 2012 about five top CEOs whose continued existence in that role was a mystery.[19] How does it happen that poor performance and poor leadership continue to survive?

Consider the case of Al, the general manager of a manufacturing unit, part of a global firm based in the Midwest. Al is neither a keen people leader nor a strategist. His direct reports often share stories of his flip-flopping on decisions resulting in lost talent and squandered dollars. But Al has held on to his position over the years in large part due to exceptional followership. As an example, consider how he handled this tricky situation.

Both Al and Ernesto had been heading up large business units while vying for the job of CEO. When Ernesto secured it, Al knew that the only part of the business Ernesto had little experience with was the unit that Al led. He also knew that it would be a tremendous help for Ernesto to gain familiarity with how Al's business operated, how it made money, how it served customers, and what the current strategy and projects were. So Al organized a two-day offsite for his executive team and invited Ernesto. The unofficial purpose was to provide Ernesto an inside look at the workings of the business unit, meet Al's impressive executive team, see Al in action with his direct reports, and gain comfort in Al's knowledge of the business. It worked brilliantly. By having Ernesto participate at the retreat rather than being presented to, Al gained tremendous credibility and latitude.

Ernesto probably doesn't realize the extent to which he judges Al's performance based on followership or the extent to which followership is masking other deficiencies. When just one skill is used to make a positive evaluation of overall effectiveness it is called the *halo effect*. You don't need Sherlock Holmes to explain Al's longevity, just an understanding of effective followership and the halo effect.

When people don't talk about followership or spend time thinking about it, it is easier to be misled by the followership halo. That is what happened with Al and Ernesto. In retrospect, Sam now sees she may have fallen prey to this, too. She had a direct report who was a terrific follower – always on her wavelength, receptive to feedback, anticipated her need for information, and fantastic to work with. She went to bat for a promotion for him on numerous occasions but never succeeded in convincing her boss. Sam now reflects that she may have been a bit blinded by his followership skills; perhaps there were specific skill gaps that she didn't see with her follower-fogged glasses on.

Carrying a Pitchfork

Two people we coached, both vice presidents, had been encouraged to take lower-level positions in their respective organizations. Each had a 20-year track record. Both had solid skill sets and were highly regarded leaders by their teams. Both opted to take a package rather than be demoted. What had happened to their careers?

The dismissals happened shortly after their boss retired and a new one was hired. The reason both employees were given was that they weren't "strategic enough." Often, when someone says, "I need you to be more strategic," what she really means is, "I need you to think outside your box and inside mine." These executives were dismissed because of the *pitchfork effect*. The pitchfork effect is when someone forms a negative impression of another person based on the presence or absence of a single skill, situation, or trait, which in turn masks the person's strengths. It is the opposite of the halo effect. Our two former executives hadn't been agile enough to transition to their new bosses.

Lack of followership is a powerful driver of pitchfork firings. We did a survey of career transition consultants – professionals who provide counseling and support to employees who have been fired or laid off – on the factors that led up to firing. Between 95% and 100% of their clients had a new boss in the last 18 months![20] It was the highest and most consistently mentioned reason.

Lynn Schmidt (2009) did her PhD dissertation on why women executives get fired. The factor cited more than any other was having a poor partnership with the boss. Here is a telling quote from one person she interviewed:

> It was really hard for me to identify in my new boss something that I respected. So there wasn't a foundation of respect for me ... I have ... strong ... principals and value set ... there were areas in which I had to be true to myself and being true to myself was not aligning. (pp. 71–72)

With awareness it becomes easier to spot the anomalies, give followership its appropriate place, and make clearer assessments.

> Followership can create a halo effect or pitchfork effect. Awareness is the best way to combat both.

Followership Is Not the Same as Managing Up

When we interviewed a former CEO of HarperCollins USA, she told us, "I used to spend more time managing my boss than I did at the rest of my job." Typically when people talk about managing up they are referring to behaviors they feel are positive and contribute to a productive environment. Despite being well intentioned, however, managing up is the wrong way to think and talk about it. Managing up is about manipulating your boss to accomplish your own goals. Followership, on the other hand, is about getting your team's goals accomplished.

For example, imagine you are interviewing two candidates for a key job on your team.

Interview with Candidate 1:

> TELL ME SOMETHING YOU ARE REALLY GOOD AT.

> I'M REALLY GOOD AT MANAGING UP. I'M SKILLED AT GETTING MY BOSS TO DO WHAT I NEED THEM TO DO TO MAKE ME SUCCESSFUL.

Interview with Candidate 2:

> TELL ME SOMETHING YOU ARE REALLY GOOD AT.

> I'M REALLY GOOD AT FOLLOWERSHIP. I HELP MY BOSS ACHIEVE THEIR OBJECTIVES BY LISTENING TO WHAT THEY ARE TRYING TO DO, ASKING QUESTIONS SO I UNDERSTAND IT, AND DELIVERING SOLUTIONS THAT HELP.

Which of these candidates would you hire?

One of our first workshops was for a conference of the HR team at a full-service insurance company. Years later we reconnected with the director of HR who brought us in. She told us of a recent hiring that had a shortlist of three candidates all pretty much equal in terms of qualifications. At the final interview the HR director asked each, "Are you better at leadership or followership, and why?" Only one chose followership and articulated a sound rationale for it. That's who got hired.

If leadership is about setting goals for the team then followership is the complementary action: the pursuit of team goals.

Followership Requires Development

Making the Invisible Visible

As with any skill, it is hard to improve at followership if you don't know what you are trying to get better at. Having open, frank conversations about followership goes a long way to helping people.

In a workshop we gave on followership was a fellow, Dave, sitting at the front right table. Dave grimaced for at least half the day. He looked positively sickened. We were fairly sure he disliked the workshop, an opinion bolstered by the fact that Dave left 15 minutes before the end. Surprisingly we got this e-mail from him the next day:

> I wanted to thank you for the workshop yesterday. It was very worthwhile. For many years I thought my difficulty in working in large corporations was due to the fact that I am corporately dysfunctional. I realize now that I am not dysfunctional. I was simply lacking followership skills. That was a lot to take in. Thanks!

It turned out that Dave had spent years bouncing from job to job. This was his wake-up call. Identifying followership was a life-altering experience for him. A few years later we caught up with Dave, and he had transitioned to being a successful employee at a large corporation.

Once you start talking about followership, and once you have a model for it, it provides consistency and rigor to building partnerships and teams. There are significant implications to this shift in perspective. Resources allocated to teaching leadership might be more effectively directed to teaching followership. Interventions that target leadership to improve engagement might be even more effective in the context of followership. Emotional intelligence training could be applied to the followership role. Hiring for leadership could be balanced by hiring for followership as well. And performance systems could assess followership contributions. These are a few ideas, but there are many more possibilities to explore. Check out Chapter 14 for more implementation ideas and www.leadershipishalfthestory.com for additional resources.

Followership Summary

Excellent followership gets more done, more effectively and efficiently. It facilitates the work of the team; makes managing easier; and extends the reach of leadership by finding opportunities, solving problems, and delighting customers. People who are great followers are happier with their work and take greater accountability for the success of the organization.

Because of this, individuals should make it a personal priority to develop followership; managers should learn to coach it within their teams; money and resources should be provided to develop it; and executive teams and organizations should make followership an area of emphasis.

As a leader, you can build and reinforce followership by acknowledging its value and distinctiveness, by making the invisible visible through using the f-word, by talking about the specific behavior's value, by giving examples to your team of how senior leaders in your company have demonstrated excellent followership, and by modeling the behaviors you seek.

As a follower, ensure that you are doing everything you can to best support your leader's goals and be a go-to collaborator for your peers. But be careful not to manage up.

Does followership ensure you will always do the right things? No. It's a set of skills, not a moral compass. But it is an essential building block in an actionable model for partnerships. It is the complement to leadership that opens up new opportunities and insights. Once those building blocks – followership and leadership – are in place, a partnership can reach its full, generative potential.

CHAPTER 3

A New Kind of Leadership

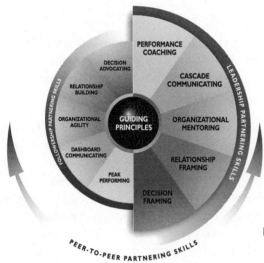

Figure 3.1 Leadership skills

A TV show we watch regularly is *So You Think You Can Dance*. In the show, young dancers are brought together to work on a variety of styles, and then the public votes on their favorite dancers after each episode. The audition process for the show always includes one team dance number. A group of four to six dancers who don't know each other are given a song and asked to choreograph a dance to be presented the next morning for the judges. Each team is self-organized. It's easy to imagine these highly motivated youngsters staying up all night choreographing and rehearsing so the judges don't send them home.

A few teams succeed, and the results can be remarkable. Many, however, implode into a mess of hurt feelings and disjointed dance moves. After watching this for more than 10 seasons, we've observed that the problems teams encounter come in two varieties (other than suffering from extreme sleep deprivation):

1. They don't know how to share leadership.
   - Sometimes no one steps up to the leadership role.
   - At other times one person steps up, only to be replaced; and their work ignored by the next.
   - Multiple people try to take the leadership role at the same time.
2. They don't know how to exercise followership.
   - Someone decides not to follow a group decision once it's made, often covertly (more on this in Chapter 9 – Decision Skills).
   - Someone refuses to acknowledge the person who took on the leadership role.

When we see this kind of ineffectiveness it is tempting to say that leaders aren't needed or that they get in the way. If only we had fewer leaders, more work would get done.

People have been talking about self-organizing, leaderless, or self-managed teams since the 1950s. Self-organizing teams emerged as a reaction to overly bureaucratic companies and the observation that the so-called scientific management principles of the prewar era were failing: management was making misinformed decisions, work was progressing slowly, and teams lacked empowerment and engagement. The term *self-organizing* is misleading – it implies little or no leadership involvement when what actually happens in these situations is *a sharing of leadership between team members*. For the dancers, this can take the form of a single leader, a succession of leaders, or more than one person trying to lead at the same time. In these groups, informal leadership and followership take place all the time. When the roles are performed well the results can be amazing, even if the dancers aren't the best in the competition.

Let's consider another company that tried to use self-organized teams. Most of us are familiar with how Google has come by its most coveted employer status over the years. Much has been publicized, lauded, and criticized about the slides in their offices, video games, foosball, piano, yoga rooms, dogs, clubs, gourmet cafeterias, and the 20% allocation of employee time for personal projects. But the real story is the progressive practices behind the games: how Google envisages the role of leadership.

Early on in Google's history the founders aimed to create an organization without managers, hoping that leadership would emerge spontaneously and equitably in teams. That experiment lasted mere months as the founders became inundated with approval requests and interpersonal issues. A number of years later, they again sought to shake up the traditional manager role in response to low satisfaction scores with some managers and a general lack of interest in taking on the role – programmers would much rather be coding! This time, augmenting the founders' vision were deep data, a high standard of proof, a people analytics team, and a groundbreaking project aptly named Project Oxygen. The project expected to find that managers didn't matter. To Google's surprise, they found that not only do managers matter, but excellent managers matter a lot. The right kind of management and leadership[1] had sizable benefits on every key metric considered:

✓ Retention
✓ Performance
✓ Happiness
✓ Innovation
✓ Work-life balance
✓ Career development

We need leadership. It is vital to success, but maybe not quite the same sort of leadership we had in the past. Google realized that leadership needed to be more responsive to people rather than processes, and that there is a greater demand for leadership than ever before. In other words, it takes:

1. Dynamic leadership
2. Greater leadership capacity
3. People-focused leadership practices

Dynamic Leadership: Who's Got the Ball?
In 1981, Michael Jordan was a freshman on an already talented North Carolina Tar Heels basketball team. Dean Smith, the legendary coach of that team, said to Michael, "If you can't pass the ball, you can't play." What is less well remembered about that time was that Jordan was al-

ready a solid passer, having averaged 10.1 assists per game in his final year at high school. So what did Coach Smith mean by his remark?

The surface meaning of Coach Smith's comment is straightforward: passing is a part of the game and you have to be solid at all aspects to be a complete player. With five players on the other side, one player alone can't do it all, and passing is how you make it a five-on-five contest. At a slightly deeper level the comment suggests that no matter how masterful you are, it is important to keep your peers engaged – pass them the ball once in a while to ensure they keep their heads in the game.

There is, however, a third and deeper meaning. Basketball is a fluid sport much like soccer, rugby, hockey, or lacrosse in that play continues unabated until a penalty or goal occurs. The coach is the primary, undisputed leader before the game starts. Once a game has started, the team captain takes on the mantle of on-field leader. With the most successful teams, however, something more takes place, something that all the best players have to learn, even Michael Jordan. When play is in full swing, for winning teams, the person with the ball has the leadership role and everyone else takes on a followership role.

When Michael Jordan had the ball he got to decide where to dribble, what play to run, whether or not to shoot, and who to pass it to. Once he passed the ball his role changed: he had to think about all the ways to support his teammates. A poor team player thinks, "Well, I'm the best player on the team so I'm going to stand in a spot that will allow me to get my shot." An excellent player thinks, "Should I set a pick, open up space in the lane, distract their defense or set up for a shot?"

The key is that while the captain is always the formal field leader, any player can assume the actual leadership role at any time. Passing the ball is a physical way of saying, "I am passing on the leadership responsibility to another, and now I am taking an equally important, active, dynamic followership role."

"Who's Got the Ball?" identifies the person taking on the leadership role.

The best people know when to lead and when to allow others to lead. When you've got the ball and you see a clear path to the basket, go for it. When you're not in the best position, pass it and stay alert to all the ways you can help.

In organizations, how do you know whom to pass it to and when? The default is often to push it up (or down) the hierarchy, but it doesn't have to be that way. Depending on the task or initiative perhaps the person with the most technical expertise may be the best choice; perhaps it is the person with the most passion or creative inspiration; or perhaps it is the person with the capability, capacity, and drive to take the lead.

The point is that our thinking about leadership must evolve to include formal leadership coexisting with informal leadership, and a shared, dynamic model of leadership prompts useful discussions such as "Who's Got the Ball?"

> Do not worry about holding high position; worry rather about playing your proper role.
>
> – *Confucius*

Leadership comes from all different places in an organization. In fact, just because you are in a senior leadership position doesn't mean what you are doing most of the time is leadership. We all take on the leadership role from time to time. Admittedly some people take on the mantle of leadership more often, and certain positions in the hierarchy demand it more than others. Regardless, we stand by the fact that Joe Team Leader needs to be as capable at leadership as Mary Technical Expert or Bigwig CEO. In fact, Joe Team Leader needs to understand when it isn't his time to lead.

Consider Kevin McKenna, for example. He is general manager of the Canadian Division of Phoenix Contact, an 80-year-old German organization with nearly 13,000 employees in 50 countries worldwide. Voted one of the top 50 Great Places to Work, Kevin's company has developed an award-winning culture.

During the meetings we've facilitated for Kevin's team he is always a fully engaged participant. He sits at one of the tables, learns any new concepts and material presented, and helps generate ideas that the team might want to consider adopting. But then he does something surprising! Just as the group is about to start powering up ideas and deciding which ones are best to proceed with, Kevin slips out to "take a phone call with a key client." He usually reappears in time to catch up with his group, see what they decided, and celebrate their accomplishments. The third time this happened we asked him, "Kevin, did you really have another key client meeting this morning or did you leave at that time for another reason?"

"Guilty as charged," he replied. "I've learned to be conscious of my position: when it's useful to be around and when it's better to be absent. I want to show commitment to advancing our knowledge, trying out new ideas, and adopting new techniques – to get things moving along – but I don't want to hold the team back, either. I want them to share leadership and take ownership and it's easier for someone on my team to do it when I'm not there."

That's just one aspect of what makes Kevin special. We have also noticed that when someone is taking on the leadership role, Kevin will actively adopt the followership role: supporting ideas, taking on some of the work, or providing additional information. He has a keen sense of when to lead (and how to do it) but also when to follow (and how to do it).

Developing Greater Leadership Capacity

The idea of passing the ball tremendously increases the leadership capacity of an organization. But to get more leadership you have to train it and develop it.

A study by Bruce Avolio and his colleagues (2009) provides intriguing evidence that leadership development is a sound investment. After reviewing data from 134 previous studies, with over 11,000 participants in total, they set out to answer a simple question: Does leadership training work and, if so, with whom and to what extent?

The results were compelling. Using a fully costed model for onsite training, the average return on investment (ROI) of leadership training was 61% for senior executives, 169% for mid-level leaders, and higher still for frontline leaders. In other words, for every dollar invested in senior leadership training you get back at least $1.61, with the biggest bang for your leadership development buck coming from investing in the most junior staff.[2]

Leadership training has the highest payback when given to frontline managers.

The military has already figured this out, having long ago having learned its lessons about the pitfalls of the command-and-control style. Our longtime friend Peter Elmenhoff has been in the army reserves for 15+ years, served a tour in Afghanistan, and regularly teaches and mentors. He shares this observation:

> There are big differences between the military and civilian life when it comes to leadership. First, in the military when they spot you've got an aptitude with people, they earmark you for a leadership position. Second, they give you leadership training *before* they promote you to that position. Third, they give you followership training too. As leaders, you have to explain and model good followership as well as leadership.

Of course, training is a small part of leadership development, which also includes coaching, mentoring, self-learning, and on-the-job practice.

One problem, though, is that not everyone wants to take on a leadership role.

A high-tech firm we worked with was undergoing such rapid growth – almost doubling in size each year – that they barely had time to fill all the programmer roles let alone do leadership development. They told us that their biggest challenge was attracting people to take on management positions. Each of their people leaders had 18 to 26 direct reports, worked long hours, and didn't get to write computer code. Not surprisingly there was little interest among the IT staff in going this route. Staff mostly aspired, instead, to move up the technical stream.

We gave workshops for them on leadership development with roughly two dozen people in each, split about evenly between managers with direct reports and senior technical professionals such as data architects, engineers, and project managers.

Near the beginning of the workshop we asked all participants to reflect on how they spent their time in an average week. What did they do? What skills did they need to exercise in order to do those activities? What is their job really like? Not a job description but a realistic account of what actually happens.

Next we had people gather into groups with their peers: project managers with other project managers, team leads with other team leads, that sort of thing. We asked them to share and discuss with each other what their jobs entailed and to consolidate/converge their individual notes. It was a loud, animated, and cathartic activity! By the end, each group was satisfied that they had captured the essence of their job.

Then we gathered everyone back into the big group to share and compare notes, using a huge chart something like this:

Table 3.1 Who Is Leading? Comparing Activities of Senior People in an Organization

Senior Technical – Activities	Senior Manager – Activities
• Example 1	• Example 1
• Example 2	• Example 2
• Example 3	• Example 3

Once we listed the consolidated activities for each group, we discussed the similarities and differences. The big "aha" for everybody (even us) was how much these supposedly separate streams did the same activities – greater than 80% overlap.

This activity demystified the leadership role for them – it wasn't all that different from the technical one. Senior technical people do nearly as much leadership as team leads. Moreover, the activities most prominent in everyone's mind, and those that garnered the lion's share of discussion, were interpersonal ones such as communicating, building relationships with people/other teams, creating and leading a decision-making process, generating collective perspectives in a meeting, and developing staff. People in technical roles and technical environments often find the technical aspects of the job easy compared to managing people, but it is the people stuff that makes the real difference. The best technical leads gave the people side more attention and were more intentional about it.

In collaborative work environments everyone on the team needs to have leadership skills. What, then, is that?

People-Focused Leadership Practices

The Gartner Group reported an increase in a working style called "swarming," in which a diverse group forms quickly to attack a problem or to power up an opportunity, then disbands just as quickly once the problem is solved.[3] Their other top trend was the percentage of nonroutine work, and that is expected to almost double over the next few years. Both of these newer ways of working make the traditional management task of organizing and coordinating – or largely focusing on process – rather counterproductive. In these settings no one person is solely responsible for coordinating the work of others.

Table 3.2 Two Approaches to Leadership: Process Focus for Efficiency and People Focus for Collaboration

Process Focus	People Focus
Power	Supporting personal agency
Control	Enablement
Command	Collaboration
Autocracy	Democracy
Uniformity	Diversity
Self-centered	Higher purpose
Hero	Humble
How can I get you to perform?	How can we best achieve together?

In today's collaborative teams, it's not always the manager taking on the leadership role; sometimes it's another team member. The key is that leadership, regardless of who is doing it, is shifting more toward focusing on people than process.

In an environment where everyone can take on the leadership role, leaders don't dangle carrots and prod with sticks. Leaders don't delegate. Leaders don't get involved in assigning work or choosing people for teams. The role is not so much to evaluate, rate, rank, review, differentiate, and recommend for promotion. Rather, the leadership job is to coach, chart the path, clear the path, and help people have awesome experiences in the process. It involves a lot of communicating, a lot of emphasis on goals, being clear on priorities, erring to "yes," and attention to the people side of things. It means taking personal responsibility for continually advancing your people skills.

$$\text{New People Leadership Formula} = \frac{\text{Passion} + \text{Purpose} + \text{Expertise}}{\text{Carrots} + \text{Sticks}}$$

Arguably, the most notable feature of what we are talking about is the shift in the burden of evaluation and differentiation. Peers are perfectly able to evaluate whether an individual is ready for a promotion, and peer evaluations work. This system works because it is a lot harder to fool a peer than a leader. It works because everyone is subject to the same scrutiny, and it is done in a culture of openness with information and feedback. Your peers typically get what you do, they can gauge how much value you are adding, and they can see the effort you put in. If you are slacking off, not pulling your weight, acting bigheaded, or making outrageous demands, you can pretty much count on your peers to call you out. At Google, for example, you are allowed to order any equipment you want: no asking your manager or writing up a business case. If you need the latest in ergonomic chairs, or three computer screens, or even a fish tank, you order it. When we first found out about this practice we asked what stopped people from being ridiculous about it? The answer we were given was, "Peers." At review time, when you are in front of your peers, you will have to explain your decisions to them.

The peer system not only keeps people aligned to the team, it does a better job of recognizing genuinely positive contributions. Joseph Fung, founder of TribeHR and VP of Human Capital Management Products at NetSuite, says that after five plus years scrutinizing huge volumes of data on kudos in the workplace, the overwhelming majority comes from peers. Peers do recognize each other – insightfully, properly, and regularly.

> Today's leadership job is to coach, chart the path, clear the path, and help people have awesome experiences in the process.

It is possible to reimagine and redesign the leadership role. Together with a carefully constructed environment, you can have a virtuously reinforcing system where empowerment looks like freedom, productivity tools look like recreation, and efficiency programs such as free, healthy food make employees feel cared about.

A Last Word on Leadership – Why Change?

Not every organization has a lot of money to spend on staff perks, or can afford to only hire the best of the best. Whatever the case, here are some decidedly dismal statistics that bear consideration:[4]

- The failure rate of leaders is 50% to 75%.
- CEO tenure at Fortune 500 companies has been steadily trending downward over the last 10 years.
- Executive derailment – getting fired, demoted, or plateauing – is at about 50%.
- Global employee engagement scores were 56% in 2010 – companies with low engagement had a total shareholder return that was 28% lower than the average.
- The prevalence of *destructive* leadership – bad for the organization and bad for subordinates – is 33.5% to 61%.
- Happiness at work has been declining since 1984. Unhappy workers are 22% less productive than happy ones.

Each of these represents a huge loss in productivity, innovation, joy, and money. None of them are solved through process improvement, although process improvement *is* valuable. While the cost of building better leadership and bringing it to the entire organization can be high, the returns make it worthwhile.

Leadership Summary

Great leadership helps people become better than they are and better together. It creates a work environment that attracts and motivates workplace partners, builds relationships, breaks down barriers to progress, and creates conditions for success.

In modern organizations leadership is dynamic: everyone takes on a leadership role from time to time. Leadership is defined not by role or hierarchy but by "Who's Got the Ball?" How do you know whom to pass the ball to? It may be the person with the most technical expertise;

the person with the most passion or creative inspiration; or the person with the capability, capacity, and drive to take the lead.

Leadership has to be trainable and, therefore, a leadership model should be about skills. Specifically, it should be about interpersonal skills: being a skilled administrator, for example, is important for managers, but that doesn't make it a leadership skill.

When you know what leadership is (and isn't), you can teach it, mentor it, learn it, and develop the appropriate skills.

Finally, all the leadership skill in the world is meaningless (or, at least, less meaningful) if there isn't a complementary followership skill. The two are a matched set.

SECTION II

Guiding Principles

Generative Partnership® Model

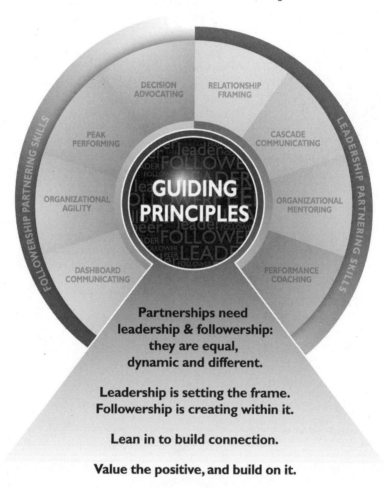

DECISION ADVOCATING

RELATIONSHIP FRAMING

PEAK PERFORMING

CASCADE COMMUNICATING

ORGANIZATIONAL AGILITY

ORGANIZATIONAL MENTORING

DASHBOARD COMMUNICATING

PERFORMANCE COACHING

FOLLOWERSHIP PARTNERING SKILLS

LEADERSHIP PARTNERING SKILLS

GUIDING PRINCIPLES

**Partnerships need
leadership & followership:
they are equal,
dynamic and different.**

**Leadership is setting the frame.
Followership is creating within it.**

Lean in to build connection.

Value the positive, and build on it.

Have deeply shared goals.

Principle 1: Partnerships Need Leadership and Followership. They Are Equal, Dynamic, and Different.

Partnerships need leadership & followership: they are equal, dynamic and different.

Leadership is setting the frame.
Followership is creating within it.

Lean in to build connection.

Value the positive, and build on it.

Have deeply shared goals.

Figure 4.1

> Nothing exists except in relationship to everything else.
>
> – *Margaret J. Wheatley*

Jennifer Harcourt and her colleagues (2009) at Cambridge University published a study on stickleback fish in the academic journal *Current Biology* a few years back.

"Why would I care about fish?," you might be wondering. "Isn't this a book on partnerships?" Yes, but humans are really complicated. Sometimes it's easier to start with a simpler example, one that doesn't have all the extra baggage to muddy the interpretation. Something like fish.

Stickleback fish are relatives of seahorses and pipefish, measuring

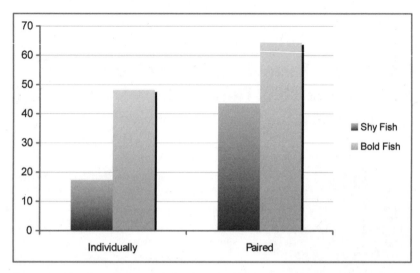

Figure 4.2 Number of trips made by shy or bold fish, depending on whether they were alone or with another fish

two to four inches in length, with gray or blue-green backs and silvery flanks. Unusually, they have no scales but they do have bony plates with three spines, hence their name.

Stickleback fish are prey. In the oceans and lakes where they live, bigger fish and birds eat them. Because of this, sticklebacks spend much of their time hiding in the weeds, only emerging to forage. The percentage of time spent foraging varies significantly between sticklebacks. Some – the shy ones – only venture into the open occasionally while others, their bolder compatriots, do so much more often. For example, in Harcourt's experiment the shy sticklebacks spent about 14.3% of the time in the open while the bold ones were out from cover 41.3% of the time, a threefold difference. Another way to measure the boldness of a fish is by the number of trips it takes to look for food in an hour – coming out from cover and back again. Bold sticklebacks took 48.1 trips compared to only 17.3 for the shy ones. However you look at it, bold fish and shy fish behave quite differently.

Now things got really exciting when a bold stickleback and a shy stickleback were paired together. Entirely new patterns of behavior emerged. When one fish left cover, the other often joined it and they foraged together. When one returned to cover, the other did the same.

Not surprisingly, the bold fish left cover first much more of the time. You might say it took on the role of leader while the shy fish took on a followership role. As a result, the shy fish foraged more often when paired up with a bold fish. What's unexpected, though, is that the bold fish did, too! If you look at the chart (Figure 4.2), the bold fish went from under 50 trips an hour to well over 60 in the presence of another fish. If it were a study done on humans you'd be tempted to conclude that the reason the bold one went out more often was to act more like a macho leader because it was being watched – "Look at me, I'm scared of nothing!"

Bold fish increased foraging by 30% when paired with shy fish.

In fact, it makes more sense to characterize the interaction as two-way. Each fish influenced the other to make the partnership mutually beneficial: being partnered made both better at foraging.

Equal Roles

What if you paired up two bold fish, wouldn't they do even better still? In a separate study done on guppies[1] it was found that groups with both shy guppies and bold guppies fed more than groups of all bold fish or all shy fish. As the authors of that study say, "not only do shy fish gain foraging benefits from associating with bold fish but there are also benefits to bold fish, too" (p. 170). In other words, it is better to have two fish that complement each other than have all fish with the same traits, even if that trait is better for a specific individual. Partnerships aren't just the sum of the parts. There is more to it than that.

Great partnerships are an easy flow from symmetry to mimicry to complementarity to individuality.

There were other complementary behaviors. When only one fish of a pair was out foraging, it was much more likely to return to cover than when it was not paired up. If both were out at the same time they stayed out longer than as individuals. You can almost hear the fish thinking, "If I am out there and my partner doesn't join me, maybe they know something I don't. I better get back under cover!" Or when they are both out, "If I am out from cover and my partner also thinks it is okay to be out, then everything is fine." There is a notion that everyone should be a leader all the time and, if leadership is so game changing, we must need more of it from everyone all the time. In fact, as our fish examples show, it takes both roles – leadership and followership – to get the best results. They are equally valuable.

Dynamic Roles
But wait, there's more!

Harcourt took a closer look at the stickleback data. Was the bold fish always the leader? Was the shy fish always the follower?

As it turns out, the bold fish did lead the excursions three to four times more often than the shy fish, but the shy fish also went out first from time to time. And when the shy fish did lead the way the bold fish was four times more likely to join it than the other way around. It was even more likely to join the shy fish than to initiate a trip in the first place. Maybe we should call the shy fish the better leader because its partner followed it more often than the other way around!

The real point is that both fish took turns as the leader. The role was *dynamic* because it wasn't always one fish doing it. Similarly, both took turns as the follower. Followership was also a dynamic role.[2]

Different Roles
On any single trip one fish led and the other followed. But there was more to differentiate the roles than just that. In a follow-up study,[3] it turned out that the leader of any given trip was less likely to respond to what its partner was doing. This effect lasted even once they were back under cover.

Finally, if you don't lump fish into the two categories – bold and shy – and instead measure boldness on a continuum, then three other differences emerged:

1. The bolder the bold fish was, the more likely its partner was to join it.
2. The bolder the bold fish was, the more likely it was to abandon a solo trip.
3. The shyer the shy fish was, the bolder its partner became!

In other words, the roles involved different behaviors and some surprising interactions. Andrea Manica, the author in whose lab these experiments took place, observed that "The behavior you get from the pair is totally different from what you see in individuals."[4] It wasn't just the followers who were influenced by the leaders; the follower fish also shaped and improved the leadership. The net effect was greater foraging efficiency.

Their behavior together wasn't just an extrapolation of what they did as individuals: it was more foraging AND new behavior. That's generative.

- Each fish demonstrated both leadership and followership at different times. Neither – bold or shy – exerted more influence than the other. Their contributions were equal.
- Leadership and followership were shared, dynamic, and temporary rather than permanent.
- Their behaviors were complementary but different, and together they produced far better results than when they were on their own.

In summary, the two fish formed a partnership that is generative.

Back to People
When you go into business, you seek partners to help you forage better – greater efficiency, innovation, resource utilization, speed – than you could get on your own. Partnerships between organizations are entered into for the same reason: to combine strengths for mutual advantage. Such partnerships are diverse and plentiful: for example, Starbucks + Barnes & Noble, Target + Amazon, BlackBerry + Alicia Keys, Nike + Herman Miller. Savvy organizations realize that in today's fast and fickle environment you need to foster interfirm relationships just to stay in the game.

Partnerships aren't about friendship, or affection, or chemistry. It is well documented that The Beatles did some of their best work together – the *White Album* and *Abbey Road*, for example – despite high levels of internal strife. Tensions were high and each member of the group spent considerable time working on individual efforts. But the group still had a partnership that was generative even close to the end. Stickleback fish don't build friendships, either. We aren't suggesting that friendship is unimportant, just that partnerships are different from friendships; and the distinction is important.

Equal – Creating a Better Apple

Steve Jobs and Timothy Cook were perhaps the most powerful one-two punch in corporate history.[5] As CEO of Apple, Steve Jobs provided the pizzazz for employees, the driving force for innovation, and the public presence. As COO, Timothy Cook made sure things ran smoothly behind the scenes. "He's the story behind the story,"[6] said one former Apple executive.

As second in command, Cook countered Jobs's quick, unpredictable temperament with a quiet, thoughtful manner. Jobs could concentrate on the big picture and ideas for snazzy new products because he knew Cook was taking care of the nuts and bolts of the business. Far from being a yes-man, Cook had his own ideas about how things should be done, and industry insiders saw his stamp on the company. Yet he was content to play "Spock" to Steve Jobs's "Captain Kirk," using his analytical and detail-oriented mind to complement Jobs's more intuitive, emotional approach. Like Spock supporting Kirk, Cook didn't hesitate to push Jobs's boundaries to help him, and the organization became better as a result. And just as Kirk never hesitated to beam down to a planet leaving Spock in charge, during his bouts of poor health Jobs confidently placed the company in the hands of Cook.

Cook took over as CEO of Apple in August of 2011, succeeding Steve Jobs. In early 2012 Apple's board of directors awarded him compensation of 1 million shares, vesting in 2021. As of April 2012, those shares were valued at US $600 million, making him the world's highest paid CEO at the time.

Without Cook being able to take charge when it was about matters of operational excellence, Apple would have been the same "almost great" idea factory of Jobs's first tenure as CEO. With Cook, Jobs formed a partnership where the contributions of both partners – of both leadership and followership – were fully valued and valuable.

> My model for business is the Beatles. They were four guys who kept each other's kind of negative tendencies in check. They balanced each other, and the total was greater than the sum of the parts. That's how I see business: Great things in business are never done by one person. They're done by a team of people.
>
> – *Steve Jobs*

Dynamic – Rocking It Like The Beatles

We perform both leadership and followership in our work lives. We often have to flip adroitly between the two. The flipping back and forth of roles – what we are calling dynamic leadership and followership – has to be present for a partnership to be truly optimized. Who better to exemplify this than our four lads from Liverpool?

In a period of eight years, The Beatles released 23 studio albums that have sold over a billion albums worldwide. While each of The Beatles had success after the band split up, it was their special partnership that fueled the greatest outpouring of popular music in our time. And they weren't just prolific. The music of The Beatles is so uniquely creative and appealing that every generation since their heyday in the 1960s has cottoned on to it. We watched an episode of *Glee*, the smash TV show and harbinger of what's hot. It was the first of a two-part Beatles tribute that kicked off with the music teacher's remark, "The Beatles are so epic that we need two weeks to do them justice."

On Rolling Stone Magazine's list of the 500 best albums of all time there are five Beatles albums in the top 15. *Sgt. Pepper's Lonely Hearts Club Band* is number one.[7] Even though Lennon was the acknowledged leader of the group, *Sgt. Pepper* was McCartney's idea. During the process of recording it, each band member brought forward his own songs and creative ideas and took a lead on them. Did the other Beatles see it that way? Well, how about this quote from Ringo: "Sgt. Pepper was our grandest endeavor. The greatest thing about the band was that whoever had the best idea – it didn't matter who – that was the one we'd use. No one was standing on their ego, saying, 'Well, it's mine,' and getting possessive." George Martin, their producer, often referred to as the fifth Beatle, concurs with this telling comment: "… in the studio the group's leader was defined by the song they were working on."

For example, "A Day in the Life" might have been Lennon's song but McCartney added a middle lick that elevated it to an instant classic. McCartney took on the role of active, engaged follower when it was Lennon's song. The *Sgt. Pepper* album might have been Paul's concept but everyone contributed his best work to make it a landmark. To show you just how far this collaborative spirit went, it was Neil Aspinall, The Beatles' long-time assistant, who suggested that they reprise the title track just before the grand finale of "A Day in the Life."

"Whose song is it?" helps define who takes the leadership role.

The Beatles created a partnership that was immensely productive, innovative, and agile. Were they simply the most talented individuals ever? Probably not. Many super-groups have been formed with stars of rock-and-roll that had as much or even more individual talent, but ended with disappointing results. And while each of The Beatles had success afterward it doesn't compare to the success they had together.

Were they the most cohesive group? No. The group had its share of conflict, especially during the later years, but still continued to produce great work. It isn't harmony (or lack of it!) that creates a partnership that is generative: it is the equal, dynamic, and different roles.

With partnerships such as The Beatles the whole is greater than the sum of its parts. These teams achieve far more than an incremental improvement in team performance, or a synergy where you get more of the same thing. The catchphrase "high-performance team" does not do them justice; rather, their performance aspires to a different level, a new bar, a new peak. It is more innovative and more productive. Generative.

We reckoned we could make it because there were four of us. None of us would've made it alone, because Paul wasn't quite strong enough, I didn't have enough girl-appeal, George was too quiet, and Ringo was the drummer. But we thought that everyone would be able to dig at least one of us, and that's how it turned out.

– John Lennon

Different Roles

Some leadership guidance espouses that strong leaders "model the way." While this is true in spirit – great leaders roll up their sleeves and get involved – it should not be interpreted literally. Followership is not an imitation of leadership, a sort of mini-leadership, or a leadership-in-training. Followership is a different role requiring different, but complementary, skills to those of leadership.

Early in his career, Marc worked in a business unit headed up by a brash, young, and extremely smart VP who confronted opinions, challenged the processes, and generally said what he thought. Marc remembers being impressed enough by the success of the VP to start imitating those same behaviors, believing this was what successful people did at the company. Unfortunately, what Marc only realized after a number of weeks spent alienating his boss and colleagues, was that the VP only acted this way in his leadership role. The same leadership behaviors that he modeled and revered were condemned in the followership role.

In 1987, Kouzes and Posner, authors of the iconic book on leadership *The Leadership Challenge* published a list of the characteristics of effective leaders based on what managers believed (Table 4.2).[8] The most important characteristic was "honesty/integrity," followed by "competence" at number two. The survey by Agho in 2009 mostly reconfirmed the original Kouzes and Posner rankings. When Agho asked managers about effective followers, they also gave honesty/integrity and competence as their first two choices. In other words, the same attributes were the top requirements for leaders as well as followers.

It suggests that there are certain characteristics to be effective, irrespective of role. Honesty and competence are important for leaders but they are not unique leadership traits. No matter what role our partners are engaged in, we'd all prefer to work with people who are honest and competent.

For followership, the third and fourth place attributes on Agho's list were "dependable" and "cooperative." That was different than the third and fourth place leadership characteristics – "forward looking" and "inspiring." The survey results found differences between being an effective follower and being an effective leader.

Table 4.2 The top leadership and followership traits as identified by 300 senior executives – Agho, 2009

Top Leadership Traits[9]	Top Followership Traits
1. Honesty/integrity	1. Honesty/integrity
2. Competent	2. Competent
3. Forward looking	3. Dependable
4. Inspiring	4. Cooperative
5. Intelligent	5. Loyal
6. Fair-minded	6. Intelligent

If you were to draw a picture of what leadership and followership looked like based on these surveys alone, it might consist of two over-lapping circles. One circle would represent all possible positive lead-ership traits, skills, and behaviors – what the Global Leadership and Organizational Behavior Effectiveness survey called "universally per-ceived leadership attributes" (Javidan, Dorfman, Sully de Luque, and House, 2006, p. 73) – while the other circle would represent the same for followership. Leadership is comprised of unique characteristics such as being forward looking, but also shares some with followership such as being competent. The overlap represents shared characteristics of excellent leaders and followers: in other words, what you might hope to have in any capable associate or employee. Precisely what belongs in each of the three categories – leader, follower, or both – is not yet known. Table 4.2, for example, is a poll of what one group of people believe, but it is neither comprehensive nor universal.

Although trait theories were marginalized after WW II, they have seen resurgence in recent years. For example, general intelligence is known to be an important predictor of success in most jobs, suggest-ing that it is in the Both category. Emotional intelligence is another trait (or skill?) that might be useful for leadership and followership. Being dependable and cooperative, however, might be better located in the follower category, although it's wise to be cautious about survey data such as this.[10] After all, it is difficult to imagine a good leader who is not dependable or cooperative.

What, then, is left over? What is specific to leadership? What is specific to followership?

The rest of the principles chapters and skills chapters answer these questions. We'll get to that shortly but first a small digression that will help orient the difference between the principles and skills.

From Fish to Birds and a Bit about Guiding Principles

Collectively, birds are far more successful when they flock. Their flying is more effective, their feeding is more productive, and they are safer. But how is it that birds can create this chaotic, sophisticated, and intricately patterned behavior?

At first blush, it seems that the birds must spend a lot of time communicating to make flocking work; when you watch gulls on a beach there is a cacophony of cries, squawks, and other noise as they fly, dive, wheel through the air, and then land. Communication, however, is only a small part of the answer. Flocking can be understood by three fairly straightforward guiding principles.

1. Avoid your neighbors.
2. Head to the center.
3. Move in the general direction of your nearest neighbors.

Guiding principles are incredibly helpful in any discipline. They establish a collective mindset and mutual understanding between parties – it allows for adaptation and complex outcomes based on easy-to-remember rules. And they help inform and guide actions, especially in new or unfamiliar situations. When in doubt, rely on a guiding principle.

For example, if you want to learn how to run better, knowing the names of all the leg muscles involved in running – hamstrings, quadriceps femoris, gluteus maximum, or iliopsoas – isn't going to help much. However, understanding the underlying principles of muscle movement and how the muscles are designed to work together will.

Marc is often asked to do talks on neuroscience and its applicability to organizations. People are endlessly fascinated by the brain and its many parts, wanting to learn the names of the areas that are related to emotions and cognition – the hippocampus, prefrontal cortex, fusiform region, or insular cortex, for example.

Funnily enough there is research to show that if you include names of brain parts in a story about behavior the story is considered more credible.[11] That's probably why so many people are flocking to add a little neuroscience into their talk or book or blog these days! Anyhow, Marc indulges this to a degree but makes it clear that understanding the underlying principles is what will help you use your brain better.

In a similar vein, Sam had a successful career as a corporate accountant. She recalls how useful principles were to learning accounting and financial statement preparation. For example, the Principle of Relevance means that a business should disclose all information that is capable of making a difference to the way investors or creditors assess its performance and future prospects. Guiding principles – such as the principle of relevance – require expertise and judgment to apply properly. As you gain comfort in applying them in different situations, their application becomes swift and habitual.

This first guiding principle has reframed how we think and see the world. We see our partnerships differently. We see organizations differently. Instead of thinking of leadership as the prime mover of everything – looking at the world through a monocle – we apply this new lens: leadership AND followership. We see opportunities for shared accountability, mutuality, and reciprocity that we didn't before.

> The real voyage of discovery consists not in seeking new landscapes, but in having new eyes.
>
> – *Marcel Proust*

The failure to have a language for the different roles we all have impedes development and progress. It means valuable discussions and development opportunities get missed. It creates ambiguity in roles – one of the top stressors at work.[12]

Far from being a theoretical point, there are many practical applications of Principle 1:

✓ Being more conscious and deliberate about the roles of leadership and followership

✓ Drawing on the right skill set in different situations
✓ Focusing on the most useful development opportunities
✓ Analyzing interpersonal situations to give more precise, actionable feedback

By distinguishing between leadership and followership behaviors we can be far more specific, pointed, and accurate in feedback giving. And receiving. Consider our personal stories at the beginning of this book: we both could have used feedback directly relating to our followership at certain points in time in our careers. Tool 4.1, on making feedback role specific would have helped us immeasurably! The value of distinguishing between leadership and followership will become even clearer as you move through the book and gain familiarity with the balance of the principles and the various aspects of the leadership skills and followership skills.

 Tool 4.1 Making Feedback Role Specific

Giving specific and actionable feedback is one of the most helpful, yet tricky, things we do for the ongoing betterment of our partnerships. The feedback has to be delivered carefully, with an understanding of how it will be received and how it might be actioned.

1. Begin by thinking of someone you need to provide feedback to. Perhaps you have observed a behavior that is holding him back. Or a behavior that is holding you back. Perhaps he has asked you for feedback about what to improve. Perhaps it is part of your performance review process.
2. Consider what behavior or action you observed that necessitates feedback.
3. Next, put on your leadership/followership lens and apply it to the situation. What role was he performing when you observed the behavior: leadership or followership?
4. Now, what feedback can you offer that will be helpful and actionable with this new perspective?

Principle #1 Summary

Partnerships become generative when a leader-focused mindset is replaced by one that embraces the roles of both leadership and followership. The roles are equal, dynamic, and different:

- ✓ There is a deeply held belief that everyone in the partnership or team is equal and an equally valuable contributor.
- ✓ There is awareness that leadership and followership shifts between people, irrespective of formal titles and hierarchies.
- ✓ There is recognition and appreciation for the different skills of leadership and followership.

Principle 2: Leadership Is Setting the Frame. Followership Is Creating within It.

Partnerships need leadership & followership: they are equal, dynamic and different.

Leadership is setting the frame. Followership is creating within it.

Lean in to build connection.

Value the positive, and build on it.

Have deeply shared goals.

Figure 5.1

Our Salsa Dancing Project – Part 1 – About Framing and Creating

Marc and I started taking salsa dancing lessons. We wanted to learn to dance together better. Moreover, we wanted to learn about partnership development and what tips, if any, could be transferable to our work.

We were surprised when we met the instructor recommended to us. Instead of a Latino with a bold personality, Jeff was a quiet, unassuming fellow in a hockey jersey. However, after telling us how he taught dance at university while studying kinesiology (the science of human movement) and how he'd developed a methodological approach that worked for everyone regardless of natural talent, we were intrigued and signed on.

We attended a human resources professionals' conference just days before our first lesson where we were invited to take a workplace style quiz. The results – I am "A Leader" and Marc is "A Performer" – foreshadowed our biggest challenge; it wasn't the salsa dancing steps, it was me learning to follow and Marc learning to lead.

If you think about it, when you watch ballroom dancing it is typically the woman (or follower) whom you watch. That's where the flair and creativity are most apparent. The lesson quickly confirmed that following is absolutely not a passive role. The level of focus and concentration required took me by surprise.

In my development as a follower I am learning to be 100% present, focus on maintaining connection, observe and interpret the different leadership signals, and figure out how to add flare or creativity within the frame that Marc sets. Oh yes, and appear relaxed. Not like I'm gripping a steering wheel driving down the highway during rush hour!

Our instructor, Jeff, began by teaching Sam and me the basic steps: the front and back and side-to-side rocking motion that is instantly recognizable as salsa.

Beyond that, our roles were different. As the leader of our dance partnership, I am learning to set and maintain an appropriate frame. Jeff is relentless about this: "Framing is the foundation of leadership." He tells me to hold the frame – by which he means my arms, hands, shoulders, and general carriage – "loose but connected" and to plan a number of moves ahead so Sam and I have ample space and time to make turns and change direction. Also, he reminds me to give enough varied opportunity for my partner to create and add flare within the frame I am setting. Needless to say, I'm worn out after each and every class!

This experience is really bringing home how important it is to have partnership principles and to practice together. When we are learning together, Sam helps me when I forget or miss something and vice versa. Without regular practice we lapse into old patterns with Sam trying to lead and me forgetting to maintain the frame.

From the Ballroom to the Boardroom

While Principle 1 articulates the nature of partnerships that are more generative, Principle 2 summarizes the specific difference between the roles of leadership and followership. Further, it supplants our thinking about delegation as THE primary leadership competency.

Here is the definition of delegation by Lominger, an organization specializing in competency dictionaries and assessments:

> Clearly and comfortably delegates both routine and important tasks and decisions; broadly shares both responsibility and accountability; tends to trust people to perform; lets direct reports finish their own work.

Expanding beyond delegation is an activity that forms the foundation of all leadership: *framing*.[1]

To use an analogy, a picture frame separates the inside from the outside, it adds to the beauty of the picture, and it provides structure. When you frame a problem or situation all the same qualities apply. A good frame enables someone to take action. It determines what are acceptable and unacceptable actions, resources, and solutions. It establishes appropriate constraints. It incorporates both the traditional ideas of leadership and management. And, it shares responsibility and accountability.

A frame is a specific type of boundary that is supple, malleable, yielding, agile and fuzzy. We talk about "fuzzy" again in Chapter 13 in reference to goals. "Fuzzy" is a recognition that the future is unknown, thus a frame must be opportunistic in nature, not too rigid.

Frames are particular to the initiative. As a leader, you want to think: new initiative = new frame; and new frame = new vision, new assumptions, new risk profile, etc. This doesn't mean that every frame has to be unique and distinct, but it does mean that as a leader you need to:

1. Assess each situation from the ground up.
2. Choose a frame that will enable the partnership to achieve its vision/mandate/deadline/challenge.
3. Figure out how the frame leverages the team's capacity and capabilities.
4. Present the frame at the right level of challenge to maximize productivity, creativity, and engagement.
5. Modify the frame as the situation changes to continually optimize the conditions for success.

Taking these points into consideration ensures key assumptions are rigorously and regularly examined, and patterns confirmed and intentional.

It often happens that a leader neglects to frame a challenge sufficiently, putting his or her team at a disadvantage. A group of senior engineers we worked with lamented that they had been given a mandate to be more creative and innovative; however, their leaders hadn't articulated what they were actually *looking for* creatively. How much risk/failure/experimentation would be acceptable? What kind of innovation was expected? Was it disruptive change, incremental change, or a product enhancement? What resources could be deployed? What could the engineers stop doing? For the first few months nothing happened and everyone thought the project to bring more creativity into the organization was a failure. It was at that point that one of the leaders started to add structure and constraints to what the engineers could and couldn't do. Within a month the first innovation appeared.

Contrary to popular belief, a blank slate does not stimulate creativity and innovation. To illustrate this, try doing the following as quickly as you can:

Think up 10 creative ideas. (Stop reading and give yourself 90 seconds to respond.)

Now look at the list you made. How many ideas did you put down? How creative are your ideas?

It is a harder exercise than you realize. Most people stumble, stop for a minute to think, and then ask, "Ten creative ideas for what?" People are far more creative and productive working within a frame of well-articulated constraints. Contrast it with this exercise:

Think up ten creative ideas for new breakfast items at your favorite restaurant.

This constrained problem triggers swift, confident responses.

People don't operate optimally in the absence of a frame or when the frame is too loose. Ambiguity is uncomfortable. Obscurity is unproductive. It is why delegating doesn't always work as hoped. Similarly, when the frame is too constricting, that quashes creativity and individual initiative.

We don't want to suggest that all the accountability lies in one direction. It is true that people don't deliver what you expect when the frame is too loose (or too tight). But followership also imposes three critical responsibilities:

1. If the frame is not articulated in a way that you can understand, ask.
2. If the frame is not producing optimal results, provide generative feedback.
3. Think and work outside the box, but inside the frame.

Thinking Outside the Box Does Not Mean Thinking Outside the Boss

This last point is worth a second glance because it appears to contradict the truism, "Think outside the box." You can do both: work within a frame AND think outside the box. For example, imagine you have been tasked to come up with a creative restaurant concept. You suggest a restaurant where the chef assists patrons in coming up with new dishes, and then demonstrates their preparation before everyone tucks in to enjoy their co-creations. That's outside the box, but still within the frame.

On the other hand, when people step outside the frame (the boss) it is often unproductive. We ran a workshop at a college in California where the students were asked to design a new way of presenting menus to patrons. One student team constructed an e-menu available at each table that provided nutritional information along with crowd-sourced suggestions from other patrons to suggest sides, drinks, appetizers, and desserts. It was an excellent example of inside-the-frame but outside-the-box thinking. An exceptionally smart, charismatic, and out-of-the-box thinker, however, dominated another team. She convinced her teammates to expand the frame and construct an entirely new type of restaurant. Sadly this creativity produced an unworkable idea that fell flat and didn't meet the objectives of the activity.

When the leader sets the frame, the followers should endeavor to work within it. Only after sufficient experience and credibility is gained, is it advisable to step outside the frame.

> Framing is about building optimal conditions for success.
> Creating within the frame is about taking informed initiative.

The Beatles are an excellent example of this. They totally understood the rules of commercial radio and making hits – essentially the frame needed to be successful. Check out an early Beatles record such as "Please Please Me" from 1963; hit songs like this are all three minutes or less as suited commercial radio at the time, highly melodic, repetitious, and easy to learn. These rules facilitated hit-making. Many albums later, they had enough credibility and experience to break the rules and alter the frame forever. In *Sgt. Pepper's Lonely Hearts Club Band*, songs ran four minutes, five minutes, or more; tempos changed from the 4/4 beat of early rock-and-roll; new instruments were used; the whole album was put together as a unified concept; and songs were reprised.

It works like this in organizations too. You need to build credibility and work effectively within the frame before you can attempt to change or alter it.

Down with the Establishment!

Marc learned about the problem of having too little structure at a very early age. He was born in London, England, to Drs. Harry and Charlotte Hurwitz. That's where his parents met, back in the fifties at Birkbeck, a college of the University of London. His father was a psychology professor teaching adults and his lab even hosted the Queen Mother (apparently they built a new water closet – British for toilet – just for her visit to the college!). Marc's mother was a student at the time and, later on, a child psychologist.

In addition to being psychologists, both his parents were bohemians – think of that as pre-sixties hippies. So, not only did they love experimentation, they also believed in imposing few conventions and rules. As a consequence, from the tender age of three, Marc was given no rules to follow by his parents. Child psychology at the time said that children needed rules (still true today), and that they can't create their own rules to follow. But that's exactly what Marc did. Much to the surprise of his parents, he established his own bedtime, what was appropriate to eat, and how to behave around others. Essentially he took the lead in building a frame so that he could create and operate more effectively within it.

Other Examples of Frames That Stimulate Generative Results

Poetry. Marilisa Sachteleben is an educator, writer on topics from autism to zoology, and a generous poet. She blogs:

> Poetry is one of the most expressive and unfettered forms of creative writing. Writing poetry can be daunting for beginners. I love to empower the inner poet. Here are free printable poetry frames and poem templates to break the creative ice ... For seasoned readers and writers, the poem template simply provides a springboard from which to launch poems.

Haiku, limericks, and sonnets are examples of poetry written in a frame. A strong and tested poetic frame enhances a poet's creativity and productivity. Everyone knows that Shakespeare wrote sonnets, for example, and that his sonnets are considered some of the best poems in the English language. One of the best writers of free verse (poetry without a specific formal structure) was Dylan Thomas. Arguably his finest work, however, veers away from free verse to its opposite: a codified French form called the villanelle. A villanelle is a 19-line poem arranged in stanzas of 3-3-3-3-3-4, with a complex rhyming scheme. The poem Thomas wrote using this form was for his dying father, and the beginning is one of the best-known first stanzas in the English language:

> Do not go gentle into that good night,
> Old age should burn and rave at close of day;
> Rage, rage against the dying of the light.

Wikipedia. Jimmy Wales and Larry Sanger launched Wikipedia in 2001. It is younger than any of our five children! Wikipedia is defined (on Wikipedia) as a "collaboratively edited, multilingual, free Internet encyclopedia supported by the non-profit Wikimedia Foundation. Wikipedia's 30 million articles in 287 languages, including over 4.3 million in the English Wikipedia, are written collaboratively by volunteers around the world. Almost all of its articles can be edited by anyone having access to the site." It is, quite simply, the largest encyclopedia of all time.

Most of us use Wikipedia daily and can't fathom not having it in our lives. Among other things, Wikipedia is a fun example of generative framing.

The leaders of Wikipedia established The 5 Pillars frame for contributors. Everyone is invited to create within this frame:

1. Wikipedia is an online encyclopedia.
2. Wikipedia is written from a neutral point of view.
3. Wikipedia is free content that anyone can edit, use, modify, and distribute.
4. Editors should interact with each other in a respectful and civil manner.
5. Wikipedia does not have firm rules.

Creating the Frame

We have asked many friends, clients, and workshop participants: "What are all the activities that outstanding leaders do?" We then ask the same people, "What are all the activities that outstanding followers do?" The answers typically fit handily into the rubric of framing and creating.

In an organizational context, framing is about building optimum conditions for success.

First, **define success:**

✓ Create a vision and purpose.
✓ Clarify objectives and expectations.
✓ Communicate constraints and appropriate risks.

Then, **build optimum conditions:**

✓ Gather appropriate resources.
✓ Support the use of good processes.
✓ Eliminate barriers to progress and reduce ambiguity.

✓ Encourage freedom to initiate and create while balancing synergy and productivity.

What Are All the Ways I Can Contribute within the Frame?

In our followership role, frames help us think generatively: a new initiative = new frame = new opportunities.

Creating within the frame is about taking informed initiative.

First, **get informed**:

✓ Probe to understand the frame.
✓ Clarify expectations, relative priorities, what success looks like, timing, and other resource investments.

Then, **take initiative**:

✓ Look for all the ways to add value and contribute.
✓ Power up ideas and bring forward new ones.
✓ Provide useful decision support.

Don't assume each frame is the same as the last one even if the project is the same. For example, if you have a new boss, she is likely to create new frames even when the situation hasn't changed or use the old frame but mean different things by it. Problems occur when a new leader isn't explicit about the frame and their team members don't probe to see what has changed. Both parties get stuck in assuming that the old patterns each is bringing to the table continue to apply.

In your followership role, don't limit yourself to what you have done in the past, or even what your job description says. Frames are fluid. They invite questions such as: What is needed *now*? What engages and excites you? What opportunities can you spot? What opportunities are there to try new things? Be careful to ensure that the choices you make are appropriate to the role you are taking in that circumstance and that there is an appropriate level of trust between you and your boss. Sometimes it is also important to take the initiative to bring forward work that is causing you problems or stress. Perhaps it was a stretch assignment that you thought you could handle; but, now that you are in deep, you need more support.

A Useful Frame: Scouting and Settling

Scouting and Settling (Tool 5.1) is a useful frame and terminology that helps get people onto the same page and bring things into focus. We refer and build on it in Chapter 9: Decision Partnering Skills.

When you go on an expedition, it generally has one of two purposes. The first is to seek out new territory – think *Star Trek*, *"To boldly go where no one has gone before."* In a scouting mission, the scouts (a followership role) have a lot of autonomy to determine direction, freedom to use resources, and a loose frame that allows for flexibility of action. The role of leadership is to remove barriers, give broad directional guidance, and provide inspiration.

Scouting missions often precede the second type of expedition, settling, by which we mean going somewhere to put down roots, *"To inhabit new worlds and star systems."* Whereas scouting is broad and expansive, settling is narrow and goal driven – there is a definite accomplishment or objective to be met. Leadership, therefore, has to be more directive, the frame tighter, and communication more frequent. The followership role in a settling mission is to keep the focus on the objective and move toward it.

Many projects and decision processes start with a scouting mission – what are all the possibilities? – and end with a settling mission on one of the directions discovered – how do we get there as a group?

Tool 5.1 details the differences between scouting and settling from a leadership and followership perspective. It is a useful way to frame projects but we have used it in many other circumstances, too. It builds on best practice management advice such as "Modeling the Way" by Kouzes and Posner in their leadership model. Modeling the way is appropriate when you are settling because the leadership job is to stand at the front of the caravan and guide everyone to a common destination. However, in a scouting mission, it is the followership role to be out front (and often out of sight) exploring! There is no sure destination and different scouts should be going in different directions. The leadership role is to point out all the possible ways and be open to the possibility that there are new directions to explore.

!FliPtips! Tool 5.1 Scouting and Settling

To use the table, start by identifying whether you are on a scouting or settling mission. If you are in a leadership role, articulate the distinction to your team. Use the top-left quadrant in the chart as a checklist for scouting missions and the bottom-left as a checklist for settling missions. Use the right-hand boxes as a mentoring and coaching tool.

    If you are in a followership role, confirm whether it is a scouting or settling mission. Then use the applicable right-hand box as a checklist: What are you doing well? What could you do more of? Less of? And, while coaching is often thought of as a leadership responsibility, if you spot something the leader of the expedition could do differently, talk with her about it.

	Leadership: Framing	Followership: Creating
Scouting	Point the way Gather suitable resources Identify the territory Understand & mitigate risk Encourage quantity & diversity of information Value & use all contributions Show commitment to the mission	Understand what you are looking for Know exactly how much time you have Scout out new information, insights, & options Return with useful decision support Build on & value the ideas of others Collaborate with other scouts Be self-reliant & engaged
Settling	Lead & model the way Gather suitable resources Set direction Communicate constraints & acceptable risks Facilitate mission with good processes & tools Set optimistic but reasonable goals Co-create the vision & inspire purpose Eliminate barriers to progress Reduce ambiguity	Probe to clarify the frame, not change it Confirm priorities & time investments Advocate the new direction Anticipate what needs to get done Be resilient to setbacks & plan for roadblocks Power up ideas within the frame Help to generate & weigh alternatives Report on obstacles & suggest remedies Ask, "What are all the ways I can add value?"

Principle #2 Summary

Partnerships become generative when specific advice – leadership is about delegation and followership is about following orders – is supplanted with expansive thinking around framing and creating.

✓ Leadership is setting a frame that builds optimum conditions for success and peak performance.
✓ Followership is about understanding the frame and maximizing contributions within it.
✓ Both roles emphasize accountability, action orientation, and adaptability.

CHAPTER 6

Principle 3: Lean In to Build Connection

Partnerships need leadership & followership: they are equal, dynamic and different.

Leadership is setting the frame. Followership is creating within it.

Lean in to build connection.

Value the positive, and build on it.

Have deeply shared goals.

Figure 6.1

We lived for many years in the city of Waterloo, Ontario. You might not have heard of Waterloo, but it boasts one of the best universities for engineering, computer programming, and mathematics in the world. Google and Microsoft are just two of the many high-tech companies located in the Waterloo region to take advantage of the talent coming from the University of Waterloo. It also happens to be where Mike Lazaridis, the engineer who built the first smartphone, the BlackBerry, went to school.

Eight years after Lazaridis founded BlackBerry, the other pillar in the BlackBerry story joined the company, Jim Balsillie. Together, as pioneers of wireless Internet and the smartphone, they built BlackBerry into a world brand. In this case, it really was together. Not only were they co-chairs of BlackBerry – it was literally a company with two heads pointing in one direction – but they also shared an office for many years.

More and more BlackBerry buildings sprung up around Waterloo, and their campus eventually sprawled over the entire city. To manage this enormous growth, Lazaridis and Balsillie moved into offices over 10 minutes away. It is far more challenging to maintain a healthy connection – to lean in – when partners aren't co-located. The result was unfortunate but predictable: what started out as a shared vision fragmented into competing directions.

Was this the only reason BlackBerry lost its dominance in the market? Probably not, although it is telling that another high-functioning partnership – Steve Jobs and Tim Cook at Apple – was the force that brought down the BlackBerry partnership.

Our Salsa Dancing Project – Part 2 – About the Generative Point

Jeff, our salsa dancing instructor, told us, "The key to a great partnership is having a great connection. I'm not talking about chemistry, I'm talking about technique." He said it was important for both of us to "lean in" just so. This meant that we each needed to shift our weight slightly forward, into our partner, and apply a bit of pressure. Too little pressure and we'd lose connection. Too much and we'd restrict movement. We needed to aim to share the weight just right.

This is the inspiration for the name of Principle 3 – Lean In to Build Connection.

Sheryl Sandberg, the chief operating officer of Facebook, popularized the phrase "lean in" in 2013 with her runaway best-selling book *Lean In: Women, Work, and the Will to Lead*. She uses the phrase to encourage women to lean in to their career and not shy away from their ambitions. While we acknowledge that our use of the phrase differs, we have decided not to change the terminology in our model. Our rationale is:

- While we use the phrase differently, it isn't different enough to be confusing or incompatible: lean in to your ambition AND lean in with your partners.
- It's a kinesthetic representation that is helpful for remembering and training.

This principle reminds us how much we benefit in both our leadership and followership roles from staying connected and being on our partner's wavelength. Doing so is effortful; it takes deliberation to strike the right balance of connectedness, and it requires ongoing exertion to maintain it. This optimal point of connectedness is what we call the *generative point*.

Of course, it is essential that **both** partners lean in to keep the connection; otherwise someone is likely to fall over!

As a leader, when you don't lean in with your team, what happens? They don't get to know you, they don't figure out what you need, they aren't on your wavelength, and you are extremely difficult to follow. As a follower, when you don't lean in your leader doesn't get to know you, they don't know how to support you, and they have no idea what's going on with your work. Without some pressure – good pressure of the rousing, reassuring, and reinforcing kind – it is hard to stay connected.

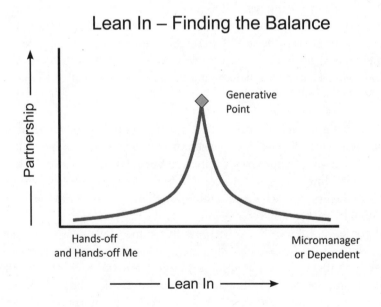

Figure 6.2 Finding the generative point with a partner

The Lean-In Curve (figure 6.2) shows the point between the two extremes of no pressure and too much pressure, where you get optimal sharing. The generative point is the level of understanding, connection, communication, and trust that creates optimal partnerships and enables *co-flow*.

The generative point is unique to each partnership and can even vary by situation or environment. However, you can count on the fact that the extremes rarely put you in good stead.

From One Extreme: Hands Off, Buster!

A hands-off approach to leadership inevitably leads to a lack of connection and the perception of questionable commitment. Experienced staff may think they want it, some will even *say* they want it, but it doesn't work. So many times we've heard people bemoan their boss then finish with a shrug and this comment: "At least he leaves me alone ..."

Tim Hurson – best-selling author, speaker, and creativity guru – recounted this telling experience to us.

> I was hired by a multi-national tech firm to help onboard a new senior vice president by facilitating a team-learning event. At the beginning of the daylong session, the new VP spoke about his commitment to his new role, and to helping his people become a truly creative and collaborative team. He then said, "Good luck with the day. I'll see you all at 5 pm." And off he went.

We had a similar experience with a client. The president hired us to hone the partnership skills of his senior management team. He stated to all that it was an important initiative but then didn't attend a single session himself, despite our continued asking. His people saw right through the lip service he'd paid (along with the dollars), and the interpersonal training fell flat as a result.

When an employee does the same thing and stays away from her boss, the results are equally damaging. Consider Mary Anne, a seasoned volunteer coordinator for a large international not-for-profit, who had applied for a position in HR as an international recruiter. Human Resources contacted Mary Anne and set up an interview between her and the VP of Global Recruitment. The interview started well. Mary Anne felt comfortable and self-assured. She was asked the standard questions: Why did you apply for the position? What key skills and qualities will you bring to the job? Why should I hire you?

Then, the VP asked, "Describe your ideal boss." Mary Anne replied, "Well, I really don't need a boss who micromanages me as I am very responsible and reliable. My ideal boss would understand that I like to work independently and that I can be counted on to get the job done. I can manage myself." We know what happened because Mary Anne contacted us for coaching shortly after finding out she didn't get the job.

We have heard the reasons for this attitude before: "I'm very independent," or "I know my job better than my boss," or even "I am most effective when I'm left alone." The truth is this isn't partnership thinking or expert partnering skill.

Someone who "manages" himself or herself isn't a partner. Being **easy to manage** is different from managing yourself.

Worst of all, when a staff member has a hands-off-me attitude, the leader doesn't feel supported, listened to, updated, or in sync. Any time or effort saved this way by the follower is more than offset by the extra time and effort her boss has to put in in probing for information and coordinating tasks.

But what if your leader is ineffective or you don't like her? It's tough. We know! But it's life. It happens. Feeling this way about your boss is, in fact, an alarm bell to redouble your efforts by working twice as hard at leaning in! Check out this sage advice by John C. Maxwell in his book *The 360° Leader*:

The first reaction to working for an ineffective leader is often to withdraw from him or her and build relational barriers. Fight that urge. If you make your leader your adversary, you will create a no-win situation. Instead, build a relational bridge. Try to get to know him, find common ground, and build a solid professional relationship. And in that process, reaffirm your commitment to the mission of the organization. Doing those things will put you on the same team. (pp. 40–41)

To the Other: In Your Face!

Too much leaning, think of it as *leaning on,* by a leader is micromanaging. Micromanaging is stifling. It restricts opportunities and consumes all the available energy in a partnership. The result is a drop in effectiveness and overall work satisfaction for both parties. Micromanaging can be a personal style; but, more often, it is an overreaction to a team member who is hands-off and not communicating sufficiently.

The dependent follower – the person who needs help to do everything and who needs your constant attention – is the flip side of the micromanaging boss. He sucks up management time and attention. We have a friend with over 30 direct reports. Yes, that's far too many but it happened because the firm was in rapid growth mode. Imagine if even one of those 30 people had dependent behaviors. Where would our friend have found time to work with his other 29 staff members?

More on Project Oxygen

In Chapter 3: "A New Kind of Leadership," we introduced Google's Project Oxygen, which was a response to employees' dissatisfaction with some managers throughout the company. The project involved the People Analytics department who mined all their HR data – tens of thousands of data points – to find out what made a good manager. They analyzed performance reviews, feedback surveys, and nominations for top-manager awards. They correlated phrases, words, praise, and complaints.

The result was a ranking of the manager behaviors most prized by employees and most causally related to success. In order of importance the behaviors were:

1. **Be a good coach.**
2. **Empower your team and don't micromanage.**
3. **Express interest in team members' success and personal well-being.**
4. Don't be a sissy. Be productive and results oriented.
5. **Be a good communicator and listen to your team.**
6. **Help your employees with career development.**
7. Have a clear vision and strategy for the team.
8. Have key technical skills so you can help advise the team.

Here's what Laszlo Bock, VP of People Operations, said about the results:

> In the Google context, we'd always believed that to be a manager, particularly on the engineering side, you needed to be as deep or deeper a technical expert than the people who work for you. It turns out that that's absolutely the least important thing. It's important, but pales in comparison. Much more important is just making that connection and being accessible.[1]

This is a fascinating list. You may think, "But these are all basics." Yes! And it shows how important it is to get the basics right. No amount of pay, progressive HR policies, or cool toys in the break room will compensate for not getting the basics of leadership right. Google took this information and rebuilt its training and coaching programs. The effort paid off quickly. "We were able to have a statistically significant improvement in manager quality for 75 percent of our worst-performing managers," said Mr. Bock.

What else do these results indicate? Technical skills are still important but less so than seven other managerial skills. These seven are people focused and include coaching, communicating, and relationship building. All the items we've bolded relate to Principle 3: Lean In to Build Connection. Item 4 in the list above will be discussed in Principle 4: Value the Positive and Build on it. Item 7 in the list above was touched on in Principle 2: Framing and Creating and will be again in Chapter 13: Performance Partnering Skills.

We are undoubtedly impressed with Google's improved leadership though we can't help but think they only uncovered half the problem. How much **more** potential could be developed by including good followership in the Google context?

Finding Your Generative Point
A few points to consider:

- Everyone has a leadership preference *between* the two extremes: hands-off and micromanager.
- Everyone has a followership preference *between* the two extremes: hands-off me and dependent.
- It is rare that both people in a partnership will have the exact same preferences and needs.

For example, Sam worked for a boss with a tendency toward micromanaging – she wasn't a micromanager, just past the middle of the continuum – whereas Sam, in her followership role, was more inclined to a hands-off-me approach. Was her boss too much of a micromanager? Was Sam too standoffish? Both felt underwhelmed with the partnership. The bigger job was Sam's in her followership role. It may sound surprising that the follower should take more accountability especially given the earlier assertion that the roles are equal, but the math tells the story. It is easier to adapt to one person (as the follower has to do) than make multiple adaptations to many people (as a leader would have to do). Both people have to change, but more of the onus falls on the shoulders of the follower. Sam adapted, and the relationship flourished as a result.

Tool 6.1, The Partnership Checkup, is a useful tool for identifying issues with Leaning In.

!FliPtips! Tool 6.1 Do a Partnership Checkup with the Lean-In Curve

Write down all your direct reports, your boss, your boss's boss, key peers/colleagues, key clients and anyone else you consider vital to your success at work. Think about who your boss would solicit feedback from if she was engaging a 360° assessment on your behalf.

Next, plot each of them on the Lean-In Curve based on your perspective of where it feels like your partnership is at.

For the partnerships farther from the Generative Point, ask yourself:

- What can I do?
- Where is there opportunity to improve this partnership?
- In what ways can I make this partnership more positive, more productive, more creative, more connected, more generative?
- What are this person's preferences and how are they being taken into account?
- What will my action steps be?

Next, take a look specifically at your direct reports and team members, ask yourself:

- Are there large differences in preferences between the people on my team?
- Are these differences causing friction on the team?
- To what extent can I accommodate the differences?
- To what extent will I need them to adapt more?
- Do I currently lean in more with some people than with others?

Consider discussing these points openly with each of your partners and establishing a partnership agreement. Strive for mutual benefit within the partnership and a sense of reciprocity. Notice that, as you move away from the generative point, partnership effectiveness drops off quickly. It can feel like you and your partner are completely out of step even if the real gap is small. Sometimes minor adjustments by both people can make a big difference. At other times the gap is large; it can feel like you haven't made any progress even though both are trying. There is no magic formula. Realizing that there is a gap is the first step.

Principle #3 Summary

Partnerships become generative when both partners *lean in to build connection* and continually work to develop the essential ingredients of mutual understanding, communication, trust, and support.

- ✓ Partners must apply a bit of good pressure in the partnership to avoid falling over! Too little pressure and you lose the connection. Too much pressure and movement is restricted.
- ✓ There is a balance point or optimal point of connectedness that we call the generative point, and it differs with every partnership.

On either side of the generative point are two extremes, a hands-off approach and a leaning on or micromanaging approach. Neither proves effective.

CHAPTER 7

Principle 4: Value the Positive, and Build on It

Partnerships need leadership & followership: they are equal, dynamic and different.

Leadership is setting the frame. Followership is creating within it.

Lean in to build connection.

Value the positive, and build on it.

Have deeply shared goals.

Figure 7.1

We participated in a fun workshop with Jennifer Spear, a "recovering corporate executive" and graduate of the Improv Program at Second City. Now in her own practice, Clean Slate Strategies, she uses improv to help organizations learn to solve problems more creatively. During her workshop we whet our chops at various theater games while Jennifer taught us some of the basics of improvisational acting.

And here are the rules we took away:

1. **Accept what you are given**. For example, if someone *throws* a line at you such as, "Look at that briefcase lying on the ground over there," you shouldn't respond with, "That's not a briefcase, that's a bomb!" Instead, *catch* it by opening up the (imaginary) briefcase and being surprised by what you find inside. That's the spirit of

this "Rule of Agreement" – respect what your partner has created and work with him to make it the best of all possible ideas.

2. **Say "Yes. And …"** After you have accepted what you are given, build on it. Make the idea better. More entertaining. More unusual. In organizations this might mean making a process more innovative, more foolproof, or more doable.

3. **Sometimes you need to lead. Sometimes you need to follow and, sometimes, you just need to be a singing tree.** It would be rare for most of us to end up as a singing tree, as happened to Jennifer in a skit where she played this wooden role in a musical forest. We are regularly offered situations that require us to play unexpected roles. Put your best foot forward even if it doesn't seem particularly important or glamorous at the time. It builds trust and often is exactly what the scene needs!

4. **Don't pimp your partner.** Don't set your partner up to fail. Saying, "Jane stands on her head at the end of every sentence," might seem entertaining until you are on the receiving end of one of those bullets. Put yourself in your partner's shoes and give him opportunities to shine, not fail.

5. **Keep track of what's happening on stage.** Always listen and be on your toes. Think, "How can I support my partner?" or, better yet, "What are all the ways that I can support my partner?"

6. **Help create the scene; don't just be part of it.** Initiate and contribute generously. Offer novel content to help define a situation rather than waiting and letting your partner(s) do all the work.

These six rules are the essence of Principle 4. They remind us when working with others to first value the positive, and build on it. These are two distinct but interrelated ideas – value, then build – and one without the other isn't nearly as powerful or generative.

But Doesn't Negativity Actually Work? No! (see what we mean)
We all know what it feels like to be constantly criticized. It is debilitating. It quashes creativity, enthusiasm, and motivation to keep doing what we are doing. Yet many people still believe that negativity works.

We were being given a tour of our new condo apartment while it was still under construction so we were suited up in steel-toed boots and hardhats. Ronald, a young employee of the condo developer, showed us around. When we got on the elevator after touring the condo, the site manager was there. He looked at Ronald and started berating him, "Why wasn't I told that you were bringing people up here? You can't bring someone up without telling me even if it is booked on the calendar," and so on. It was a rather standard, negative approach to "improving" Ronald's performance. Was it more effective than a positive approach? We may never know for sure but all the evidence says it isn't and as customers, we were stunned by the display.

This sort of behavior by managers is all too common and here is one reason why.

How often have you seen someone do poorly, get resoundingly criticized for his performance, and then improve shortly afterwards? Or the reverse: someone does well, gets praised for his efforts, and then doesn't do as well the next time?

Does this mean that negativity is an effective way to manage? No. It doesn't. Rather, it is an example of a perceptual error known as regression to the mean.[1] To get a sense of this error, do the following experiment: get out a six-sided die and "try" to roll high numbers. There are only two rules to the game:

Rule 1: Whenever you roll a "1,"criticize the die for its bad performance. Shout at it!

Rule 2: Whenever you roll a "6," praise the die. It did a good job and deserves your support!

What happened? When you criticized the die's performance, was the next roll usually better? When you praised the die's performance, was it usually worse the next time? Of course, the reason for the change in performance of the subsequent roll was that the die listened to you. Praise made it worse, and criticism made it better.

Wait a minute, that's dumb. Dice don't think!

All kidding aside, the real-life version of the dice experiment is the basis for a lot of superstitious behavior. At gaming tables people blow on dice, shake them a certain way every time, have good luck charms, or perform all sorts of other pre-rolling rituals. Why? Because at one time, during a run of bad results, they tried something different and their results improved.

The real reason praise appears to fail and criticism appears to work is that when we praise *top* performance, odds are the next performance won't be as strong regardless of what we did. Exceptional events are just that – they don't happen often, including unusually good performance. When we criticize poor performance, odds are the next time it won't be as bad irrespective of our reaction to it. Ascribing the outcomes to praise or blame is a wrong cause-effect relationship, but one that is easy to make.

The fact is, when you do experiments ensuring that regression to the mean and other biases are eliminated, praise and positivity improve performance whereas negativity and criticism don't. In fact, every measurable aspect of performance gets better with positive feedback.[2]

This is not only true when you are in a leadership role. Negativity from a follower reduces the performance of her boss and teammates, as well as damaging personal effectiveness. Been Kim and Cynthia Rudin of MIT analyzed data from 108,947 separate dialogues recorded during the course of 95 meetings. They found that:

> Judging from these and similar dialogue segments … framing a suggestion as an agreement with a previous suggestion increases its chances of being accepted. That is, if the idea comes across as if it were in line with previous thoughts by others, the suggestion has a higher chance of being accepted. This applies either when attributing the full idea to others, or just the line of thought. (Kim & Rudin, 2014, pp. 18–19)

Ethan Burris investigated how managers responded to employees based on how the employee communicated an idea, what is known as "voice."[3] Employees who used a challenging voice were given lower performance ratings, thought to be less loyal, and had their suggestions adopted less often than staff who had a supportive voice. In other words, challenge led to a reduction in effectiveness and personal success.

Does that mean you should never challenge the boss? We think the answer is no for three reasons.

1. First, most challenges can be reframed supportively. Consider the first two rules of improv: "Accept what you are given," and "Say yes. And." If your leader proposes an incremental change you have

concerns with, first position your response as acceptance of what is being suggested, then build on it with your refinements and ideas. This is a shift in voice from challenging to positive, helpful support. In addition, pay attention to timing. Untimely suggestions can be particularly irritating. Consider whether the train has already left the track. If you aren't sure, ask, "Is now the time to voice concerns?," or "Would ideas that build on this be welcome at this time?"

2. Second, as we will see for feedback in general, there is a ratio of positive to critical feedback that is most effective. While positive feedback should be more frequent, if it is never tempered by critique it can be interpreted as suck-up behavior, or even the sign of weak character.

3. Finally, there are times when challenge is essential. If the airplane is about to fly into a mountain, or the organization is about to do something that is illegal, or your moral/ethical health is at stake, then you must challenge.

First, Value the Positive

While walking around the university where Marc worked, we noticed unusual posters tacked to the bulletin boards in the hallways of the buildings. It was the kind of poster you often see on campuses, with tear-offs on the bottom advertising furniture for sale, someone looking for roommates, or an upcoming concert. This one, though, was different. Instead of an advertisement, each tear-off piece had a simple message written on it:

Take a smile!

Most of the tear-offs were gone. This fun project is called The Smile Epidemic (http://www.thesmileepidemic.com).

A few years ago we met Jim Moss, the founder of The Smile Epidemic by Plasticity Labs. Jim was a former elite athlete – one of the best lacrosse players in the world and a star in the NLL (National Lacrosse League). In 2009, with a young son at home and his wife pregnant with their second child, Jim felt some tingling in his hands and feet. Over the next two days his condition worsened; he became unable to use his legs and had lost feeling in his hands. Jim found himself confined to a bed in the hospital. The doctors said he might never walk again and a nurse even suggested he get used to it as this could last a lifetime. Soon after, however, a night-shift nurse who was helping Jim get to the bathroom said, "Don't you worry about it, sweetheart. You'll be back on your feet in no time!" Her positive attitude boosted Jim's spirits incredibly, helped him out of his funk and, six weeks later, in part due to a newly found positive attitude, he was at home rehabilitating the use of his limbs and walking with the help of canes.

This life-altering experience led Jim in a new direction: he began The Smile Epidemic. Its mission is to make people and organizations more positive. Being positive may sound fuzzy and unimportant, but positive teamwork, positive work relationships, and positive leadership have been shown to improve organizational outcomes.[4] It increases innovation, enhances work coordination, improves performance at every level, reduces turnover, and supports individual reliance. It can have a huge impact on health. And, it is contagious – the more positive you are, the more positive your coworkers will be regardless of whether the person is your boss, a peer, or one of your staff. This is called upstream reciprocity.[5]

Positive teamwork, positive work relationships, and positive leadership have been shown to improve just about every organizational outcome imaginable.

A Strength-Based Approach

Gallup scientists have uncovered evidence that people respond more positively when they are given the opportunity to play to their strengths rather than focusing on their shortcomings. For example, people who can focus on their strengths daily are six times as likely to be engaged in their job, have 12.5% greater productivity, and are more than three times as likely to report having an excellent quality of life.[6]

Dr. Greg Evans is the founder of the Happiness Enhancement Group in Toronto. He says, "People are happier when they are largely playing to their strengths rather than focused on getting rid of their weaknesses. We can even look at fMRIs (brain scans) and tell: happiness looks different."

Gallup's research[7] suggests that having a manager who regularly focuses on strengths can make a dramatic difference. Looking at employees who were deemed negative or actively disengaged, they discovered that it was strongly associated with managers who either ignored their staff or focused on their weaknesses.

Table 7.1 Results of Gallup research on the impact of managerial focus on employee engagement

If your manager primarily	The chance of being actively disengaged is:
Ignores you	40%
Focuses on your weaknesses	22%
Focuses on your strengths	1%

The Pygmalion Effect

Marc often remarks that Sam is a strong people leader to which she responds with, "Thank you, but I've always been fortunate and had a fantastic team." That type of response is characteristic of leaders who genuinely believe they have great people working for them. What is the result of this attitude? When leaders have such a deep belief in the abilities of their team, their people rise up to meet those beliefs. They end up being much better than they otherwise would. This is called the Pygmalion Effect.

In an important experiment by Rosenthal and Jacobson (1968), researchers told teachers that some of their students were "spurters" and could be expected to make significant gains during the year. By the end of the year, the students identified as spurters had a measurable increase in their IQ.

In other research, this time a meta-analytic review, Bruce Avolio and his colleagues (2009) found that one leadership training technique outperformed all others. This technique produced the best affective, cognitive, and behavioral outcomes in staff. If you guessed that it was the Pygmalion Effect, you would be right. Leaders were given evidence that their staff were better than they initially thought; in other words, the Pygmalion Effect was evoked by transforming the beliefs of the leader. The performance results based on this simple intervention turned out to be greater than any other training method studied including sessions on transformational leadership, authentic leadership, servant-leadership, or situational leadership. When leaders believe and behave like they have their A-team it translates to more engagement and productivity than anything else. The "we can do it" influence we are talking about is not mindless cheerleading but, rather, a key that unlocks personal and partnership potential.

The best leadership training of all is getting leaders to genuinely believe they have great staff.

We've rarely encountered more exemplary Pygmalion leadership than the Seth family's. This family's history as restaurateurs began when their father and mother, Deepak and Punam Seth, immigrated in the 1960s from India to Canada. They lived in a small basement apartment below a pizza restaurant, where they dined as often as slim pocketbooks allowed. Those pizza dinners provided much more than simply the best pizza they'd ever had. They provided a thoroughly nourishing experience – comforting, heartening, and inspiring. Eventually, after a lot of hard work and years of saving, Deepak and Punam bought their first restaurant, a Tim Hortons coffee shop (arguably Canada's most iconic brand),[8] and then another, and another, and another. The operation is now run by the next generation of Seths: the eldest son Amit, wife Rachana, and younger brother Anik. They have rapidly become a highly successful Tim Hortons franchisee.

Amit and Anik Seth are CPAs by training, but rather unusual ones. In the hypercompetitive industry of quick service restaurants, they believe that nothing trumps customer service. The family also believes that nothing leads to an awesome guest experience more than employee engagement and development. Not only do they believe it, they measure and reward it, just as accountants are trained to do.

We were invited to the annual employee recognition evening for Seth Hospitality Services. It was a gala event for their more than 400 team members. The Seths handed out awards for length of service, best service scores, top Sethpitality, best team manager, going above-and-beyond on a key project, being a rock star at work, and more. Positive contributions were recognized in countless unique, heart-warming, and innovative ways. The Seth family put tons of effort into planning the event. Even Punam and Rachana stayed up all night to make fresh Cold Stone ice cream in custom flavors – chai and cardamom – for everyone at the feast. If there were Olympic medals given for employee appreciation, this would have won the gold.

The Seth family hires all their restaurant managers from within. These are people who start off working at Tim Hortons for relatively low wages, many with little formal education. Nevertheless, the Seth family have faith that their managers can take each and every restaurant to top-of-class levels of guest service, employee loyalty, revenue, and profitability. It works. Their restaurants significantly outperform the average! For example, their director, Rosy Pal, who has been with the company 17 years, started as a part-time cake decorator, and now oversees the entire group of management and operations.

At the gala, the Seth family celebrated all their staff's successes and, in grand value-the-positive-and-build-on-it tradition, Amit emphasized, "Now that we're doing all these amazing things, let's do even more together next year!"

Then, Build on It

Senior engineers at one of the world's most prominent theme parks were presenting a proposal to the executive VP of customer experience. It was for a new ride they had been working on for some time. Afterwards, the executive responded with kudos and specific remarks about what he especially liked about the ride. Once the engineers felt comfortable that they'd succeeded and met expectations, the executive said, "Now, pretend you had more time and more money to take this to the next level. What would you do next? Where would you take it? What would make it even better?"

The park executive used Principle 4 well. First, he provided positive feedback. Next, he asked the engineers to build on it.

In this case, the engineers did a solid job. But what if they hadn't? What if the design the engineers had come back with wasn't acceptable? There are many techniques for dealing with this situation in a positive way. For example, if the ride wasn't exciting enough, the VP could have asked the engineers, "What are all the ways to make it more exciting?" He also could have asked what the engineers personally found exciting in a ride or what made other rides popular, or even asked them to collect customer feedback on the proposed ride.

When something needs improving, criticizing the faults rarely helps. For example, imagine you are struggling to get your latest smartphone to work. So you ask a teenager to help. That help often begins with something to the effect of, "OMG, you've done it all wrong!" Then, a few frustrating seconds later, she takes the phone from your hands, does some inscrutable things, and hands it back with a, "There you go. All fixed!" in a self-satisfied way. How does that make you feel? Mostly like you don't want to ask her the next time a problem arises. Teenagers have yet to learn that this is a terrible approach. Competent coaches and consultants don't do that and neither should people in a leadership or a followership role. With the wisdom of practice there is a better way.

We aren't suggesting, however, that you should never criticize. Because the critical approach can be so disengaging, it is easy to believe critique of any sort is wrong. That's not what we are suggesting.

We did some work with a research initiative called REAP (Research Entrepreneurs Accelerating Prosperity) at the University of Waterloo. REAP is a program to bring academic and private sector partners together to explore new technologies and foster entrepreneurship in undergraduates. We were brought in to do some upfront training, be available for mentoring on an as-needed basis, and conduct interviews at the end of the term to identify what was working and what could be improved upon from the student's perspective. First of all, consider that each student was handpicked for her assignment; paid handsomely; received specialized training; had mentors who were some of the most successful and talented local entrepreneurs; was given a beautiful technologically advanced "playroom" to experiment in and the program was spearheaded by two of the most caring, conscientious, passionate professors we've ever encountered, Drs. Jill and David Goodwin. What could the students possibly be looking for improvements on, you ask? Well, there were certainly a lot of positive comments about the program from the students. but a fair number also admitted that they could have achieved more if they were encouraged to work even harder, continuously improve, push the envelope more, and stretch for a higher bar.

We all need constructive criticism to improve. In fact, the ideal ratio of encouragement to critical feedback is about 4:1.[9] The combined approach of valuing the positive then building on it produces higher performance, greater learning and development, and contributes to happiness and well-being.

The right ratio of encouragement to constructive criticism is about 4:1.

Implementing positivity while still building and providing constructive criticism takes skill and practice. For instance, how do you:

- Help someone develop without focusing on what they did wrong?
- Ignore weaknesses?
- Prevent serious errors?
- Give feedback in a way that gets results?

A tool that can positively help is PIP, which stands for Positives, Improvements and Plans (see Tool 7.1). Note that the PIP approach differs considerably from the "hamburger method" of feedback that begins with a compliment (fluffy bun), proceeds with criticism (the meat), and ends with another (fluffy bun) compliment. A more colorful name for this technique is the "sh%t sandwich" because that's how most of us feel by the end of it.

Whatever you call it, when compliments are only given to soften the blow of criticisms, it doesn't fool anyone. Cynthia Rudin, the MIT researcher we met earlier, notes in her analysis of meetings that[10] "Positive social acts (such as compliments) are almost never advisable if immediately preceding or following negative assessments (criticism)" because "positive social acts can sound disingenuous when accompanying a negative assessment."

A natural tendency to react to and remember negative comments

!fliPtips! Tool 7.1 Positives, Improvements, and Plans

There is a best practice methodology for giving feedback, supporting team development, and even problem solving derived from research in human behavior as well as practical experience on increasing creativity, performance and work satisfaction. We call it Positives, Improvements and Plans or the PIP approach.

1. Point out **positives** first.
   ✓ Consider the positives in terms of the situation, the person, their current development, their capabilities, resources and any potential outcomes.
   ✓ Be specific and ensure the positives relate to the area of needed improvement: "What's good about this is ..."; or "Your strengths in this area are ..."; or "This is good because ..."; or "This helped me learn to ..."
   ✓ Seek agreement on the positives.

2. Generate discussion about **improvements**.
   ✓ Paint a vivid picture of an even better future, "Wouldn't it be lovely if we could ..."
   ✓ Plan for the future by identifying how to get there.
   ✓ Share rationale, "This would be even more valuable if it was ..."
   ✓ Stimulate ideating with generative questions, "What are all the ways we could ..."

3. Develop actionable **plans**.
   ✓ Come up with a plan for progress.
   ✓ Conduct a pre-mortem[11] to identify possible roadblocks and include ways of overcoming roadblocks in the plan.[12]

far more than positive ones is called the automatic vigilance effect. Once someone hears criticism, any words of kindness uttered previously disappear like a puff of smoke; the brain then tunes itself for fight or flight so it fails to register any further praise. This happens to us all the time – we do a training session and get terrific reviews from everyone but one person who writes that it was "a waste of time." Guess what we focus on and remember! It takes a conscious effort to orient back to the positives and look at the situation from a more objective perspective.

PIP reduces this strong emotional reaction by making the positives relevant to the improvements. It provides for feedback that is collaborative, genuine, and actionable, which supports stronger coping behaviors and outcomes.

Mistakes Happen

PIP doesn't point out mistakes and errors except to show where and how improvements are possible. If someone has done something wrong, it is more effective to focus on how to do it right than to launch into criticism on what she did wrong.

Similarly, when someone has a problem to solve, it is better to help her solve it than solve it yourself.

Marshall Goldsmith, in his best seller, *What Got You Here Won't Get You There*, cautions leaders against trying to "add too much value." There is a temptation when someone brings you an issue to come up with a solution. The problem, he says, is that while your input may have improved an idea by 5%, you have reduced commitment by 50% because it becomes your idea, not your staff's.

Leadership is about winning through helping others be their best, not by doing it all yourself.

Principle #4 Summary

Partnerships become generative when both partners value the positive aspects of the partnership while also investing energy and time to build on it and take it to the next level.

- ✓ Humans have natural negativity biases. It's important to fight against the bias by reinforcing positivity, creativity, and well-being instead.
- ✓ When all people get is the positive without encouragement for enhancement, it saps energy and drive.

✓ When all people get is criticism without first valuing the positives, it is debilitating and destroys creativity.
✓ It's the combination of both that stimulates ongoing peak performing.

CHAPTER 8

Principle 5: Have Deeply Shared Goals

Partnerships need leadership & followership: they are equal, dynamic and different.

Leadership is setting the frame. Followership is creating within it.

Lean in to build connection.

Value the positive, and build on it.

Have deeply shared goals.

Figure 8.1

Most of us in organizations already understand the importance of goals and of goal setting. We would like to build on this and emphasize a critical feature of goals that lies at the root of any high-functioning partnership. Specifically, goals must be shared. *Deeply shared.*

Think back to the beginning of this book when we mentioned the enormous successes of The Beatles during their heyday: many hit songs, many lauded albums, many rules broken, many boundaries scrambled. Quite the revolution! Then what happened? Why did they drift apart and ultimately disband? The answer is that their goals were no longer deeply shared.

Early in their careers when they felt down and out, as they toiled night after night to get noticed, they'd have the following exchange:

[John would say] "Where are we going, fellas?" And they'd go, "To the top Johnny!" And I'd say, "Where's that fellas?" and they'd say, "To the toppermost of the poppermost!" and I'd say, "Right!" Then we'd all sort of cheer up.

– John Lennon

But by the late sixties, each Beatle was beginning to move in different musical directions and work on his own projects. George was spending more time on his own music and had become a devotee of Indian culture, mysticism, and Hare Krishna. John was pursuing avant-garde and experimental music, and had become committed to political and peace activism. Ringo was starting to compose more and receive critical acclaim for his acting. Only Paul remained interested in pop music and, frankly, wished to do more of the same. He wanted to *Get Back* while everyone else just wanted to *Let It Be*. They no longer had shared goals, and the group broke apart.

Shared goals drive collaboration rather than competition. They increase teamwork and help ensure that resources are available and pulling in the same direction. It sounds like a simple proposition, but many goals and goal-setting processes miss the mark. It is because goals can easily *appear* shared yet are not.

Shared has three implications:

1. Goals have to be shared *with someone*.
2. Goals have to be shared throughout *teams* and organizations.
3. Finally, *shared goals* are different from *same goals*.

Let's examine each of these perspectives in detail.

Shared with Someone

A personal goal is important – whether a goal of mastery, a level of hoped-for success, a new skill, a significant impact, a preferred level of wealth, or something else. Personal goals drive individual performance. It is hard to imagine a vibrant, competent person who doesn't regularly set and strive for personal goals. But personal goals don't provide the impetus for better partnerships – only for personal action.

Partnerships require commitment, a commitment that comes from wanting to achieve common objectives. Imagine, for example, that during a meeting you and your manager decide you should develop better negotiation skills. The plan the two of you develop includes taking a course in a few months and then gaining additional practical experience, perhaps renegotiating a supplier contract coming up for renewal later in the year. A few months pass. Just before the negotiation course starts, a large new piece of work hits your department. Everyone is working flat out to complete this assignment. What do you think would happen? Would you be asked to cancel the course and make your priority the new assignment? Or, what if, when the supplier contract came up for renewal, a senior manager told your boss that getting the best deal was essential to his performance evaluation this year? Would you still be allowed to conduct the negotiation? Would your boss decide it was too important or sensitive to pass along the opportunity to you?

If you and your boss have a truly shared goal, the answers would be obvious. If it was a priority to your boss that you develop negotiating skills, then you would still get the opportunity. However, if the boss was not committed to the goal, the likelihood of getting sufficient support for you to meet the goal is low.

Some companies take personal goals very seriously and treat them as shared goals. For example, it is well known that Google has a 20% rule: employees are encouraged to take 20% of their time to work on their own projects. It is a strategy to boost innovation adopted from 3M who implemented a 15% rule way back in 1948! We asked a manager at Google what would happen in a situation like the one we just described. He answered this way:

> Let's assume we have a big project launch next Monday. Lots of people have been working for months on it. Now, Joe comes over and tells me that he wants to take some 20% time this week, which means his work on the project won't get done and the launch will be delayed. That's okay. We support that. Joe can take the 20% time.

Google balances long-term goals with short-term goals of expediency. It works because everyone is given the information to make solid choices: choices that align with the needs of the team, the organization, and the person.

Shared throughout the Team and Organization

A few years ago we were brought in to help a cross-functional product team made up of people from the engineering and operations departments of a large electronics conglomerate. The problem they had been wrestling with was the length of time it was taking to bring new products to market. The existing product development (PD) process was averaging two years whereas the market was demanding more like an 18-month turnaround.

When we arrived, the team had already tried many tactics to reduce the length of the PD process – agile teams, streamlined processes, parallel development, innovation training – and some gains had been made but not nearly enough. After extensive discussion with the engineers, it became apparent that, to them, excellence in new products meant the company delivered technological advancements along with new, exciting features. Engineers were rewarded by their peers and in more formal ways such as pay or promotion for producing cutting-edge technology.

Members of the operations team, however, had different goals: excellence meant the ability to ramp up to full production quickly, have a small manufacturing reject rate, and be able to offer extensive warranties.

The PD process map had unfortunately morphed into a product development *cycle*: engineers would send a product prototype to the operations team. The prototype would contain new features and advances in technology, and the operations team would return it with suggestions on what to cut to make it easier to build, more reliably. After many iterations and a lot of frustration, the entire team would ultimately come to an agreement on a final design.

Although both teams had a shared goal of creating innovative, new products, each also had goals specific to their areas. Exposing the goals that weren't shared helped them have a healthy dialogue over ways to trim the PD process. After developing shared goals, new products are now delivered in under 18 months.

Shared, Not Same

Here's a situation that we ran into at a large insurance firm: a business unit IT team was told by their VP to get the work done 10% faster. As a result, the project director of one team assigned each person the *same* goal of completing his or her personal tasks 10% faster.

The IT architect managed to get her design done 10% faster and tossed it over the wall to the developer. The code warrior speeded up his production of code to make the new 10% target and then tossed it over the wall to the quality assurance person. Do you expect that the quality assurance person was also able to do his part 10% faster? No way. Not with hastily written code built on a quickly assembled design. The real result was an overall increase in code production time!

This is the dysfunction a *same* goal can create as opposed to a *shared* goal. Same goals are goals that use the same language and promote similar outcomes as shared goals, but which can be completed without input by the rest of the team. Shared goals have two features that distinguish them from same goals:

1. Goals are not shared if an individual can accomplish them without the partnership.
2. Goals are only shared if they require true interdependence. Sequential interdependence is not enough.[1]

Only by working together toward a *shared* goal could the IT project team have reduced turnaround time by 10%. Doing so might have required quite different approaches to solving the problem such as the architect taking longer in order to build in more opportunities for reusing code, or conducting meetings to include input from the quality assurance person up front.

Generative relationships are built on a foundation of deeply shared goals.

Shared goals are a systems approach to goal setting that naturally encourages collaboration, creates opportunities, and shares accountability.

Personal, Individual, and Team Goals

There is one more point that relates to the discussion of shared goals we have to make; and that is the distinction between personal, individual, and team goals.

Personal goals are not shared with anyone. While they may drive individual excellence, personal goals rarely encourage collaboration and partnerships.

Individual goals are personal goals that require the help of someone else, but may not be completely shared by that other person. For example, a real estate salesperson may set an individual goal to join the Million Dollar sales club. As discussed earlier, that's fine as long as the manager also helps out. A sudden drop in support can readily derail individual goals of this sort.

Only shared team goals reliably stimulate collaboration and build partnerships that are generative. Managers we have worked with tell us that they are worried about introducing shared goals because it can lead to greater shirking, social loafing, and other problems that can arise when team goals replace challenging individual goals. Further, according to a lot of the research into goals, setting challenging individual goals does improve performance.[2]

We have two responses to those concerns. First, individual goals increase individual performance. If that is all you need, then set individual goals. But, a collection of high performers does not necessarily make for a terrific team, and individual goals may not support getting the best results at the team level. Second, individual and team goals can coexist. For example, a team goal relevant to the IT example above could be something like, "Project X needs to be completed 10% faster. Results will be measured on the basis of total project time, as long as cost and quality objectives are also met." A separate, individual goal could be added to this, "You will also be assessed on how well you have contributed to the team's objective of 10% faster delivery. The measure for this will be a peer review of your helpfulness to others in meeting the team's target." Now both types of goals – team and individual – are included in a way that works together, building a platform for success.

While many tools are available for ensuring effective goals setting, the most useful one for building stronger, more collaborative teams is

FliPtips! Tool 8.1 Deeply Shared Goals Audit

A Deeply Shared Goals Audit is a team-based process for making goals more shared. It helps people unpack and articulate ALL their expectations - agendas, aspirations, any project vs. home team priorities – prompting good, open dialogue. Then, teams can share, compare, negotiate and reframe.

First, make a huge chart like the one below on a white or black board or paper. Have **each** team member write down their personal, individual and team goals for a particular project or period on sticky notes, one goal per note. Have everyone share their goals by pairing up or in small groups and working together to place them in one of the categories on the chart: SHARED, SAME, CONFLICTING, UNRELATED based on how they relate to all the other goals presented.

Shared	Same	Conflicting	Unrelated	How might I make it more shared?

Next, have the team work together to find ways to move the majority of goals into the SHARED category. Do this by looking at the underlying principle or purpose of the goal and reframing it. For example, change "I'd like more work/life balance" to "everyone on the team has their personal work-life balance needs met"; change "I'd like job satisfaction" to "we would like to create a sense of team spirit and purpose that rivals any other team we've been part of."

the Deeply Shared Goals Audit (see Tool 8.1). We have used it often for project teams, functional teams, and management teams – new or old – and have always come away with insights and resolution of issues.

Principle #5 Summary
Partnerships become generative when there is a foundation of deeply shared goals.

✓ Shared goals are a platform for collaboration rather than competition. They ward off interpersonal and intra-team conflict.
✓ Shared goals ensure that resources are available and are pulling in the same direction.
✓ Goals must be shared with someone, throughout the team and organization, and be truly shared as opposed to a same goal.

SECTION III

Skills

CHAPTER 9

Decision Partnering Skills

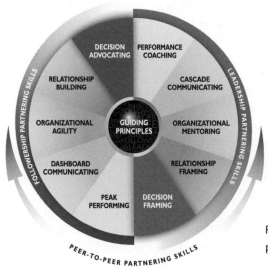

Figure 9.1 Decision partnering skills

Kirk vs. Spock: Whom Would You Entrust with Your Decisions?

One night we met friends at a restaurant to celebrate a birthday. During pre-dinner drinks we posed this scenario and question:

> Imagine you are on the USS Enterprise. You've lost 90% of your power, deflector shields are down, and an attack by a Klingon Bird of Prey warship is imminent. The situation looks dire. Your options are limited. Whom would you entrust with the life and death decision of what to do next, Captain Kirk or Science Officer Spock?

It turned into a fun party game as each of us made a choice, explained our rationale, and tried to guess what the rest of the table would say.

While Kirk was the favorite, a significant number picked Spock. One couple, both in the legal profession, split their votes. It led to an interesting debate: Who is the best choice? Kirk or Spock?

For those without exposure to the fictional world of *Star Trek*, Spock is a genius who can determine the exact probability of every possible outcome to five decimal places! He always makes the most logical decision based on probabilities. Captain Kirk, on the other hand, is all gut feel and emotion, with a steely determination that often ignores inconvenient truths. Nevertheless, he has the uncanny ability to overcome even the most improbable odds.

Whom should we trust: the intuitive Kirk or the rational Spock? And what does this mean for how each of us makes decisions both individually and as a team? The answer to this last question is an active research topic in neuroscience, neuroeconomics, and psychology.

In this chapter, we will first focus on useful best practices for decision making that apply irrespective of what role you are taking on in the decision-making process. Next, we'll discuss how to ensure you are taking on the right role. Then, we'll satisfy your curiosity about what you've no doubt pondered by that point: who is the better choice, Kirk or Spock? After that, the balance of this chapter is organized into the two essential aspects of collaborative decision making – the leadership role of Decision Framing and the followership role of Decision Advocacy.

Honoring Our Brain and Body

Making a decision is tough – we rarely have a complete set of facts, and there is often no clear right or wrong answer. To make matters worse, our brains are wired to loathe ambiguity. This causes us to make too-quick decisions, to base decisions on heuristics (rules of thumb), or to avoid making them entirely. We put up with bad situations because the "good unknown" is scarier than the "bad known." We claim to like change but do much to avoid it.

Fortunately, our bodies and minds already have awesome decision-making tools, they just require harnessing. Five steps to making better decisions are:

Step 1. Gather and organize the information
Step 2. Let your unconscious do its job
Step 3. Mind your body

Step 4. Listen to your feelings
Step 5. Confirm your quick responses

First, gather and organize information. Study the decision to be made in detail. Bring in all the information you can and reorganize it into meaningful categories. This important step provides the essential raw material for your brain to process.

Then, let your unconscious do its job. Ap Dijksterhuis is a professor at Radboud University in the Netherlands. The area is a hotbed of soccer (or football, as it is called outside North America) and predicting the outcomes of matches is a popular pastime. When students were tested on the accuracy of their soccer predictions, it turned out that:[1]

1. Experts were better at predicting outcomes.
2. The greater the expertise, the more useful it was to have time for the unconscious to sift through the data.

It probably isn't a surprise that experts make better predictions than punters. The second finding – that experts benefit from unconscious processing time – is more surprising, but also highly useful.

Why do we need the unconscious? Well, the problem is that the conscious mind is very limited; it can only evaluate about five items at once.[2] For example, watch how long pre-readers take to sound out a word – about 10 letters per second if they know their ABCs well. They consciously process words one letter at a time. One way our brains cope with such limited capacity is by chunking information into words. We no longer have to sound out letters. Put another way, with expertise we stop reading letters and start reading words – this isn't just about being better at the same thing, it is a new skill handled completely at the unconscious level.

To see an example of this, quickly say out loud the common object referenced below.

Figure 9.2 One letter or two?

If you said The Car, that is because your brain is chunking information without reading each letter. Is the middle letter an H? An A? It doesn't matter to your ability to read it as long as it is close enough to both. It took no effort to recognize the middle letter as either because you are an expert at reading. In fact, we can even write words without vowels and mst ppl wll stll b abl to read it perfectly well.[3] Imagine asking a young child to do this!

Because its capacity is so very limited, conscious memory is not productive at sorting through complex data. By contrast, just one system in your unconscious mind – your visual system – can digest 200,000 times more information per second than your conscious mind. If the conscious mind is like counting on your fingers, the unconscious is a massive, supercomputing powerhouse!

Once that supercomputer is fed with data and left alone to process it for a while, it can sort through and organize large amounts of complex data, finding the crucial threads needed to make the best decisions. That's why experts benefit from thinking time, because their brains are tuned to find the crucial threads, but novices' brains aren't.

Your unconscious processes over 200,000 times as much information as your conscious.

For unconscious processing to work, however, you need to distract the conscious brain and stop it from interfering. Useful techniques include going for a long walk, taking a shower, meditating, or just sleeping on it. These all allow the unconscious to process data fully and arrive at an optimal solution. A useful motto is, "Feed it, then leave it."

Always mind your body. Our whole body gets involved in a decision. That gut feel you get before making a decision is one way your body helps attaches preferences to choices.[4] The gut feel is essential for making high-quality decisions, but you also have to be careful that too much caffeine, anxiety, sleeplessness, or other misleading inputs don't unduly influence it. Be sure that your body is feeding your mind relevant data.

What are your feelings telling you? Emotions are important, too. People with brain lesions in areas that regulate emotion such as the amygdala, insular cortex, or ventromedial prefrontal cortex have a difficult time making good choices: they don't know how to weigh the consequences of different options or make trade-offs based on the likelihood of something happening.[5] It is popular to suggest that the best decisions are made by emotionless, logical processes, or should be. In other words, Spock is the right choice because he relies only on logic and rational argument. The problem is that this isn't true for humans and there is very limited evidence on whether it applies to intergalactic species such as Vulcans! Emotions are important information even though they can, at times, mislead.

Want to make better decisions? Feed it (your brain), and leave it.

Confirm your quick responses. We naturally develop and use heuristics to shortcut the decision-making process. A heuristic is a "fast, frugal, and simple" (Goldstein & Gigerenzer, 2002, p. 75) way to solve problems when there isn't enough time, information, or ability to work out the best answer. Heuristics are most useful when there is a moderate amount of ambiguity and considerable expertise with a certain situation. In other circumstances, these quick-response systems can easily lead us astray. **Use heuristics carefully and consciously.**

These five steps apply any time you participate in decision making, whether it is yours alone to make, whether you are part of a team doing so, or whether you are leading the charge.

But first, however, be sure you are taking on the right role.

Who Is Leading and Following? The Accountability Rules

Every day we face dozens of decisions, big and small, from those that feel like intergalactic warfare to the everyday. Sometimes we are leading and it's our decision to make. Sometimes we are following and it's not. We can add tremendous value either way, but what we do depends on our role: leadership or followership.

How do you decide which role to take on? When do you lead, and when do you follow?

Marc once worked with a consultant with a tremendous ability to sort through seemingly complex organizational challenges by applying a simple maxim. He abided by, and shared, these rules for decision-making accountability:

Rule 1 – Determine the core purpose of the decision and who deeply shares that core purpose.

Rule 2 – Ensure decision-making authority is as close to the frontline as possible.

Rule 3 – If after applying the first two rules, the outcome still points to more than one person or department, push responsibility up the line until it fits under a single person's purview.

 At the time, I remember the organization's new product development was in trouble: decisions were stalling because it was considered the joint responsibility of marketing, IT, operations and customer service as each area was *affected* by the introduction of a new product. We were brought in to help and could quickly see that the *core purpose* of new products was to increase product revenue, which was core to marketing's mandate. Therefore, marketing should be accountable for making the decision. Now if marketing wanted to build something that couldn't be implemented because they hadn't consulted the right people or didn't have the resources to complete development they were equally accountable for its failure. Competing priorities and agendas are common in organizations. Getting decision-making accountability right and having deeply shared goals (Principle 5) goes a long way to aligning efforts. That organization got much more done once the accountability rules were firmly in place.

Whether you are given a decision to make, you initiate a decision, or you brush up against one, first recognize who has the accountability. Once that is sorted out you can assess whether your role is leadership or followership.

When Should You Question a Decision?

When a decision crosses your path, first confirm whether or not it has already been made and by whom! Consider an experience Sam had when she was controller. Meet May-Ling:

I was waiting for two team members to join me – Charles, my director, and May-Ling, his new senior analyst – for a conference call with department heads in other locations when I received a meeting decline from May-Ling. Charles came in soon after and told me that May-Ling had decided not to come.

"Decided not to come?" I asked. "What's up?" Looking sheepish, he explained, "She decided to stay at her desk and work." Charles knew we had expressly invited May-Ling as an opportunity to learn about the varied perspectives of our internal customers.

There wasn't time to go to her desk and explain our reasons just then but, afterwards, the three of us met to discuss what had happened. May-Ling explained that she thought three of us attending a meeting seemed inefficient. The problem was I'd already made the decision that she should attend. It would have been fine for her to clarify the reasons for my decision, but not to overrule it at the last minute.

Now that's not to say you can never disagree with your boss or the person assuming the leadership role. Sometimes you must. But if you disagree, do it *before* a decision is made and not after. The only exceptions to this are when a decision is immoral, unethical, illegal, or so important that there is no room for error – all rare situations.

Kirk vs. Spock: Redux

Now, back to the original question in this chapter: who should we entrust with decision making: the intuitive Kirk or the rational Spock?

Thankfully in real life it's rarely a choice we have to make. Instead we can partner for truly generative decision making, by which we mean getting a better, more creative decision efficiently.

- Spock excels at providing decision support – facts and assessments. He makes wholly accurate evaluations based on all the available evidence.

- Kirk excels at providing a different kind of decision support: he creates new realities. In other words, he doesn't take situations at face value but imagines new options.
- Finally, in his leadership role, Kirk excels at creating a strong decision-making frame, one that sets up the team for success. He gathers the crew to examine a situation, encourages diverse opinions and rationale, values the contributions of each crew member, and harnesses their collective wisdom to see new pathways. More on this in the next section of this chapter!

Overall, then, Kirk is the right choice ... at least as far as humans are concerned! But the optimal situation is Kirk leading the process with Spock as an integral contributor.[6]

Decision Framing: The Leadership Role

Let's say it is your decision to make. You are in the leadership role. What now?

Decision making is much more than the event of making a decision; it is about creating an effective decision-making *environment and process*. That is, it's about framing the decision. An effective environment is a safe place for ideas to flourish: the right people are brought to the table, and the right information gets on the table at the right time. An effective process is a structured one that has clear, definable objectives.[7]

Decision Responsibilities Extend from Making to Implementing

Karen is the HR director of a U.S.-based scientific foundation with a worldwide mandate to nurture projects with the potential for groundbreaking social and environmental improvement. The foundation employs more than 80 research scientists along with a small administrative team. Staff generally have advanced degrees, many with PhDs, and are highly committed to the vision and mission of the organization. Not surprisingly, the scientists are passionate about the projects they personally uncover and bring forward for funding. When we first met Karen she was frustrated with progress on a key organizational change initiative that had been underway for a couple of years.

Karen had been on the job just three months when the situation first came up. She was the third HR director the foundation had since the initiative started, reporting to the president, Bill, who asked that she complete an organizational restructure he had personally initiated. The foundation was growing, and Bill believed reorganization was crucial to sustain that growth. He had involved the scientists and support staff in designing the go-forward organizational structure using a time-intensive, collaborative process and, by the end, they had reached a consensus on what they wanted to do.

Fast forward two years and Bill was frustrated. Reorganization efforts were in limbo. Karen described the project to us as herding cats: "Each time we start to implement something, one of the researchers comes up with a new, even better idea. We never get anything done!" The solution everyone had agreed to initially became an ever-moving target. The problem was that while a process had been put in place to make the decision, there wasn't an equivalent one to implement it. The foundation staff, including Bill, hadn't made the mental transition from one stage to the other; they continued to loop back and tackle the problem rather than moving forward into implementing the solution.

This situation highlights the reality that a decision-making process must extend all the way from making it to implementing. It should include a timeline, phases, milestones, and role expectations. Without this, even the best-intentioned, most consensus-driven decision is likely to fail.

A structured decision-making process puts everyone on the same track. It supports making and implementing decisions that are objective and evidence based. If used consistently, it is also more efficient, cost effective, and repeatable than ad hoc methods.

The leadership role in this is to frame the decision-making process, communicate it to all the stakeholders, and oversee the implementation. We have used a model to frame the process we call the Decision Lifecycle.

The Decision Lifecycle

We often draw this on a white board when we train or consult with teams on how to get better decisions. Then, we walk everyone through the lifecycle distinguishing the leadership role and followership role at each stage, discussing deliverables, effective and ineffective behav-

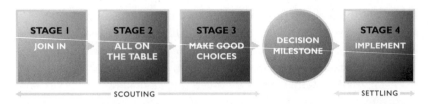

Figure 9.3 The decision lifecycle

iors, and challenges. A common problem is when people try and go backwards on the path or stall at a certain stage, such as the foundation example earlier.

In Principle 2, we introduced a useful frame called Scouting and Settling (Tool 5.1). A scouting mission is to seek out new territory – to boldly go where no one has gone before. A settling mission is to put down roots – to inhabit new worlds and star systems. Here we've built on these concepts and integrated it with decision making. Distinguishing the scouting/investigating phase from the settling/implementing phase, articulating the different roles in advance, and allocating sufficient time to each stage can inoculate decisions (and organizations) from getting stalled.

Note the diagram is a one-way path: don't backtrack unless it is absolutely necessary. There is always an additional fact, issue, idea, critique, or roadblock to give pause to the direction chosen. But, if the potential gain from revisiting a previous stage is less than 20%, you are likely using time poorly. The foundation would have fared better with a completed 80% solution than with its 100% of nothing. The old adage, *a poor decision well implemented is always better than a good decision poorly implemented*, reminds us that there is always further opportunity to make anything better upon implementation.

Stay committed to your boss's and organization's decisions, but stay flexible in your approach.[8]

Stage 1: Aim for a "Join In" Rather Than a "Buy In"

Key Leadership Ideas

- Consider decision making an interpersonal skill.
- Err on the side of engaging people as often, as early, and as broadly as you can.
- Gather a group to be truly creative.

You don't get quality decisions from having all the information on the table so much as by getting all the *people* to the table. When that is done right, you barely even have to make a decision. Solutions often present themselves – picture Captain Kirk sitting in his command chair in the center of the starship bridge harnessing the collective intelligence of his crew.

In your leadership role, if you aren't spending the majority of your time and effort on the people side, you will want to start doing so. Consider decision making as an interpersonal skill: strong leaders engage others as early and as often as time permits, giving them ample opportunity to feed into the process. Strong leaders toss a wider net to scoop in anyone who might have information, concerns, perspectives, and interdependencies or anyone who might simply be affected. We know that early involvement facilitates buy-in and commitment. Moreover, early involvement preempts the need to get buy-in later. People need to have a voice and feel they are listened to. Without that opportunity, a leader runs the risk of decisions being blocked or even sabotaged when it comes time to implement them.[9]

Recognize that the best support typically comes from your team and that it can enhance decision quality, agility, productivity, and commitment. Early and frequent engagement helps build their decision support capability and capacity.

An even more persuasive reason to take a team approach and collaborate is perhaps the surety of arriving at a better, more creative answer.

When Should We Collaborate?

Tool 9.1 provides practical advice on when to collaborate. The vast majority of the work we grapple with today is moderately difficult,

❗FliPtips❗ Tool 9.1 Collaboration Guidelines

How do you decide whether to collaborate, or work alone?
Here are some useful guidelines.

Individuals are best at problem solving and generating decisions when **ALL** of the following are met:
1. The problem is simple or extremely hard;
2. It only requires the expertise of one person;
3. The solution is straightforward to execute.

Teams are best at problem solving and generating decisions when **ANY** of the following apply:
1. The problem is of moderate to hard complexity;
2. It requires the expertise of many people;
3. Buy-in from multiple stakeholders is required to execute the solution.

requires a wide range of expertise, and depends on many different people to implement it. The nature of work has changed dramatically, which is why collaboration and teams are what makes sense much of the time.

Group creativity and decision making require strong individual contributors and capable leadership. The leader must leverage the valuable diversity of the group and not allow it to succumb to *groupthink*, a natural psychological phenomenon that emerges in a group whenever the need for harmony or comfort outweighs other objectives. When groupthink happens, people become reticent; they don't voice minority opinions and the leader often believes consensus has been reached even if it hasn't. For example, an award-winning video reenactment of the landmark decision to launch the Space Shuttle Challenger illustrates how groupthink can lead to catastrophe.

A diversity of participation and consultation can help to avoid a few other common decision-making errors and biases:

1. Functional Specialty: taking too narrow a perspective

2. Confirmation Bias: seeking out positions that confirm our own
3. False Consensus Effect: overestimating the degree to which others agree with us

Aiming for a "join in" rather than a "buy in" with diverse expertise and perspectives will get you to a better, more creative answer. And, even if it feels less efficient at times, using a group process improves end-to-end productivity and quality.

Stage 2: Put It All on the Table

Key Leadership Ideas

- Clarify the real problem or opportunity.
- Create intelligent constraints.

Many times, someone comes up with a groundbreaking solution only to discover it solved the wrong problem. For example, how often has a new product been launched to great fanfare only to fall completely flat because no one wanted it. There are many examples of this: Harley Davidson perfume, New Coke, bottled water for pets, and lemon mint toothpaste, to name a few. Of course there are also examples of companies launching highly successful products that customers did not know they wanted. Steve Jobs famously said, "It's really hard to design products by focus groups. A lot of times, people don't know what they want until you show it to them." Another visionary, Henry Ford, had a similar sentiment, "If I had asked people what they wanted, they would have said 'faster horses.'" Of course, Ford and Jobs were both very clear on the underlying opportunity.

In your leadership role, frame the underlying issues and be open to the prospect of having to dig deep to uncover them.

A story that exemplifies this is the *Tale of Two Sisters and an Orange*. It goes like this: two sisters wanted an orange but there was only one in the fruit bowl. Framed this way, the only equitable answer seemed to be to split it and each take half. That's what they did but neither ended up satisfied with half an orange. Later that day the sisters discussed why they needed the orange. One said she wanted it to make marmalade using the peel. The other said she wanted to juice it for the Vitamin C as she wasn't feeling well. If only they had spent time articulating their needs by putting the real issues on the table, each could have had 100% of what they wanted.

Once a problem or opportunity is identified, intelligent constraints – a frame, in other words – enables a more creative and viable solution to be found.

Stage 3: Make Good Choices

Key Leadership Ideas

- Select decision criteria early.
- Create more choice.
- Turn choice into possibility.
- Delay decisions ... make them just in time.

In the movie *Freaky Friday*, a controlling mother (played by Jamie Lee Curtis) drops her daughter (played by Lindsay Lohan) off at her high school. As the daughter leaves the car and walks toward school, her mom leans out the passenger window and yells in an annoying mom-voice, "Make good choices!" Poor daughter, the start of another day and already publicly embarrassed. Soon after, with the help of a little mystic mayhem, FLIP! mother and daughter have switched bodies. It is time for them to walk in each other's shoes. Would you be surprised if, by the end of the movie, the daughter understood that making good choices was brilliant advice? Too bad her mother didn't tell her *how* to go about making good choices.

How to make good choices begins with choosing decision criteria, and doing so well *before* decision time. Why? Because there is a strong tendency to come up with decision criteria that justify the decision after it is made.[10] People are more objective early on, before getting vested in a specific decision and before emotions run high. Appropriate decision criteria can be the "voice of reason" to resolve disagreements.

There's another reason to bring up decision criteria early: the unconscious mind is most effective when it is working toward specific goals.[11] Make a goal clear,[12] frame it with criteria, motivate its achievement, and then … do something else for a while![13] When the criteria are known and time is given for reflection, you get the best results.

Decisions take time to incubate, develop, and ripen. John Cleese, the beloved English comedian, actor, writer, and producer of *Monty Python* fame affirms this brilliantly in his humorous 1991 video on creativity. He opines that while we revere leaders who are decisive and act quickly, we ought to admire instead those who wait until the very last possible minute to decide. They are the ones who have taken the most time to think, reflect, and explore all the implications of a decision. This sounds easy to do, almost like procrastinating, but it isn't. To excel at giving each decision the fullness of time, you must be able to tolerate the discomfort that comes with having an unresolved situation, continue to use energy to keep thinking about it, and have impeccable timing to know when you have delayed long enough but not too long.

Along with decision criteria, you want to foster as much choice as you can.[14] The first workable answer is rarely the best. To surface many choices on the table early in the decision-making process:

✓ Encourage diverse opinions, ideas, and rationale.
✓ Reinforce the right kinds of contribution.
✓ Value everyone's individual ideas and the collective wisdom.
✓ Don't reject options too early as their merits aren't always immediately obvious.

One series of steps a generative leader can employ to make good choices is:

Step 1. Discuss and agree on how long you can wait to make a decision.
Step 2. Use creative thinking tools and techniques to get ideas on the table.
Step 3. Use a tool to develop ideas into workable solutions.
Step 4. Evaluate the solutions against pre-determined decision criteria.

There are many fun, flexible and functional tools a generative leader can have in their toolkit. Brainstorming is commonly used for step two, although there are many other options. One we particularly love for expanding ideas (step 3) is POWER[15]. POWER stands for Positives, Objections, What else (the parking lot category), Enhancements, and Remedies. Applying each of these categories to an idea can turn any idea into a viable solution. For example, start with the base idea and ask, "What are all the Positives about it?" Then for each positive ask, "What are all the Enhancements that will make it even better?" Systematically going through all five letters helps turn a raw idea into a full solution, one that maximizes the benefits while decreasing the impact of any objections. Only after you have "POWERed" up each option and there are a number of valuable suggestions on the table should you evaluate the most promising against your decision criteria.

The Decision Milestone

Key Leadership Ideas

- Make the decision.
- Record and communicate generatively, sharing rationale.
- Celebrate the milestone to signal it's time to switch gears.

Making a decision is both an event and a milestone. It is an event because it can be as simple as a personal choice or as complicated as a team vote. Regardless, the effort you have put in prior to this point will pay off in making a better decision.

The decision milestone is also an important signal for a shift from one frame to another. Up to this point, the leadership responsibility has been to create a frame for a scouting mission. Like any scouting mission, you might find a new path to travel or a more valuable goal than the one you started out on. However, once a decision is made, both the leadership and followership roles have to quickly shift to a settling mission.

At this point, if either the leader or follower doesn't shift from scouting to settling, problems arise. To avoid this, mark the milestone by recording it and celebrating it. Communicate the decision to all the people who need to know and would like to know. It is not about selling; it's about sharing rationale. And it's about signaling to your team that it's time to switch gears.

Stage 4: Implementation

Key Leadership Ideas

- Stay the course.
- Honor the intention of the decision.
- Continually tighten the frame but not like a noose! Think strengthen, and focus like a funnel.

A decision has been made and communicated. Now it has to get done. This may require different resources than the first phase, possibly even bringing in new leadership such as a professional project manager. There was plenty of advice in Tool 5.1, Scouting and Settling, so there are only a few points we want to add.

First, resist the temptation to change course. Carefully weigh the costs and benefits of doing so. It's rare that benefits of change outweigh the costs if enough time was given to make a decision initially.

Second, keep the decision criteria front and center. Too often, during the implementation of a decision, wrinkles emerge, adaptations are made, and the final result no longer satisfies the original goals. Just as bad as coming up with a great decision about the wrong problem is implementing the wrong solution to a great decision.

Third, the frame should get more defined as the implementation phase progresses. In formal project management methodology, project cost estimates narrow as you pass key milestones – it often starts as $x plus or minus 50%, and, by the time the project gets all the formal approvals and is well underway, the allowed variance should be more like plus or minus 5%. Cost, however, is just one aspect of a frame. Everything should be specified more completely over time including:

- Resources
- Scope
- Time to completion
- Risk
- Reporting (which needs to get increasingly granular and detailed)

If there are documents such as a project charter, consider making them living documents: in other words, subject to frequent modification. In the IT world, this idea has been embraced by the Agile community who believe in continual, rapid, and iterative development. Goals are constantly adapted by the frequent engagement of customers. The process becomes the frame and, within it, the details get constantly refined.

Decision Advocating: The Followership Role

As we noted earlier, sometimes you have decision-making accountability; often, however, you don't. Without decision-making accountability, some people become hedgehogs: "I'll unroll from my defensive posture when it's over," they say. Others think it's the time to give their opinion because, when they offer advice, they believe it is so obvious or they have such insight into the problem that the rest of us should accept it ipso facto.

How can you avoid these mistakes and reliably make a positive contribution? Be a decision advocate! Take the initiative to contribute by asking yourself the generative question, *"What are all the ways I can add value to this process at this stage?"*

Continually find ways to contribute and add value throughout the process. Ask yourself, "How can I make it easier for {insert my boss, our client, a prospective investor, my peer, my staff} to make a decision?" Once a decision is made, how can I contribute to implementation in a way that makes it look like a brilliant solution, but not MY brilliant solution?

Here is more followership advice for the different stages.

Be Passionate For, Not Against

Key Followership Ideas

- Be a *decision advocate*, not a devil's advocate.
- POWER up ideas and their implementation.
- Adopt a "yes, and" approach.

When discussing possibilities it is wonderful to be passionate about results. Care about getting to the right answer and invest in those results.

Passion pushes people to excel, as long as it is passion *for* something. Passion *against* something, however, is seen as emotional: as hanging onto the way things were or opposing change.

We know it's popular to talk about being a devil's advocate – like that's a beneficial thing. But we disagree. Playing devil's advocate is to take an opposing position for the sake of argument.[16] It can expose weaknesses in a given position but most often, in our experience, it quashes the germ of an idea along with the creative energy surrounding it. More potentially brilliant ideas fail to get a fair hearing because of this common behavior than for any other reason. Worst of all it's easy to be devil's advocate – criticism is trained into us from our earliest days to the point where the responses are almost automatic: "It's been done before and yadda yadda yadda," or, "It's too expensive/hard/cheap/risky." Defending a novel suggestion against this onslaught is almost impossible.

On the flipside, playing decision advocate is to take a suggested idea and power it up, offering ways to make it even better. Apply *generative judgment* – consider what is advantageous and what is disadvantageous about an idea, enhance the positives, and see what you can do to remedy the objections. This *building on ideas* using a tool such as POWER prior to judging them heightens energy and excitement within a team, which in turn enhances collaboration and innovation. Only after you've made the most of an idea is it worthwhile being critical.

When you weigh the pros and cons of adopting the role of devil's advocate versus decision advocate the scale tips heavily to decision advocate. Let someone else be the devil's advocate. Better yet, in your leadership role, reinforce decision-advocating behavior on your team and eliminate devil's advocate behavior altogether! We've tried it … the results are remarkable. It is the more fruitful path to collaboration.

Finally, consider if you are reacting negatively to a person rather than an idea or decision. Are you looking at it with a balanced perspective? Has the group put all the options on the table before evaluating them? Are you feeling frustrated or tired? Are you listening more than talking? Have you fully clarified other perspectives? Are you defending turf?

One trick we have found useful when any of these destructive behaviors arise is to take a cue from improvisational acting (see Chapter 7 for a more complete list of the basic rules of improv acting). Try saying, "Yes, and ..." or "Yes, let's ..." rather than "No, but ..."

Be a Decision Support Expert

Key Followership Ideas

- Be a true "thinking partner" and strive for Level 3 Contributions.
- Cookie-crumb your reasoning by sharing the steps that led to your response/idea/option/solution.
- Always consider whether you are giving complete information.

An opinion is less important and less useful than data. And information is less important and less useful than decision support. Consider the following three levels of support you can provide in evaluating a decision.

Level 1: Opinions

When you give an opinion without accountability, or when you deliver it without reasons, that is all you have contributed: an opinion. It is no more than a straw poll of *what* you think rather than *how* you think or *why* you think it. Some people attempt to support their opinions by appealing to personal expertise – this is called an *ad hominem* argument and its value is limited to very technical and specific sorts of questions where you might honestly expect *every* expert to come to the same conclusion. Alternatively, some people appeal to the value of their intuition; this is fine if you are the decision maker, but it doesn't help when someone else is trying to make the decision. Opinions have limited use in decision support.

Level 2: Data/Information

Some people *think* teachers make too much money, some people *think* they make too little. If you were in charge of deciding on teachers' salaries, would these opinions help you make a decision? Maybe, but more likely you'd want other information: how much do teachers make and how hard do they work compared to other jobs; what responsibilities do they take on outside classroom hours; are there specialized skills to acquire in becoming a teacher; how long does it take to acquire such skills; is there a scarcity of teachers; how does this compare to other jobs; how much money is in the budget, etc. Offering this quality of information provides stronger support than an opinion.

Level 3: Decision Support

Even information, however, is only part of the story. After all, there is more information and easier access to it these days than any thousand people could know in a lifetime of study. We are living in a world super-saturated with information – simply possessing or passing along facts no longer provides great decision support. It's not that hard to find out how much teachers make or to itemize their responsibilities or even to look at their workload, nor does this give you the right information to make a decision. In a business situation, facts also don't give you any special competitive advantage because facts are everywhere – Wikipedia provides faster access, more articles, and greater access to resources than any encyclopedia in history. *The people we seek out when making a decision don't just give us facts, they support our ability to make decisions.* Generative followers bring forward new facts and then help organize the information into a framework for making a decision. They participate in powering up solutions, look for opportunities, and figure out how to overcome objections. They put context to the decision including who is affected, what constraints may be placed on a solution, and what the solution must accomplish or avoid. They are a true "thinking partner": an advocate for a great process and ultimately a great decision. These are the skills that get noticed.

Marc has a tongue-in-cheek example of how he changed a personal behavior from a Level 1 opinion giver to a Level 3 decision supporter. Let's step out of the office now and into the mall …

Ever been clothes shopping with your partner? If you're a guy it can be an intimidating experience … that moment in the mall when, after watching her riffle through rack after rack of clothes in the interminable and largely indistinguishable (at least to my guy eyes) clothing stores, she comes up to me with a dress in hand and asks, "What do you think?" Years ago, the conversation would go something like this:
She says: "What do you think?"

I reply: "I like it." Or maybe, "I don't like it." (stuck in Level 1: the mud's deep and I'm fairly sure I'm sinking!)

Once I'd discovered that giving an opinion wasn't going over too well, I figured I could sound flattering if I said I liked the dress. Any dress. Yeah, that clearly didn't work for very long. My next attempt was to try and figure out the "right" answer. I'd ask Sam, "What do *you* think?" Equally uninspired. Equally unsuccessful.

So I tried to be useful instead: She says: "What do you think?" I re-ply: "Well, the mall closes in a half hour." (At least I moved to Level 2, better than nothing.) I think you can imagine the result. Sigh.

It's only in the last couple years that I've finally got it right: She says: "What do you think?" I reply: "When are you planning on wearing it (work, parties, casual)?" Probing questions help to *contextualize the decision.* (Yay! Finally at Level 3!) I'd comment on specific colors in the dress or the style or pattern and how they match her other outfits. I inquire about the fit: "Are you comfortable sitting down in it, or dancing in it?" I invite her to talk about what she likes about the outfit. Finally, I'd try and refine choices: "Perhaps you could consider …?" The point is I *organize* the options to help her make the decision. I feel much more confidant now that I answer the question well. Wouldn't you say so, Sam?

 Yes, terrific points! And, I must add that sometimes I'm also looking for your gut reaction. When I first walked out of the change room, did you think: "Wow! That looks great on you." Or "Gee, your turquoise dress at home looks nicer." I guess what I'm saying is that your honest aesthetic reaction or assessment can also be useful decision support. So, to add to our guidance, *it isn't always clear why your opinion is being solicited.* I recommend clarifying that first. Sometimes a leader simply wishes to challenge her best people to give them practice at putting a stake in the ground and articulating their rationale.

Cookie-Crumb Your Reasoning

Expose your thinking by sharing why it's relevant, where it came from, and how you are interpreting it. Reasons provide a cookie-crumb trail of your thinking.

Rebecca Thacker and Sandy Wayne have spent their careers studying the impact of employee behaviors. They note, "Perhaps the most potent means subordinates have for influencing impressions of their promotability is through the use of reasoning. Results indicate that reasoning was significant and positive in its effect upon supervisors' assessments of subordinates' promotability" (Thacker & Wayne, 1995, p. 750).

In other words, reasons not only get results, they make you look good.

Always Consider Whether You Are Giving Complete Information

If you give someone the full story, mostly she makes good decisions. Ask yourself: Are you holding anything in reserve? What are you protecting and why? Do you have sacred cows and are they really sacred (it seems appropriate somehow that "scared" and "sacred" only differ by a pair of *flip*ped letters)?

Commit to the Decision

Key Followership Ideas

- Know when the decision has been made (and behave accordingly).
- Probe to understand the decision.
- Make it better through implementation.

"But what if it is a bad decision?," people say to us. "How can I commit to the decision if [insert excuse below]!"

1. It is in my area of expertise and I know it won't work.
2. I should have been consulted first. If I had been, a better decision could have been made.
3. The decision maker should get my buy-in because I am affected by the decision.
4. There are consequences that weren't considered.
5. The decision is bad for morale.
6. The decision contradicts other objectives.

And finally, the phrase heard in meetings around the world,

7. It's been tried before and it didn't work!

That's a lot of excuses.

There are times when you can't accept a decision: it may be immoral, illegal, violate professional standards, or contradict your deeply held personal beliefs. We understand that. But we also know those situations are rare. Most of the time people oppose a decision for all sorts of other reasons that, frankly, are irrelevant. The cost of opposing the decision to you, to the leader, and to the organization is almost always higher than any benefit that might be obtained.

Sam once overheard a humorous example of senior executive followership. It sounded preposterous but was probably spot-on organizational mentoring. The CEO informed his executive team that expenses were going to have to be cut, and that this was a directive from the board. One newly hired executive who'd come from outside the organization piped up: "We're not going to do anything stupid, are we?" A peer pulled her aside and said, "Look, I've been here for over a decade and I've seen these expense cuts come down the pipe every so often. There is no sense arguing. It's happening. We **are** going to do stupid things. I suggest you get on the stupid train and spend your energy figuring out how to make it work."

> If it's not life-threatening then it's just life.

Most of the time – whether you agree with a decision or not – the best followership action is to pitch in, make it work, and be an advocate. Doing so can be hard, though, when you haven't been consulted.

Some decisions are made without consultation or accommodation, and sometimes that's appropriate. Sometimes the pace of work demands it: there is no time to consult. Sometimes decisions *have* to be made confidentially such as an HR issue involving a specific person or when a financial disclosure is at stake. Also, not every decision originates with your boss. Perhaps it was decided by her boss or higher up still and she isn't keen on it either. Maybe her support is only a sign that she is being a good follower.

Once a decision is made you become its message-bearer to your staff, the advocate of it. If you can't explain it well, why should the boss believe you would implement it well? And if you don't follow the intent of the decision, how will your staff know what they should do: should they follow the decision of your boss or follow you?

Probe to Understand the Decision

Understanding a decision deeply lets you implement it more effectively.

Colonel Phillip S. Meilinger of the United States Air Force in his wonderfully pithy article on followership says,

> One colleague with whom I served several years ago would indulge in periodic gripe sessions with his subordinates at which time he would routinely criticize the commander and his decisions in front of the youngest troops. When asked why he was undermining the boss, he would reply sanctimoniously that his integrity would not allow him to lie; he thought the policies were idiotic, and he had a duty to tell his people how he felt. He said he was exercising "good leadership" by telling the truth as he saw it.
>
> Rubbish. Leadership is not a commodity to be bought at the price of followership. If a subordinate asks you whether or not you agree with a particular decision, your response should be that it is an irrelevant question; the boss has decided, and we will now carry out his orders. (Meilinger, 2001, p. 99)

The only point we'd like to add is that your job is much more than carrying out orders; you can have a critical impact on what ultimately gets done and therefore what new reality the order creates.

Make It Even Better with Implementation

After the decision is made, it is time to stop exploring other options and digging up new data, and get on with the work of implementing the decision that was made. Even if you don't agree with the ultimate decision you can still aim to improve upon it through the implementation process. That's the power of true decision advocacy.

Decision Partnering Skills Summary

Leadership Skill: Decision Framing
Decision making is a lot more than the event of making a decision. In your leadership role, focus on creating an effective decision-making environment and process:

- ✓ Create an environment for ideas and input to flourish.
- ✓ Engage people early, aiming for more of a "join in" rather than a "buy-in."
- ✓ Use sound techniques to reduce natural decision-making biases and errors.

Followership Skill: Decision Advocating
Sometimes you have decision-making accountability; often you don't. Regardless, you can add real value to each step in the decision process:

- ✓ Introduce new facts, ideas, and alternatives at the right time during the decision-making process.
- ✓ Expose your thinking by sharing why it's relevant, where it came from, and how you interpret it.
- ✓ Be a decision advocate rather than a devil's advocate: POWER UP ideas and their implementation.

CHAPTER 10

Relationship Partnering Skills

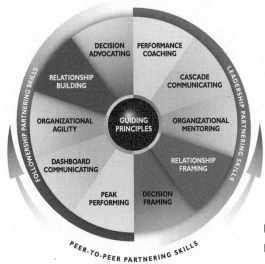

Figure 10.1 Relationship partnering skills

Relationship Checkmate and How to Avoid a Stalemate

At the turn of the 20th century – long before computers existed let alone vied for supremacy at the board – chess was one of the great battlefields of the human intellect. It was a time of rapid advancement in the theory and practice of the game with great players such as Lasker, Janowski, and Capablanca dominating the field. At one tournament, a game was organized between two teams of three grandmasters on each side. The grandmasters were supposed to collaborate on each move. Given the level of talent, it was expected to be a game for the ages: something future generations would study endlessly.

Was the game the paragon of collaboration it was predicted to be?

No. You probably won't be surprised to learn that the game was a mess.[1] It wasn't grandmaster level. It wasn't even chess master quality. The reason for this has to do with collective intelligence. It turns out that the intelligence of a team is not a straightforward calculation based on the general intelligence of each team member. A team is not as smart as its smartest person, nor the average intelligence of the members, nor as dumb as its weakest link.[2] What, then, makes a team smart? Smart teams have a high average *social* intelligence: they are sensitive to interpersonal matters and take turns letting everyone talk. Chess grandmasters are notoriously lousy at both.

This chapter delves into how to build relationships in a way that honors leadership AND followership as active participants in its co-creation – the leadership role of Relationship Framing and the followership role of Relationship Building.

But first, please, indulge us with this rant ...

You're Not the Engager of Me!

At workshops we hold, we get asked, "How do I build greater engagement in my staff?" Some of the other questions include, "How do I build trust? What leads to respect? How can I get people to care about work? How do I get people to align to the vision and value the right things?" These are great questions because achieving any (or all) of them leads to better workplaces: happy, productive, innovative, agile, focused, and with higher customer satisfaction. But the way each question is worded has the causal arrow backwards. **You don't build engagement to create a relationship; you create a relationship that leads to greater engagement.**

Engagement and these other good thinking and feeling states are a combination of what a person brings to the table (followership) and what the workplace fosters through factors such as leadership and institutional climate.

A 30-Second Rant!

There is a bit of mind-bending logic that permeates leadership guidance that drives us batty. It goes like this:

1. Leaders (alone) create relationships;
2. Followers are passive recipients of relationships;
3. Therefore, if a relationship is poor, it is the fault of leadership.

This chain of reasoning leads to two hard-to-swallow conclusions. First, it assumes everyone who is not a leader acts like a child, unable to take charge of their actions or fate. If you want a bunch of kids at work, hire them, but don't infantilize followership and the people who actively engage in it. Second, what about people who have both leadership and followership roles? Are they passive in their follower role but active doers in their leadership role; relationship builders at one moment and waiting for a relationship at another? It doesn't make sense to us, especially since we are talking about the CEO, CFO, CIO, COO, vice presidents, and everyone else all the way to the shop floor. How many good CEOs wait for their board of directors to engage them, or align them to the organizational goals? None of the successful ones we know.

In any partnership, relationship building is a shared accountability. All the partners have to build and nurture a comfortable, respectful, and productive working relationship. However, the roles of leadership and followership have differences that are important in understanding how to be effective in each.

Rather than waiting for relationships to develop organically we recommend more of a hard skill approach that emphasizes practical actions you can implement straight away. Using this approach shortens the time it takes to create a relationship – important for today's rapid pace of interpersonal change – and increases the likelihood of success. You wouldn't leave your technical role up to chance and time to develop, why do so with the people side, expecting good things just to happen naturally?

Relationship Framing: The Leadership Role

Key Leadership Ideas

- Equity is Job #1.
- Trust is tenuous: no violations are allowed!
- Relate to the team as an entity.
- Relate to each person on the team.
- Scrap the golden rule – you are not leading you – and use the Platinum Rule instead.

People work for people not companies or systems. A bad relationship with their direct boss is a major reason people leave a job.[3] Why? Because relationships count more than anything else. Remember Principle 3 – lean in to build connection – and the results of Google's Project Oxygen? It was a lot about relationships.

Relationships are the lifeblood of organizations: the heart, the soul, and the fuel. Everybody wants to work with people whom they know, contribute to their growth, and support them. Everyone wants that sense of effortless belonging. When relationships work, it results in optimum job performance and job satisfaction for both partners. When it doesn't work, a relationship can be distracting, disturbing, or dysfunctional for individuals and teams.

In your leadership role, you must *frame* the relationship building activities for your team: create and nurture an environment that is supportive, collaborative, respectful, professional, and where everyone feels they belong. Your job is to set an example and set the tone. At the top of this list is being equitable.

Equity Is Job #1

In the mid-1970s researchers realized that leaders didn't have the same relationship with every employee: they form stronger bonds with some people than others. We know it sounds obvious – it took researchers how long to figure this out? – but in the researchers' defense, up to that point, leadership theory had been based on the traits, behaviors, or situations of one person: the leader. All of these factors disregarded relationships.

This obvious incongruity led to a strand of leadership research called *leader-member exchange* (LMX) theory that considered the relationships between leaders and followers from a more mutual perspective. Leaders typically develop some high or favorable exchange relationships with an in-group – people who get more support, honest communication, and consultation by the leader. The in-group shares in more responsibility but is expected to work harder. Leaders also develop some low exchange relationships characterized by less mutuality, a more rules-based management approach, and less access to resources. This out-group suffers lower morale and reduced opportunity in all aspects of work.

Two researchers in the area of LMX, Terry Scandura and George Graen, wondered if training managers on building stronger one-on-one relationships with their out-group would improve employee outcomes such as productivity, morale, and satisfaction. They trained managers for a total of 12 hours over a 6-week period on active listening skills, being individually considerate, and initiating a mutual sharing of expectations. Within three weeks of the training, employees in the out-group of the managers improved on every measurement including a 19% gain in productivity – estimated to be worth about $5 million to the organization studied.[4]

Improving the weakest relationships between leaders and followers improves productivity by 19%.

Scandura and Graen didn't make a fuss over the fact that, as part of the change in behavior, the manager sat down with each employee in his out-group for a series of half-hour meetings. We think this change was critical; without knowing for sure, we suspect that in the past this group of employees got less face time and less interpersonal equity than their peers from the in-group. The last thing anyone wants to do in a leadership role is to play favorites or treat people differently because of how they treat you, but it happens. It is harder to be equitable than most of us like to admit. There are always going to be team members with whom you connect more easily, those you handpicked, those you relate to or those who work harder. They probably remind you of yourself, and we are hardwired to prefer people we see ourselves in.

Commit to making everyone part of the in-group! Give them face time, actively listen, exchange expectations and working style preferences, and the team will do better.

It doesn't mean that you have to, or should, treat everyone the same all the time. But it does mean that when you treat someone differently you must be conscious of it and careful to ensure that the rest of the team understands why. For example, people understand why a brand-new team member needs extra time. If explained, people also understand why a team member with a high-profile, complex project requires more of your attention. The point is that equity has a huge impact on results.

A simple tool to check in on the quality and condition of your current relationship activities within your team is an Equity Checkup.

An Equity Checkup (Tool 10.1) is a log of the one-on-one time you spend with each team member over a period of a week to a month. The objective is not to justify your actions but to evaluate your normal behavior and find opportunities for improvement.

Review the results to ensure you are being equitable in how you invest your time. Be sure that any extra time you spend with a team member is reasonable within the context of a circumstance such as being new to the team or engaged in a high-profile assignment. Be sure that reduced time is temporary, as in a vacation or an outstanding reschedule. Most of all, if there are inequities, confirm with each team member that your reasons are clear to them as well.

!FliPtips! Tool 10.1 Equity Checkup

A sample format:

My Team Members	One-on-One Time This Week	Rationale for More (Less) Time	Understood by Team Members?	Understood by Team?
Jane	1 hour	New to team	Need to explain	I should talk to them about it*
Lorraine	½ hour	Long-time team member	Yes	Yes
Bill	2 hours	Team lead	Yes	Maybe not*
Jill	none	*	No*	No*

* Items I have to follow up on …

Sucked In by Suck-Ups

If you've been skimming ahead, you will know that the #1 recommendation we have for the followership skill of relationship building is the exact thing that sucks us into the trap of playing favorites. The more initiative a follower takes in building a relationship, the more likely the leader is to favor him with a good relationship.

Marshall Goldsmith, one of the world's leading executive coaches and business thinkers, points out that we all get unwittingly sucked in by suck-ups – he gets taken in by his dog because dogs are expert at being man's best friend! Although most of us claim to abhor derriere kissers the truth is we easily succumb to and reinforce their adoration. This is Goldsmith's Habit #14 – Playing Favorites – from his best seller, *What Got You Here Won't Get You There*.

In our manager role, how can we recognize and discourage the hollow praise dished out by the suck-ups on our team? Goldsmith recommends ranking direct reports on three criteria: (1) how well they appear to like you; (2) how much value-add they bring to the organization; and (3) how much recognition you give them. His advice is to ditch the yes men. Excellent advice, to which we add be careful not to torpedo legitimate followership at the same time. When you are making a decision you want people to debate with you, give you honest opinions, offer alternatives, and provide dissenting perspectives (not be yes men). Once a decision is made, however, you want your team to execute creatively without disrupting the process. If we are brutally honest with ourselves we should be able to spot the anomalies in either situation and redirect support to legitimate followership.

Not Too Soft, Not Too Hard. Appropriate Is Just Right

Remember Goldilocks trying the three chairs in the bears' house? It may seem a bit fussy but she had to get just the right chair to be comfortable. When setting the tone for appropriate relationship building on your team, *equity* is the #1 way to get it just right, with *appropriate* as a close second.

A friend of ours, John, was complaining about his new leader. We hear complaints about leaders all the time – too demanding, too micromanaging, not around enough, doesn't get it – but we rarely hear "too nice"! John says his leader is really friendly to everyone but soft on performance targets and doesn't make the tough calls necessary for the success of the team. He says that everyone on the team recognizes this and the boss is rapidly losing credibility.

At the end of the day, the purpose of fostering strong workplace relationships within your team is to build partnerships that increase performance and satisfaction, not to find your next golf buddy or drinking buddy or best friend. While you want to create a fun and spirited environment it can never be at the expense of getting the job done.

Appropriate, comfortable, "just right" workplace relationships must also be professional. We heard about a female manager who was throwing a party for her whole team of about 25 people one summer weekend. It sounded rather fun and generous until we found out it was a hot tub party. Her two supervisors were very uncomfortable, not knowing what to do. Their instincts were that this wasn't appropriate. They were right: they were put in a tricky quandary between staff who were freaked out by the nature of the party and the manager who was acting freaky in thinking it was okay. We should mention that this happened at a very conservative organization. Admittedly the definition of what's appropriate varies between industries, professions, and company cultures. However, unless you are employed by a hot tub manufacturer or by Hugh Hefner, the nature of this team-building activity is probably inappropriate.

The Tenuousness of Trust

At times, trust seems both mystical and motherhood. When you read up on relationship building guidance, trust comes up again and again. Often trust is cited as the basis or fundamental *input* into a strong relationship.[5] We propose that trust is actually an *outcome* of a strong relationship. Regardless of which of these perspectives you lean toward, there are some aspects of trust that are useful to know.

First of all, trust develops through a process of mutual interaction. Ferrin, Bligh, and Kohles (2008) suggest that it works like a spiral – cooperation leads to trust, which leads to further cooperation, which leads to greater trust, and so on. The good news is that most of us begin new workplace relationships – an increasingly frequent situation – with fairly high levels of trust.[6] The bad news is trust can either spiral up or down from that point. Much as we wonder about the long-term effectiveness of training programs that take teams down river rapids in a raft or have them rock climbing together, there is a point that sometimes a downward spiral has to be halted and reset. A new start, if you will. Of course, because it is a spiral, a trust-building event is just a new beginning … it then needs continuous reinforcement back at work to keep the spiral moving upwards.

New workplace relationships usually start with a high level of trust.

Where does our initial high level of trust come from? It is a blend of personal beliefs about others, implicit beliefs that particular people in particular jobs are trustworthy, and that organizations punish untrustworthy behavior. This is critical. If an organization acts in ways that are untrustworthy, it sours not only existing relationships but also the agility and adaptability of its employees to form interpersonal relationships in the future. Initial trust becomes much lower and is harder to coax into an upward spiral.

We were privileged to stay with a lovely Austin, Texas, family for a few days. When we arrived, it turned out the husband/father had recently quit his job: he worked for years as the top architect at a firm that had been taken over by a larger competitor. The acquiring company made a variety of promises including that the acquired firm be able to keep its structure and culture, a promise that was quickly broken.

It is not as though the acquiring firm had a culture that was immoral, unethical, or toxic. Had our friend been hired rather than acquired by them, he probably would have enjoyed working there. Instead, however, he quit. We suspect that the owners of the acquiring company were baffled, not realizing that how this violation of institutional trust soured relationships so significantly. In a corporate acquisition, if the acquiring company miscalculates the challenge of people integration, it can destroy the initial (institutional) basis for trust that is most needed to develop relationships, teams, and partnerships. It is a big reason many takeovers fail to deliver value.

So far we have been talking about trust as if it were a singular concept. It isn't. Trust comes in two flavors: trust in someone's competence (that he can do the job) and trust in someone's integrity (faith in his intentions).[7] These two types of trust are quite different. For example, the occasional lapse in competence is easily overlooked if there are some positive experiences to counter the negative: good deeds outweigh bad ones when it comes to competence.[8] There is evidence that taking prompt action to remedy a situation after a competency failure can even lead to higher levels of trust.[9] A lapse in integrity is much harder to remedy, and it takes an entirely different set of strategies to recover from this type of violation.[10]

What are the elements of trust in a business relationship? Trust that your partner has your best interests in mind and at heart. Trust that your partner holds your confidences and keeps your needs, vulnerabilities, and worries safe in the partnership vault. Trust that your partner will be honest and upfront with you. And, trust that your partner will deliver what she says she is going to deliver and does so with a high level of competence. Only the last point was about competency; all the rest are about integrity. That's a lot of expectations, and a lot to go wrong that is hard to fix.

The only way to meet these expectations is to ensure they aren't violated in the first place. Some expectations are universal – be honest, do what you say you will do, etc. But others are person dependent. Help your staff understand what you and the organization expect and how they can demonstrate it. This is the main reason that building a relationship with each team member is a critical Generative Partnership® skill. In fact, do everything you can to ensure your team members avoid lapses of integrity while spending less time fussing over the occasional lapse of competence.

> Do everything possible to avoid lapses of integrity.
> Fuss less about occasional lapses of competence.

Relate to the Team as an Entity

It might sound a bit peculiar – to develop a relationship with the team as an entity – however, doing so is important and multipurpose. Consider it one part efficiency, one part equity, and one part identity. Some activities a leader does are simply better with the whole team at once such as communications, goal setting, welcoming new team members, and other types of networking. It is wildly more efficient and generally viewed as more equitable: no one feels that he or she are missing out on anything.

Other than for efficiency and equity, relating to the team as a whole creates a sense of team identity. Having that sense of team, of belonging, is a real pull for a lot of people going into the office. It also stimulates collaboration. Foster a spirit of fun and camaraderie. Have team learning events and learn with them! If you are swamped, it is okay to nominate a team event planner. Sam had one of those on her team years back: Carin loved coming up with creative ways to stimulate team spirit and she was great at it. When Sam first acquired the team as part of a large merger, they had the lowest morale in the whole division. Within six months their spirit was the envy of the whole floor thanks to Carin. As Sam says about that time, "I had the sense to recognize Carin's potential, get out of the way, and let good things happen."

Relate to Each Person on the Team

Sam read an article, "Team leadership lessons from the field," in an HR publication. One manager interviewed said his biggest mistake was calling people into the office one-on-one. His feeling was that it isolated everyone and fueled the rumor mill. Instead, he "evolved" to having impromptu meetings with all of them at once. This is a common yet unfortunate response: if something isn't working we do the opposite in the hopes that it will fix the problem.[11] We are in favor of impromptu meetings; team huddles can be useful, productive, and energizing. But there is also a place for planned team meetings. And there is a place for planned one-on-one meetings that encourage personal discussions and valuable face time. Done well, one-on-one meetings can be your secret weapon as a leader – a lot can be accomplished in just one hour every week or every other week, and you will be appreciated for it. You can give 100% of your attention and all your genuine interest to the team member in front of you.

Lest you think the need for this practice is changing in our increasingly interconnected, digital world, think again. The Millennials now entering the workforce are the most team-oriented generation to date. They are extremely social, love interacting with their peers, and are used to being constantly connected with their circle of cohorts through social media: soliciting advice on anything, giving advice on everything, confirming the merits of ideas, or confirming lunch plans. They will want time with you.

Millennials aren't unique in this respect. Sam once had a senior vice president remark to her that she loved having executives report to her (as compared with analysts, supervisors, managers, or directors) because at that level she could just leave them alone. We wonder if her executives were similarly contented with the SVPs hands-off approach?

In order for your team members to feel your genuine support and for you to get it just right with each of them, you need to get to know them individually. Ask questions, actively listen – by which we mean listen to understand, not to provide a response – and be genuinely interested in the answers. It is not essential to get to know everyone personally, but it is useful to find things in common. Tread carefully, though, as each person has a different comfort zone with how much personal information he or she chooses to share in the workplace and with his or her leader. Sam is basically an open book. Marc less so, but he is forthcoming when the right question is asked (you have to know to ask).

Scrap the Golden Rule: You Are NOT Leading You

Recall the golden rule you were taught as a kid: do unto others as you would have them do unto you? Toss it out the window. You are NOT leading you.

Replace this thinking with the *platinum rule*: treat others the way they like to be treated. Don't assume or pigeonhole your team members. Ask them about their work preferences: what makes them tick, be successful, be unsuccessful, be challenged, how they prefer to be recognized, what's important to them. Ask them about their interests: what they enjoy in their job, what other activities would they like to explore, what skills would they like to develop, what growth areas are they currently working on, what do they aspire to do in the future. And re-ask regularly.

The Platinum Rule: Treat others the way they want to be treated.

You can't always accommodate every team member's needs and requests, or dreams and aspirations, but your genuine interest and attempt at doing so will go a long way.

Relationship Building: The Followership Role

Key Followership Ideas

- Take the initiative for relationship building with your leader.
- Forget the golden rule: you are NOT following you.
- Help your leader get to know you.
- Pay attention to the little things.

Bank of America has one of the most extensive and impressive executive onboarding programs we have heard of.[12] It is an 18-month process that starts with a customized plan put together with input from key stakeholders followed by a team relationship exercise. A trio of coaches is assigned to facilitate the onboarding process: a senior advisor (for career mentoring), a peer coach (for organizational mentoring), and a dedicated learning and development (LD) partner (for the onboarding process). It continues with a series of events to unpack critical information including a New Executive Orientation Program with an informal panel discussion and presentations by many of the bank's senior executive team, all of whom reveal their personal experience and lessons learned. This is followed by a key stakeholder check-in for verbal and written feedback in time for corrective action before the formal 360° feedback and performance review. You get the picture. Extensive!

Given that the potential cost of executive derailment to an organization is upwards of $2.7 million per person and that the probability of derailment is 40%,[13] having a deluxe "prevention policy" is a smart idea. In fact, executive derailment at Bank of America fell to 12% after this program was introduced – a net savings of around $750,000 per executive. So the new onboarding program works, and it pays a handsome return on investment. But that's not why we wanted to mention it. One stage of the program includes a stakeholder check-in scheduled after 100 to 130 days into the new executive's tenure. The check-in is booked and facilitated by the LD partner after having interviewed "peers, partners, stakeholders, and direct reports" (Conger & Fishel, 2007, p. 453). The LD partner interviews everyone **except** for the new executive's boss. This is because Bank of America considers it the responsibility of each new executive to follow up independently with his or her boss in a timely fashion. But the new executives aren't told about this expectation. As the authors of the study say, "This independent act of initiative (by the new executive) is a critical characteristic of those who go on to be strong leaders in the Bank of America culture" (p. 453). How telling! The bank covertly introduced a followership relationship "final exam." Executives who succeed – the keepers, in other words – made the effort to build a relationship with their boss.

Successful executives are adept at followership.

The message from this is clear. **Don't underestimate** how important relationship building is, and **do take the initiative** when it comes to building your most important workplace relationship: the one with your formal leader. A key feature of the followership role in relationship building is taking the initiative more regularly to build a strong working relationship within the frame set by the leader.

Take the Initiative

We knew two senior executives who were vying for the top job after the CEO of their organization retired. One of them, James, did not win the CEO job. His peer, Bill, did. After an arduous two-year competition,

James found himself reporting to Bill. The relationship didn't go well and James left the company after six months.

Years later, James took part in one of our followership focus groups. Reflecting back on what happened, he had an epiphany. James realized that he had not made sufficient efforts, or taken the initiative to mend that key relationship. He had been too busy licking his wounds and waiting for the winner, Bill, to make all the moves. It didn't happen and the consequence was sadly predictable.

This isn't just another example of alpha males butting heads. Lynn Schmidt's 2009 research on derailed female executives contains quotes that reveal similar blind spots:

> If you don't have a positive relationship with your boss it's never gonna get better. You can't fix it, you know. People are gonna ... click with people they click with ... you just need to clear out. You need to go spend your life doing something else. (p. 75)

In her study, 75% of the women Schmidt contacted mentioned a poor relationship as one of the primary factors behind getting fired (or quitting). In some cases there was probably nothing the executive could have done. But there are also many people like the woman in the quote who take a passive approach to their most important working relationship. We can't concur with the person quoted above as we believe: (1) it can get better; and (2) you can be the reason.

In his best seller *The First 90 Days* Michael Watkins advises that, in your followership role, you should "take 100% responsibility for making the relationship (with your boss) work." While this may overemphasize the followership role in building relationships, it does so because much of the advice out there today suggests it is solely a leadership responsibility.

Why should the follower take the initiative more often? The math tells the story. Managers have multiple followers. In many organizations one manager can have 10, 20, or more direct reports but each person has only one formal leader (or perhaps two if they work in a matrix structure). It stands to reason that the onus should be on the follower to spend more time on relationship building – it is the practical solution.

Poor relationship building is implicated in 75% of firings.

There are other benefits to focusing on relationship building in your followership role:

- Bosses are impressed by the initiative.
- It demonstrates a high level of engagement.
- It shows an appreciation that the boss's job is often more demanding and more time consuming.
- The care and conscientiousness that goes into deliberate relationship building gives the impression of confidence and trust in the boss, which is often reciprocated.
- Having a strong relationship with your boss and other upper management comes with benefits. Not only does it increase your chances of promotion, but it helps you put other people at ease.[14]

Forget the Golden Rule: You Are NOT Following You

Every year we attend MindCamp, one of the premier creativity conferences in the world. It is four days of morning-to-midnight creativity held at a YMCA facility a few hours north of Toronto in the heart of Ontario cottage country, the Muskokas. The scenery is magnificent, as is the choice of workshops – everything from graphic facilitation tools to meditation to the neuroscience of creativity. It is such a unique event that it sells out early year after year: attendees come from Australia, Africa, Europe, Latin American, Mexico, the USA, and Canada. Many are consultants, but there are also representatives from organizations including Disney, U.S. military, United Way, and many more. It is a who's who of creativity.

We held a workshop there a few years back on leadership and followership, in particular on how to be more agile with new partnerships. One attendee, Jim Ridge, a graphic artist, declared at the beginning of the workshop that he was stressed because the day after MindCamp ended he was going to be reporting to a new boss at work, someone he didn't know and hadn't heard much about. During the workshop Jim created a plan. Rather than wait for a relationship to just happen, he decided to take the initiative. Jim prepared a list of 20 questions to ask his new boss and a strategy to ask the questions over a period of the first month, just enough to keep developing the relationship bit by bit but not too much to be intrusive or seem needy. We got a lovely note from Jim not long after (Sept. 10, 2010). It is still pinned up on our message board to remind us why we are passionate about partnerships and also because Jim happens to be a fabulous illustrator. The thank you note was pure art! Not only did taking control of the situation reduce his stress but the strategy worked superbly: the two quickly built a positive relationship.

Ideally your manager will come with an operating manual. If not, we encourage you to do what Jim did and create your own. Think about all the things that would be relevant to know about him or her. Learn everything from her pet peeves, best time of day for thinking, best time for meetings, how she takes her coffee, what she has on her plate that she loves to do, and what she dreads. You can get more great tips from books and articles, albeit it is rarely called *followership* advice.[15] Once you have that advice, it is your responsibility to adopt it.[16]

Help Them Get to Know You

By the same token, be easy to build a relationship with. Be clear about the things that help you be successful at your job. Work to know yourself well, what you do best, and how you do it best.

 Looking back on my corporate career, one of my best team member relationships was with Bessie. Bessie was the manager of an accounts receivable and payable department. She was very experienced in her role. I acquired the team and initially felt a bit sheepish being her leader given her many years of experience vs. mine (zilch!). However, thanks to Bessie's self-awareness, confidence, and enthusiasm for building a strong partnership with me, it worked really well, really quickly. I remember Bessie being totally clear about what was working, what could be improved, and how I could add value. She was forthcoming with what she needed and could really use help on. I did the same. She taught me how to lead an admin-

istrative department, and I brought more technical accounting standards and rigor to the team which, in turn, boosted the credibility and respect the team members received from their internal and external customers. A definite win/win.

When we were discussing this topic I actually thought about Sam first. Not only is my relationship with her the most creative, productive partnership I've had, she is the first girlfriend, wife, or life partner who does this effectively with me. When I make a relationship mistake – yes, being a guy it happens with a certain predictability – Sam is always quick to tell me what I did wrong in the right way, and how to fix it straight away. Then she waits for me to do so. For example, if she has written something awesome and asked me to edit it (often how we work), I might return it with a few corrections and no other comment. To me that means, great: the draft was so strong there was little for me to change. But Sam wants to hear that the effort she put in was appreciated. So she clarifies her expectation and what she was hoping for. It makes for an incredibly productive relationship both in business and as a couple.

Ideally you want to create a work environment that enables you to really get into your work (what we described at the beginning of the book as co-flow). It may mean minimizing interruptions, blocking out times in your schedule, or scheduling brainstorming time. In his book *How to Be a Star at Work*, Robert Kelley says, "the biological and personality quirks that make us individuals don't make the difference between the stars and their average coworkers ... you need to remain true to who you are" (p. 22). If you are a night owl and not a morning person, fess up. Your leader will want you at your best so may be absolutely fine to accommodate (no guarantees but hopefully).

Sam once had a boss, Kathy, who was terrific at onboarding herself, making it easy to get to know her and her expectations. She essentially came with an operating manual such as the tool described in 10.2: my favorite treat is a Kit Kat Chunky; I don't like to hold meetings before 10 a.m.; I don't like surprises ... tell me bad news or about errors right away, not after you've solved it; I really appreciate being kept up-to-date on team events and accomplishments; and I hate excuses. This was

FliPtips! Tool 10.2 How to Write a Personal Operating Manual

Know and express what you need to be successful in both your leadership and followership roles. Articulate and communicate your operating style. You can't expect your workplace partners to read your mind and magically get it right. Figure out how to describe how you work well and what you really need, then differentiate between critical things and nice-to-haves.

- What are all the relevant things to get to know about you that help you put your best foot forward?
- What do you need to be your strongest individual contributor?
- What do you need from your leader/manager/team members to do the best in your followership and leadership roles?
- What are the dimensions to have in your Operating Manual? Consider your communication preferences, how you think best, how you make decisions, your risk/mistake tolerance, your strengths/preferences/weak spots, how you prefer to structure your day, etc.

Critical: _____

Nice-to-have: _____

such an effective strategy that we turned it into a tool (10.2). The tool can be used in your leadership role and in your followership role.

Pay Attention to the Little Things

When someone is important to you, you take the time to do the little things that create a better relationship. In our followership focus groups the number one way we were told followers build rapport is by bringing coffee to their boss on occasion. It sounds cheesy, but it is a nice touch that gives you a chance for small talk and demonstrates that you care about personalizing the experience.

There are many other ways to enhance rapport: follow up on something your partner casually mentioned she was interested in, be a safe zone by keeping confidences, save a seat or food for your partner at meetings if she was late. When you take the time AND it isn't expected, it is more likely to be ascribed to your character; much more value is placed on it. For example, executive assistants might be expected to fetch coffee so the relationship benefit of doing so is minimal. However, when an assistant is on vacation and a junior executive steps in to pick up the boss's favorite latte at Starbucks, it's a big deal.

Finally, display the ability to work well in groups and teams because mediating conflicts saps time and energy. It is a poor use of leadership effort. Being a team player means not only being cooperative and a decision advocate (a term and concept introduced in Chapter 9: Decision Partnering Skills) but also displaying strong leadership ability when it's appropriate. The next time a conflict arises within your team take the initiative to mediate. When you find your team getting stuck in a project, take the lead to move things forward. And what if you don't normally work with a team? Try to be more collaborative in the work you do and build professional relationships with your coworkers.

Relationship Partnering Skills Summary

Leadership Skill: Relationship Framing
Create an environment and rapport with your team and each team member that is comfortable and professional:

- ✓ Set the tone for relationship building on your team that is respectful and culturally appropriate.
- ✓ Ensure equity and fairness across the team.
- ✓ Mobilize and coordinate each team member's strengths and styles.

Followership Skill: Relationship Building
Take accountability for building and maintaining an excellent working relationship with your leader(s):

- ✓ Purposefully learn and adapt to your leader's style, preferences, and abilities.
- ✓ Express your own needs and what helps you be most successful.
- ✓ Be a team player.

CHAPTER 11

Organizational Agility Partnering Skills

Figure 11.1 Organizational Agility partnering skills

Don't Be a Sea Squirt and Eat Your Brain!

Sea squirts are the great transformers of the sea. A sea squirt – *Urochordata*, to give its scientific name – starts life looking like a tadpole with gills. It has a primitive nervous system, a whip-like appendage that helps it move called a notochord, and a small brain – really just a cluster of neurons. When the juvenile sea squirt finds a cozy place to settle, it attaches to the rock or other surface with the adhesive papillae on its chin and then proceeds to eat its eye, its notochord, and its brain! There it happily stays, one of the most beautiful undersea creatures you will see. Of course, since it no longer has a brain or means of movement, any change in the local environment means that it dies in the place it lived. It *adapts* perfectly when it settles in, but subsequently loses its *agility*.

Not having agility is rather like settling down in one place as a sea squirt. You can continue to do your job as long as everything remains the same. But when change happens – and it always does – you no longer have the sensory organs or mobility to make an agile response. Of course, people aren't sea squirts: they don't eat their brains; and they can adapt over time. But adaptation is a slow process. Adaptation works best when the (new) situation is stable and consistent – it is hard to adapt to flux. That makes adaptation most useful for incremental change but not so much when change is disruptive, quick, or when you have to continuously move from one environment to another. That requires agility.

Agility connotes a sense of speed, ease, and nimbleness: both physically and mentally. As such, agility is today's essential workplace competency, not adaptability or resiliency (which is the ability to return to one's original form).

This view emerged loud and clear in the 2012 IBM CEO Study, *Leading through Connections*. The more than 1,700 CEOs interviewed gave their opinions on what it meant to be a future-proof employee.

> Across industries and geographies, CEOs consistently highlight four personal characteristics most critical for employees' future success: being collaborative, communicative, creative and flexible. Given their intent to create greater openness, CEOs are looking for employees who will thrive in this kind of atmosphere … It's virtually impossible for CEOs to find the future skills they will need – because they don't yet exist. Bombarded by change, most organizations simply cannot envision the functional capabilities needed two or three years from now. (p. 20)

We work in an unprecedented era of speed and interpersonal change – organizations need to be agile, as do the people within them. Agility is the ability to move from situation to situation quickly and surely. The question then is, "How do I develop greater agility and help others do so, too?"

First, always be learning. Continually seek new information, gain new skills, build more self-awareness, and try new things. Seek both breadth and depth. Taking a multidisciplinary approach and encouraging leading-edge thinking stimulates mental acuity and agility.

Second, develop Partnership Agility. This is the focus of the previous chapter on Relationship Partnering Skills, and much of the rest of the book, too. Be intentional in your partnership building by using tools, checklists, schedules, and other methods that enable you to develop the skill as you would a technical skill. Your relationships will flourish as will your partnership agility.

Third, develop Organizational Agility. Whereas Partnership Agility enables you to build and rebuild partnerships swiftly and surely, Organizational Agility enables you to move from team to team and across the organization. It is the focus of this chapter.

Another question that needs addressing is whether people should be expected to learn the ropes themselves, or is it a leadership responsibility to provide organizational agility for their staff? The answer is both (of course!). The role of leadership is to mentor and the role of followership is to actively engage in learning by observation, networking, asking questions, and testing assumptions. That is how the partnership gold is unearthed.

The leadership and followership roles don't depend on where people are in the organizational hierarchy. For example, the well-known chocolate and confectionery treats company, Mars, implemented a formal *reverse mentoring* program where frontline staff had an opportunity to mentor senior executives. Even "[the] president is mentored by one of our students on Millennials and social media."[1] GE did the same when Jack Welch required his executives get mentoring on the Internet by junior staff. This role reversal can also happen when a new manager takes charge of a team: the job is to mentor them in what's important to know about the team and organization including typical department expectations, deadlines, customs, history, and hot issues – this is informal leadership at its best. Just be careful to share it as your personal experience, and don't expect everything to stay the same after.

While it may be incredibly difficult to prepare ourselves and our organizations for the future skills we need, by focusing on agility skills we will get there more swiftly regardless of where *there* will be!

Organizational Mentoring: The Leadership Role

Key Points

- Create a comfortable, co-learning safe zone.

- Get "the village" to help.
- Be clear about what's being given and received.
- Use a framework to guide the learning experience.

The quickest way to develop agility is with the help of people who already have it, and that's the leadership role. Organizational Mentoring is the activity of helping others navigate and thrive within the workplace.

Agility comes from understanding the culture. It isn't the only aspect of it, but it is the part that is really difficult to get without mentoring. That is why we take a brief dive into culture first before unpacking the key points of Organizational Mentoring.

> Culture should be clear and explicit. Leaders must be continually conscious of the culture: conscious that it's intentional, conscious that it's meaningful, conscious that it's effective, and conscious about helping others thrive within it.
>
> – *Cindy Gordon, Culture Shock Coaching*

The role of leadership is to influence the culture, to decode it, to transmit it, and to mentor it. However, it becomes increasingly challenging to unravel, differentiate, and communicate an organization's culture the longer your tenure is at one place. It's natural: the more you've been drinking the water, the more you underestimate your culture's influence and how challenging it can be for newcomers to decode. It also makes it harder to adapt to a new or different culture.

In your role as a manager or a team member, take time to do Organizational Mentoring with new team members. Share your insider's knowledge, be explicit about why things are the way they are, and walk the talk. As you help newcomers become effective quickly, also remember to listen and remain open to new ideas and insights.

The longer you are in a culture, the harder it becomes to distinguish and articulate its unique features.

Mentoring is not just for newcomers, top talent, or junior staff. Everyone can benefit from it at different points in their career even if they are already successful or experienced. With team members who are more established, invite them to talk about what's changed, what they noticed across the organization, and ask them to consider mentoring others. Then help them discover the right questions to ask and how to reinforce the culture while celebrating diversity within it.

There are many benefits to mentoring; the obvious one is that it helps newcomers get up to speed more quickly and comfortably. Mentoring can also play a big part in attracting talent to an organization, fostering engagement, celebrating diversity, building organizational learning, supporting succession planning, and leveraging the subject matter expertise of an aging workforce. Finally, mentoring forces the mentor to examine and put into words how the organization works. As any teacher could tell you, having to explain something to others often enriches your own understanding.

Organizations are often concerned, however, that mentoring is too expensive and that senior people don't have the time to spend mentoring.

The Value of Mentoring

Anne Lavender, executive director of leadership, Waterloo region, recalls:

> One of the best mentoring experiences I ever had was when I was a mentee and was invited to the table as a full participant in the learning process. She (my mentor) made me feel like she was getting just as much out of the time we spent together as I was.

The fact is this: mentoring is one of the most cost- and time-effective development activities for organizations. It doesn't just benefit the mentees, either. A study of chief financial officers conducted by Robert Half Management Resources revealed that 22% of CFOs found the biggest reward of being a mentor was improving their own leadership skills.[2] Research consistently shows the positive impact of mentorship for both the mentor and the mentee.[3]

The biggest reward of mentoring is improving leadership skills.

As mentors unpack what they know and articulate it, their thinking crystallizes about the behaviors and actions that drive success. This learning loop is bolstered by prompts from the mentee. Done well, it is a positive growth experience for both partners. With engagement scores at an all-time low and executive derailment at an all-time high, mentoring turns out to be one of the least risky investments you can make.

The Mentoring Safe Zone

Keep mentoring moments confidential and non-evaluative. For example, don't link mentoring to performance evaluations. This creates a safe zone where learning can flourish. If you engage in a mentoring relationship with someone other than a direct report, establish an agreement that includes confidentiality, expectations both ways, and what the ground rules will be. Consider how to make the mentee feel that it's a level playing field. Success depends on both partners being highly self-reflective.

It is important to stimulate reflection right off the bat at the first mentor-mentee meeting. Consider beginning any new mentoring relationship with a discussion of shared goals (see Chapter 8 – Principle 5: Have Deeply Shared Goals).

Get "The Village" to Help

When people think about mentoring they picture a wise, seasoned master advising a keen, young apprentice. As we're both *Star Wars* fans, we inevitably picture Yoda advising young Luke Skywalker how to harness the power of the force with his legendary, pithy words of wisdom such as:

> Secret, shall I tell you? You will find only what you bring in.
> Do, or do not. There is no try.
> Always pass on what you have learned.

This makes mentoring seem daunting to us mere mortals or, at least, for us non-muppets! How on earth can we live up to the mentoring prowess of Yoda in our leadership roles? Fortunately, the answer is simple: we don't have to. Perhaps it doesn't quite take a village, as the expression goes, but when it comes to organizational mentoring go ahead and call in the village. The mentor role can be carried out by various people in an organization: sometimes one's (formal) leader, sometimes another senior person steps in, sometimes a seasoned peer, occasionally as in reverse mentoring it is a junior staff member, and sometimes all of the above. No single person has to do it all. Encourage and help facilitate the mentoring that all your team members need and desire, whether you take it on personally or farm it out. In particular, frame the mentoring by clarifying what it is for (and isn't for), who should be involved, and when it is taking place.

Be Clear about What's Being Given and Received

Years ago Sam received surprising feedback from her direct reports as part of a formal 360° assessment. Five of the seven responded that she was "a highly generous and useful mentor"; but the other two of the seven, her most junior staff, said that she didn't do any mentoring at all. Sam was puzzled by the divided feedback, especially as she had hour long, weekly one-on-one meetings with each person on her team. She began to suspect that the two junior staff didn't realize they were being mentored. So Sam tried being more explicit with them after that, literally saying, "I am now about to give you some mentoring." Happily, it worked: six months later Sam got feedback that all now appreciated her mentoring.

In the leadership role of Decision Framing, we discussed how crucial it was to have a milestone separating the exploratory, pre-decision period from the execution-oriented implementation phase. The frames in each were different because the followership role changed with the phase. Don't forget to make the mentoring frame explicit, too. Not only does it ensure that the conversation isn't taken as a casual, "By the way, this might be of use to you, ignore it if you want," sort of discussion, it also gives the mentee license to ask questions, probe for more information, or contextualize the information. With so many ideas competing for attention, those little flags we put up to signal "Stop! This is important!" helps distinguish the nice-to-know from the act-on-now. That's what Sam had to learn in her leadership role.

Use a Framework for the Learning Experience

While it is the mentee's role to drive his or her learning by setting the agenda,[4] it is the leadership role to *frame* the learning experience. Some of the framing is environmental – we've talked about being explicit about the mentoring, creating a safe zone, and ensuring a co-learning experience. We would now like to recommend the use of a specific frame for the *topics* of conversation (Figure 11.2).

Diving deeper into the mentoring framework, Tool 11.1 provides specific questions that can be used for *any* mentoring opportunity, so some of the questions will fall outside the scope of Organizational Agility; but that's okay.

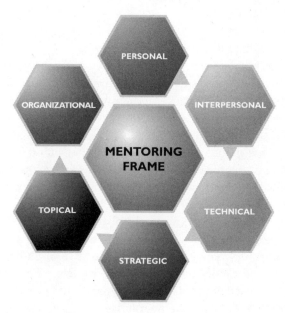

Figure 11.2 A mentoring framework

FliPtips! Tool 11.1 The Six Dimensions of Mentoring

This framework comprises six topics with suggested questions to stimulate mentoring discussion.

Personal	How am I feeling? What am I working on/just been assigned/and do I feel confident in my abilities? Are my career aspirations a good choice for my strengths and the organization?
Interpersonal	How am I getting along with my leader/peers/team? How might I build even stronger relationships? How might I handle a sticky situation or adapt better to a situation I'm in? How might I expand my internal networks? Am I taking on both leadership and followership roles within my peer group?
Technical	How comfortable am I with the fundamentals of my job? What about preparation for my next job or the next level? What are considered best practices, and when/how do I apply them?
Strategic	How might I develop or demonstrate my strategic thinking/planning/perspective? Do I understand the big picture: the environment, the customers, the business drivers, the competitors, and the marketplace?
Topical	What's hot in my field? What's relevant in the news, in R&D, and in current books? What trends, changes, and controversies should I know about?
Organizational	What can you share with me about the company's culture, the pulse of what's happening now, the way communication happens? How has history shaped today? How do the following factors influence decisions, where people spend their time, and how success is defined: people, customers, deadlines, scope/objectives, revenue, expense management, short- vs. long-term thinking? What variations are there across the organization in different areas? How does the organization promote life balance, learning, collaboration, social responsibility, and opportunities for leadership? What are the learning hazards, roadblocks, and things to beware of? What are typical career paths, and how does that progression happen?

Organizational Agility: The Followership Role

Key Points

- Honor the organizational culture, and take your cues from it.
- Network to work.
- Drive your own discovery and development.
- Practice Organizational Agility.

The followership role is to understand and adapt to the many different cultures and subcultures you encounter in an organization and outside it if you interact with customers, suppliers, or other external people as part of your job. Some people are naturally adept at understanding new cultures. They have a high cultural intelligence or CQ: a combination of innate and learned abilities:[5]

1. Knowing how to think about culture – metacognitive CQ
2. Wanting to learn more about culture
3. Knowing the rules of a specific culture – cognitive CQ
4. Being able to use the rules in appropriate ways – behavioral CQ

The first of these abilities is mostly innate although you can get better at it over a long period of time. The second is solely a followership responsibility. Similar to engagement, it is something strong followers bring to the table. The last two are the natural domain of partnerships, where the leadership role is to mentor and the followership role to learn, absorb, and become more culturally agile.

In mid-career, an MBA colleague of Marc offered him a job and a promotion. Marc had been working as a quant in the actuarial department because of his math credentials and ability to think outside the box, both useful skills for pricing complex financial products. Prior to being offered this new job, Marc had been coming to work in wacky, colorful T-shirts, challenging the status quo yet producing excellent results. His MBA colleague was the head of the marketing department looking for an injection of creativity and Marc was just the outgoing, innovative person to get the job done. As part of the hiring process, Marc was interviewed by most of the senior executives including the general manager.

The GM had one last question for Marc:

We are looking for someone to rock the boat, but not tip it over. Can you do that?

It was a great clue and question, letting Marc know he had to be both creative and culturally appropriate.

When you are aware of the culture it helps ensure your boss never has to defend your actions, and it shows that you care enough about your boss and the organization to make the extra effort. Strong followership entails working hard to learn the ropes, developing a deep understanding of an organization, and using this knowledge to thrive within it.

The expression "learning the ropes" is from the days of sailing ships. When a new recruit came aboard he would take the initiative to climb the ship's ropes, tie all the knots, and haul the sails. This helped him get a feel for the ship – how it handled, how it resisted, how to create balance, which sail was what, where you had to pull and push. After all, you don't want to tip it over!

Knowing the ropes in an organization gives you the confidence to get things done in a way that reflects well on yourself and suits the environment, regardless of whether you are in calm waters or being buffeted by foul weather.

In case you are wondering, Marc did get the job, rocked the boat, but didn't get anyone wet!

Honor the Organizational Culture and Take Your Cues from It

In his best-selling book, *The 48 Laws of Power*, Robert Greene suggests that you should "Think as you like but behave like others." He cautions that if you flaunt your unconventional ideas too much, people will think you only want attention and your ideas will fall on deaf ears. We all want our ideas to flourish, our contributions to matter, and our input to make a difference; so getting things done in organizationally appropriate ways yet still distinguishing oneself is key.

We're not saying you should change your personality or beliefs. And we're not saying that you should simply suck it up and fit in if the culture is toxic or unethical. We are saying that you need to embrace different roles. Consider yourself an actor in a very important play and, when you change departments, companies, locations, or bosses, keep in mind that you are now acting in a different play. Learn your new lines, the costume changes, and the cues.

Speaking of costume changes, one executive vice president we interviewed, Jonathan, had reported to four different bosses in six years. We asked him about agility and "getting on the bus" as it was obvious to us that he was an expert at it. Jonathan told us about how each boss he had worked for influenced the culture of the team with his or her norms and preferences. Often, the more senior the boss, the faster and broader the cultural influence. Here is one of his stories:

> When I first reported to Fred, shortly after he landed as President, he held his first leadership team meeting with all his direct reports. At the end of the meeting Fred asked me to stay a bit. He said,
>
>> "Jonathan, I notice you are wearing a golf shirt and khakis today."
>> "It's casual Friday," I replied.
>> Then he asked me, "What am I wearing?"
>> I answered, "A jacket, dress shirt, dress pants and tie."
>> My new boss was clear with his expectations: "I realize that the company recently implemented casual Fridays across the company but I'm afraid I'm from the old school. I still want my senior leadership team to look professional, in proper business attire. Got it?"
>
> I got it. I never wore a golf shirt into the office again. What's more, it signaled the way Fred wanted to run things.

To understand what the appropriate norms are, analyze what typically happens. For example, ask yourself which of these two statements more accurately describes meetings at your workplace?

1. People generally arrive early to meetings.
2. People are often late to meetings.

Next consider whether the answer varies by seniority, job, or team? Is it situational or do you see the same thing over and over again? Finally, present these observations to your mentor, boss, or peer. What is her take on it?

It's rather complicated when norms differ in your area from the company as a whole. How do you decide which set of norms to follow? Here's our suggestion: consider the primary audience and if it consists mostly of people from your area, follow those norms. If it is broader – which happens as you become more senior or find yourself on a cross-functional team – then follow the generic organizational norms rather than those of your area or team. If you have the opportunity, confirm expectations with your manager as what managers expect and what others do are not always consistent. Agility is all about sizing up situations and being able to switch it up in different situations.

Be observant and listen for all the cues. Some of the most profound learning can be done by simple observation. Keep a journal and document what you have noticed about the organization so far. Make reference to the Six Dimensions of Mentoring Framework and set about diarizing the many norms and behaviors. How do people behave with one another in specific circumstances such as meetings? What emotions do you observe? What is upsetting or pleasing people? What rituals can you spot? What stories are told? What does the physical space and how people react to it say about the culture: the office layout, how space is allocated and to whom, what's on the walls, how common areas are used (or not), where people walk or avoid? For example, at many companies the senior executives sit in a single area and very few other employees walk there, even if there is no official rule against it. That says a lot about the importance of hierarchy, how decisions get made, and who needs to be influenced to get new ideas approved.

Network to Work

In today's complex world of work, it is important to develop a cadre of people to learn from and trust, and on whose opinions you can rely.

Recognize that informal mentoring happens outside of formal mentorship programs and formal reporting relationships: for example, "Joe's the expert around here so spend time with him and he'll show you the ropes." Mentoring can be formal or not. Mentoring can be one-off, situational, or part of a program. You may sit down with someone for an hour and get exactly the guidance you need at that time.

Go out and develop resources for finding answers and addressing concerns. You may find you've developed a long-term mentor or even a friend in the process.

You also want to network for social reasons. Being in a new organization can be isolating if you don't make the efforts to lean in (recall Chapter 6, Principle 3 – Lean In to Build Connection).

Network, network, network. It's the main advice you get when you are out looking for a job. Everybody out there job hunting is either wishing he'd built stronger networks within and outside his workplace or is relieved that he did so. You may not enjoy networking, and hopefully you are not looking for a job, but you still need it to improve the job you already have.

 **Sam's story:** I remember getting great mentoring advice by my boss, Kathy, to "get out there and get known." It had been about a year and a half since I'd taken the position and the hard slog of integration work was well underway. I was quite literally unburying my desk. I held networking meetings with each CFO across the organization, asked lots of questions, listened, and got better known. Not long after, I was selected to chair a cross-organizational committee to revitalize a talent management program for finance professionals. I have no doubt the networking was instrumental. **People can only visualize you doing something if they've met you.**

Whether you are an extrovert or introvert is also irrelevant. Extroverts have just as much to learn and develop with their networking skills as introverts. Aim to develop an expert network and a social network to complement your formal network, and aim for networking to be purposeful and reciprocal.

Drive Your Own Discovery and Development

A mentee must take accountability for her discovery and development. Come prepared to mentoring meetings (refer to the Six Dimensions of Mentoring Framework). Create an agenda and provide it ahead of time. Delve deeper in between meetings to practice and explore what's been discussed. This also helps prompt questions for the next time. Your enthusiasm and engagement in the learning will reward your mentor for her precious time and attention; just be sure to use your mentor's time wisely.

Better than a thousand days of diligent study is one day with a great teacher.

– *Japanese Proverb*

Practice Agility

Our final piece of advice is, "Don't be a sea squirt and eat your brain!" It's easier to be a sea squirt than to be agile, and there are always reasons to do nothing: I do a good job and that should be all that matters (it never is, by the way); things will change again so why bother doing anything now; I'm too old to change; I'm not sure what is wanted so I'll wait and see what happens; if this doesn't blow over in x days/weeks/months/years then I'll change; the new direction is a bad idea; or, the excuse for inaction used most often: we've done this before and it didn't work.

None of these excuses stand up to scrutiny. If you think of yourself as having a Global Followership System, make sure to turn the power on when a new destination has been given. There is always a time during the journey when you will wonder if the benefits of the destination are worth the trip? It usually is, so stay committed to being agile.

Be conscious of the culture, big picture, pulse, vision, and your unique team(s). Think about what you would do if you were switched to a different team, were suddenly promoted to CEO, worked on the frontlines, or changed partners. Remember that you can still be true to yourself while learning to thrive in most organizations. The guidelines we've given for interpersonal and social engagement are there to facilitate better partnerships, not make everyone the same.

Together, the decision to persevere with change along with a deliberate, conscious awareness of the broader organizational context, will serve you in good stead. Over time it is the best way to develop greater agility.

Organizational Agility Partnering Skills Summary

Leadership Skill: Organizational Mentoring

Take time to mentor others on how best to navigate and operate in your unique organization:

- ✓ Generate dialogue about cultural norms and share your insider's knowledge.
- ✓ Be a role model for the right organizational behaviors.
- ✓ Relentlessly reinforce, evolve, and support the culture while celebrating individual diversity within it.

Followership Skill: Organizational Agility
Learning the ropes of your organization is critical for your personal and organizational success:

- ✓ Seek mentoring and be observant.
- ✓ Develop a social network and an expert network to complement your formal reporting relationships.
- ✓ Among other things learn how customers are served, markets are targeted, innovation happens, and money is made. Work on learning how culture varies across the organization and at different levels.

CHAPTER 12

Communication Partnering Skills

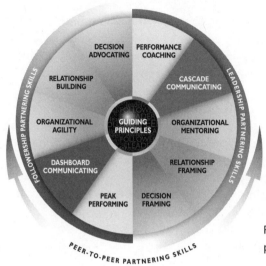

Figure 12.1 Communication partnering skills

Four-Way Communications, Barriers, Biases, and Blunders

There was quite the brouhaha at a British university: a year into her job the provost abruptly resigned.[1] She left very soon after meeting considerable resistance to the changes that she had initiated; not surprisingly, there was chaos in her wake.

The vice-chancellor of the college called a town hall meeting. Attendance was high as everyone was dying to know what to make of the resignation, what to do with initiatives that had been started and others she had canceled, and what to expect next.

Instead, the vice-chancellor talked about the successes that the college was having, the changing higher education environment, and the new strategic direction they were embarking on. Not a word about the provost. The vice-chancellor didn't address the one topic on everyone's mind. Instead he attempted a sidestepping maneuver, providing extraneous information that, research shows, is the least appropriate communication strategy.[2] Employees spent the next few days doing little other than talking about it among each other and even to us, the hired consultants!

This sort of communication is symptomatic of top-down, leader-focused thinking – you should go/think/do whatever I tell you. It is one reason that the single biggest complaint employees have about their workplace is poor communications.[3]

We've unfortunately observed and worked with a number of organizations that have created a really guarded communication environment: executives behave like campaigning politicians and evade discussing what matters most to people. It often starts with good intentions such as preventing panic or upset, but the problem is that culture is built on behavior not intent; the prolonged guarding of information has a nasty habit of sneaking its way into everyday behavior. It reinforces the natural tendencies we all have to avoid talking about problems.[4]

Nobody wants a partner who keeps things from them.

We spoke with Jose Tolovi Neto, a managing partner at the Great Place to Work Institute, where they assess, rank, and report on employers based on employee surveys of respect, fairness, pride, camaraderie, and credibility of leadership. When asked what advice he would give employers who want to do better – either making the Best Employers' list or ranking higher on it – he said, "Communicate better! Give your employees the courtesy of reality: let them in on what's really going on. Employers who communicate openly and honestly, even if the messages are of troubled times, stimulate employee understanding, loyalty, and engagement."

A Framework for Productivity

Most workplace communication fits into one of these three categories:[5]

1. Building relationships and providing personal support
2. Developing organizational agility
3. Providing a framework for productivity

Doing these three types of communication well is associated with a 45% increase in perceived effectiveness, a 40% increase in satisfaction with the communication, and a 12% increase in job satisfaction.[6] Huge numbers.

We've covered categories 1 and 2 in the previous two sections, Relationship Partnering Skills and Organizational Agility Partnering Skills. This and the next chapter, Communication Partnering Skills and Performance Partnering Skills, discuss category 3, providing a framework for productivity. The question that should precede every workplace communication is this: "In what ways will my communication improve productivity?"

There are many ways to make communications more productive and successful. We begin by looking at how to make communications more robust. We then examine some of the most common barriers and biases to organizational communication, as these could threaten to thwart even your most valiant efforts. The remainder of this chapter distinguishes planned communications in both our roles – Cascade Communicating in our leadership role and Dashboard Communicating in our followership role.

Going up? From One-Way to Two-Way Communications

Imagine an elevator that only travels from the top floor to the bottom floor.[7] No going up. Just one way: *down*. Oddly, that's how many employee communications are designed, as a straight drop from the top to the bottom. No stopping to add relevance and context along the way, and no feedback going back up.

Consider the company newsletter. The intention of this communication staple is to provide employees with greater context for their jobs, help them feel involved in the goings-on of the broader organization, and inform them of key changes. How do you know when it is working? How do you know that people are getting the context they need and desire? How do you know if it is increasing productivity?

The open rate, that is, the percentage of staff opening the newsletter, only suggests the newsletter has been looked at, but has it changed what people do as a result? How they think? How they feel? You don't know unless you ask. Getting feedback is vital to making a newsletter effective.

Open communication is even more important to motivation than building a good relationship[8] and it significantly improves job satisfaction.[9] What, then, stops people from doing it? One barrier is the fear of negative feedback. For example, an HR business partner at a large construction firm wrote of her company's experience:

> We tried a company blog to encourage conversations about topical issues within the company. However, the results were not encouraging. Only a few employees understood the blog concept and felt safe enough to put their opinions and ideas out there if they had to self-identify. We weren't comfortable having anonymous comments so we backed off on blogs. (Campeau, 2011, p. 26)

Reading this, we can't help but recall that memorable line from the 2001 cult-comedy *Zoolander* where Will Ferrell's character screams, "... I feel like I'm taking crazy pills!" First of all, the concern expressed here – that employees will post negative comments – is ill-founded. Few comments on internal company social sites contain direct attacks on people or the company. Overwhelmingly, postings are about how something affects employees. These sites provide upward feedback that can be used to clear up wrong impressions, refine messages, and communicate better in the future. Second of all, as far as any negative feedback that is expressed, well, at least you know.[10]

All organizational or leadership communicating should have genuine feedback channels built in: in other words, a dialogue. The word *dialogue* comes from the Greek, *dia logos*, literally translated as "a free-flowing of meaning through a group, allowing the group to discover insights not attainable individually" (Senge, 2006, p. 10). True dialogue requires both partners to expose their thinking and be open to the influence of others.

From Two-Way to Four-Way Communication

Communicating is a big part of management responsibilities: about 40% of management time is spent communicating in one form or another.[11] This is roughly divided evenly between getting information and giving information. Rarely, though, is it acknowledged that healthy dialogue is actually a *four-way path*.

In any partnership – leader-follower, peer-peer, business partners, spouses – each partner is accountable for *initiating* communications and *responding* to the other person's communications through active listening and feedback. In other words, each partner has two distinct communication roles.

Two partners with two roles each = four-way communication.

We call the two roles Cascade Communicating (the leadership role) and Dashboard Communicating (the followership role). In our leadership role, we *cascade* key information to our teams to keep them well informed and, in our followership role, we deliver a *dashboard* of information to keep our leadership well informed. Both are essential for the other partner to execute their roles well. Both use distinct skills.

While the results we are aiming for with both communicating roles is productivity, the primary purpose of the leadership role is to unleash the right kind of followership initiative whereas the primary purpose of the followership role is to stimulate the right kind of leadership action. Researchers from Cornell and the University of Texas at Austin found that feedback given to the person able to act on it improved organizational effectiveness.[12] However, the same feedback given to anyone else actually damaged effectiveness. Understanding the differences between leadership and followership communication enables you to craft messages that are more productive, appropriate, and influential.

More on these subtle but essential differences in the next two sections of this chapter. For the rest of this section we will look at barriers that either impede communication or alter it in ways that harm productivity and reduce agility.

Communication Barriers, Biases, and Blunders

Unleash the Elephants!
Perhaps the number one barrier to healthy organizational and leadership communicating is having elephants in the room. The expression "the elephant in the room" refers to an unwritten agreement **not to discuss** certain issues, often what's foremost on everybody's minds. We've been at meetings where you felt like a herd of invisible elephants was trampling you to death! Ironically, you often get what you are most afraid of. When organizations and their senior executives purposefully avoid discussing the issues everyone is concerned about, it causes even greater concern. When people can't confront the elephants openly, the conversation moves behind closed doors into the hushed corners and corridors where the unruly beasts get fed an unhealthy diet from the rumor mill, and trumpet misleading information.

Healthy, open communication leads to organizational success, greater personal authority, greater credibility, and trust.[13] The more people understand what's going on, the higher their morale.[14] But when information is concealed and treated as if it doesn't exist people come to believe that management doesn't care, are scared of tough conversations, or lack trust in their teams.

Deliberately acknowledging the elephants makes them a whole lot less scary for everyone. For example, people probably already suspect a tightening of the belt is coming if a big client recently departed, sales are down, or a grant wasn't received. Talk about it! It is the best solution. And if you can't do so because of serious legal or business reasons, publish guidelines so people know what can't be discussed along with the rationale. Unleash the elephants!

Without healthy, open workplace communications, people stress, guess, and fill in the gaps in actual information with rumors from the grapevine.

Shooting the Messenger: The Fundamental Attribution Error

Louis XIV was known for being a man of very few words. He was famous for replying to all sorts of requests with the phrase "I shall see," and he used this catchphrase to great effect.

All of us are subject to the fundamental attribution error – the belief that other people communicate negative messages because they *want* to rather than because they *have* to. One way of overcoming this barrier is to get into the habit of saying thank you first, or pulling a King Louis by saying "I shall see." Even small delays before responding give you time to reappraise the situation, think about why the person felt he had to give you that information, and what are all of its implications.

Reacting to the Negative: The Automatic Vigilance Effect

People react to and remember negative experiences far more than positive ones.[15] How often have you arrived at the office late because all the traffic lights were against you? How often were you early because all the lights were in your favor? We'll bet you've never even heard someone make the early excuse. Even though the probability of the two events is exactly the same, you are much more likely to remember getting held up by a bad string of traffic lights. This memory bias is the same one that causes us to misestimate the frequency of criticism and fuels our desire to avoid it.

On average, people need more positive comments than negative ones just to have a sense that feedback was balanced.[16] A simple one-to-one ratio of positive to negative might sound fair and equitable, but that ratio leads to a poor long-term relationship and decrease in performance. The actual ratio should be closer to 4:1 or better. What's more, managers tend to only spend about 5% of their time giving positive feedback, showing appreciation, or simply listening to their staff.[17] When there is a choice between a negative and positive communication choose the positive, and do it often.

Being Too Polite: The Ingratiation Effect

People have a natural tendency to exaggerate the extent to which we agree with someone in a position of power or authority. The greater the power differential between people, the more likely a politeness strategy gets used by the lower-power person. The consequence is an inaccurate view of what's really going on. To combat this, set aside time in a meeting for each team member to provide one or more criticisms so that the burden of doing so is fairly distributed. Another option is to ask the question: "I know you agree with X, but what are all the ways to make it even better?"[18]

Being Too Passive: The Abilene Paradox

One of our children experienced the Abilene Paradox firsthand while dating. The couple had been together for a few months during which time their dates had grown quite routinized: go out for ice cream, then return to one of their apartments to watch a TV show together (they were in school at the time so on a tight budget). Eventually, one of them reached a point of exasperation and burst out with the truth that they were actually sick and tired of ice cream. The other responded with equal exasperation saying that they never really liked ice cream in the first place but that they were just eating it to please the other. This sudden release of honesty must have been so cathartic that another release was triggered. "Well, I don't actually like any of these TV shows we've been watching." "Me neither," was the response. Together they had started doing something – eating ice cream and watching certain TV shows – neither would have chosen alone. That's called the Abilene Paradox. It is when a group of people engages in behavior none of them wanted only because everyone thought someone else wanted it. Obviously this wasn't a relationship with a future, but it provided a valuable lesson on developing better partnership communications.

In your leadership role, solicit feedback relentlessly. You may be surprised by the answers, but you will never regret asking and having the opportunity to make a situation better. In your followership role, don't keep doing a task over and over such as producing a particular report without checking in to ensure it's useful and relevant.

Being Too Confident: The Self-Efficacy Bias

People generally believe that they are better at doing something than they are. For example, managers generally believe they communicate well.[19] Furthermore, they report providing the same level of communication to all their subordinates.[20]

Wrong on both counts! Subordinates aren't nearly as sanguine about the communication skills of their managers. Worst of all, the poorer someone is at communicating, the less likely he is to realize it. This self-efficacy bias leads to less motivation for improving communication behaviors and protocols, and reduces awareness of communication problems. Training on best practices and maintaining a focus on continual improvement are two remedies.

> The only things you can't learn are the things you think you already know.

We have discussed the essential element of feedback in effective communications and have a sense of what to avoid in both our leadership and followership roles. Next we will distinguish the roles and how to excel at both.

Cascade Communicating: The Leadership Role

Key Leadership Ideas

- Know your purpose and know your audience(s).

- Reinforce the right kind of contributions.
- Be action oriented and time considerate.
- Communication advocacy is a leadership role.

In your leadership role, one of the most important jobs is to cascade information to your team. Share with them the vision, strategy, priorities, and results – in other words, communication is the medium for the frame, leaning in, celebrating positives, and realizing improvements. When communication expands and enriches the work experience, it enables people to be more productive, more innovative, make good choices, and be ambassadors for the organization.

The purpose of Cascade Communicating is to unleash the right kind of followership initiative. This is achieved by clarifying priorities, sharing challenges, and suggesting opportunities, all to trigger the followership response, "What are all the ways I can add value?" Sometimes when the messages are negative or difficult, it's easy to lose sight and fall prey to one of the barriers or biases we explored in the last section.

Great communicators steadfastly stick to two communication rules: know your purpose, and know your audience.

Know Your Purpose

Consider this communication misstep reported to us by three people at a large Midwest manufacturing firm. They worked in different departments and at different levels – an executive, a manager, and a frontline analyst – yet they had a remarkably consistent reaction to a communication event. Months into a company-wide efficiency initiative, staff were invited to attend a town hall with about a thousand other employees.[21] The general sentiment was that layoffs were imminent so people were naturally concerned about job security. Many departments were already under huge strain – people working overtime, nights, and weekends – just to keep up.

The RSVPs for the town hall were very low so attendance was made mandatory. The meeting ended up lasting two hours, and it also required staff to travel a half hour or more to attend.

We talked with the three people after the meeting and they were upset. Very upset. Some of the comments were: "What a waste of time";

"I literally have more questions now than I did going in"; and "I feel angry AND had to miss my son's baseball game to do work after." No one was able to articulate the real purpose of the meeting.

The senior VP running the town hall had talked about global restructuring, and then he said that people would have to be patient and wait a few more months to find out about their jobs. Next, he introduced a consultant who proceeded to talk about the neuroscience of dealing with change – your amygdala; fight or flight; natural feeling of resistance; yadda, yadda, yadda – mostly neurobabble the consultant had learned at a 10-day course on change management.[22]

The communication session certainly achieved something. Management offended staff even more! What was the purpose of the town hall meeting? Was it to quell nerves? To help people do their jobs better? Cope with change more effectively? If we asked three attendees and none of them could say what the core message was, strike one. In both cases the people we talked to felt less productive after the meeting, strike two. It made people mad; strike three, you're out: communication failed!

The purpose of every communication you engage in should be front and center. If you can't articulate it in your planning, keep thinking until you can.

Know Your Audience(s)

A nurse we interviewed works for a health-care agency undergoing ever-deepening expense cuts. This sad reality is that it heaps a pile more stress on the nurses – a job already rife with tough challenges in the best of times – who are continually getting stuck with longer shifts, more paperwork, and mandatory overtime, all while enduring salary freezes and benefit scale backs. Turnover at this nurse's agency was escalating as were stress leaves. Everyone was called to the annual Christmastime meeting, hoping for the usual Christmas bonus but fearing another cutback.

Rather than a bonus or open, honest communication such as a heartfelt thank you and apology, management offered the Nurse's Survival Kit as the gift. Each nurse received a sandwich bag with the following list and contents:

Nurse's Survival Kit

Lifesaver – a reminder of the many times others will need your help

Snicker's Bar – to remind you that laughter is the best medicine

Candle – to remind you that you can light up someone's day

Tissue – to dry tears: your own and someone else's

Starburst – for that burst of energy at the end of the day

Button – to remind you that sometimes you need to button your lip

Bath Salts – to take you away at the end of the day

Marbles – to replace the ones you will lose

Playing Card – to help you be a better mind reader

Lollipop – to help you lick everyone's problems

Mint – to remind you that your compassion is worth a mint to your patients

Penny – for your thoughts

If you search for Nurse's Survival Kit on the Internet you can see it. It's also referred to as the "Nurse's Survival Gag Gift." Cute? Perhaps. Appropriate? Maybe for a new nurse or for a lighthearted event. In this case, no way. Is it any wonder that most of the nurses promptly threw the kits in the garbage then called each other to lament over how insulted they all felt?

In your leadership role, be effortful in planning communications, confirming that you understand your audience. If you have *any* doubts about how your communication will be received, do a pilot test to ensure efforts aren't misguided. The time invested upfront pays off when your communications appear effortless upon delivery. We suggest auditing every communication before delivery using four criteria:

1. Is it "adult-to-adult" communication?
2. Have you added the 's' to audience?
3. Is it reinforcing the right kind of contributions?
4. Is it action oriented and respectful of people's time?

1. Adult-to-adult communications

The style and approach to all communications should be adult-to-adult to use the vernacular of transactional analysis. Psychiatrist Eric Berne developed transactional analysis in the late 1950s as a way of describing the three primary modes of communication we engage in: parent-to-child, child-to-parent, and adult-to-adult. Parent mode is dictatorial and patronizing for adults in a work setting. Nevertheless, because leadership is still thought of as a heroic act,[23] parent-to-child communication is fairly common between leaders and followers. Child-to-parent mode is emotional, reactive, and needy – it is the "you have done this to me" or "you need to fix this for me" style. Berne suggested that communicating in one of these two ways often leads to a reply in the other.

On the other hand, adult-to-adult communications emphasize respect, equality, objectivity, and transparency of information. It recognizes that you are speaking to other adults, collaborating in the best interests of the organization.

2. Adding the 's' to audience(s)

A refinement to the know your audience rule is to know your audiences. Communications these days rarely go to one person or one group of people. Be sure that you think through all the places a communication might end up: Do my direct reports know how to turn around and communicate this to their staff? Might anyone be offended or misunderstand it? How much explanation is needed to understand the context and key messages? What if this communication fell into the hands of people writing a book? (It happens more than you might think.)

3. Reinforce the right kind of contributions

It's not uncommon for people to be systematically and consistently rewarded (or not corrected) for withholding information. The same can be true for too much sharing of information. In your leadership role, engage in discussions with your team about the trade-offs between information safeguarding and sharing, and give clear examples of both. Endeavor to model and apply those guidelines by reinforcing the right kind of contributions.

4. Be action oriented and considerate of people's time

Another reason staff at the town hall meeting felt so offended was the cavalier approach to their time. The communication should have been streamlined and action oriented: what should staff do, or do differently, and why?

People are busy. Most would report to being busier today than 5 or 10 years ago. Exacerbating this is information overload: we get bombarded with 5,000 advertising messages a day, which is 10 times what would have happened just a few decades ago.[24] As a consequence, we cope by getting better at tuning out and ignoring messages, especially long ones, because they "cost" a lot more to take in. As a result we may not receive important information, we may struggle to distinguish what's important and what's not, and we may miss essential messages entirely. Savvy communicators know this and think deeply about how to capture our attention so that relevant information can get heard over the noise.

The average person gets 5,000 advertising message per day.

Review your existing communications and decide what can be eliminated, streamlined, or changed. Use best practices to ensure all communications are concise, contextualized, and relevant to the target audience. Make communications action oriented; specifically, what do you want the receiver to do? Most of all …

Be candid.
Be clear.
Be brief.

Communication Advocacy Is a Leadership Role

One of the hardest parts about leadership communicating is when you don't agree with or like the message you need to convey. This is an incredibly tricky lesson to learn and to live with, especially for those of us who never want to be seen as out of touch. In fact, after being a manager for more than 20 years, Sam says she only fully understood this lesson once she'd left corporate life and became a consultant.

 I was 24 when I was promoted to a supervisory position and remember feeling a bit sheepish leading people who had been in their roles for years. I did learn early on to listen more than I spoke, and to show respect for others' years of service and experience. However, the tension between being seen as relevant by my staff and

having to sell a message I didn't agree with was challenging. I now see that delivering the message properly, clearly, and with context (even when you are opposed to it) is simply a part of the leadership role, albeit not a pleasant part. Aiming to side with your staff by poo-pooing the communication is really an abdication of responsibility. It's no good to sacrifice your leadership role for your followership (or friendship) role. You should be helping the team make meaning and be productive rather than worrying about how relevant you look.

One leadership myth is the belief that resistance is something to be overcome; the strong leader, through force of personality and persuasion, can sell a message that people don't believe in or agree with.[25] It doesn't work that way. It is far better to understand the resistance, acknowledge it as helpful feedback, and respect its meaning and intent.

FliPtips! Tool 12.1 Cascade Communication Planner

For each leadership communication activity you are engaged in such as town halls, team meetings, weekly huddles, or one-on-ones, fill out the following:

What is the purpose and intended action? Try and articulate it in a single phrase.

_____

_____

Who is the audience? Think about how they feel receiving this communication.

_____

_____

Is there a channel for feedback? Is it used? Is it working? What can you do to strengthen it even more?

_____

_____

That doesn't mean the feedback is always right, but it does mean you must deal with it.

The Cascade Communication Planner is a tool (12.1) that can help you communicate more generatively.

Dashboard Communicating: The Followership Role

Key Followership Ideas

- Know your purpose and know your audience(s).
- Your work doesn't speak for itself: Communicate!
- Dashboard Communicating is the best antidote to micromanaging.
- Be the messenger.
- Be brief: inform, don't inundate!

An interview we held with a fast-rising executive went like this:

> Sam and Marc: A big part of being a leader is communicating. Describe one of the communication activities that you engage in that makes you so successful.

> Senior executive: One thing I do is give Don (the CEO) a call right when he's about to receive the quarterly financial package. I tell him what three things I think he's going to want to focus on in the report (pointing to a stack of paper two inches high). Then I share my rationale for why I've singled out those three things as being the most important for him to be aware of and to be comfortable with. We talk about them in depth. I answer all his questions. I make sure he feels comfortable talking about these things with the board and with the analysts.

Notice that the top-of-mind communication activity this senior executive mentioned when asked about successful leadership communication was actually followership. He instinctively knew that keeping his manager well informed was one of his key tasks. We should tell you that he has been promoted since the interview and is now next in line for the CEO job. Not a big surprise.

Many jobs require greater expertise at followership communication than leadership communication. Perhaps we are extra sensitive to this because project management and accounting are two areas where expert upwards communication skills can make all the difference, and both professions were a big part of Samantha's background. Indeed, anyone whose job involves responsibility for management information likely spends more time on followership than leadership.

This oft-neglected skill is a real difference maker to people's careers and to the productivity of partnerships. Roughly 20% of a manager's time is spent gathering information,[26] but that percentage would be a lot less if excellent followership communication were the norm. It is a wonder that it is afforded so little discussion in workplaces.

Know Your Audience(s)

Fortunately, the same communication rules that apply to Cascade Communication also apply to the followership skill of Dashboard Communicating: know your purpose and know your audience(s). However, we'll flip it around and focus on audience first because of its overriding importance to Dashboard Communicating.

If your boss loves lists and you write paragraphs, you have a recipe for bad communications. If your boss likes drive-by meetings, be prepared to deliver take-out. When Dashboard Communicating in your followership role, remember to put the 's' in audience(s). Your audiences typically include your boss, boss's boss, maybe their peers, or even a key client. Ask yourself, "Can my boss forward this? What would happen if someone outside this group saw it? How might this communication be misunderstood?"

If even one of those audiences changes, be prepared to have to change the communication. Sam once had a very nice young accountant working for her who held the position of expense analyst and who also happened to love creative writing. Over time the analyst took the opportunity to hone her craft by providing a monthly "story" to accompany the variance analysis. It was a fun, conversational piece about the organization's spending replete with relevant observations, comical asides, and rather quaint verbiage. Sam's boss, the CFO, loved it as did her peers. It was wonderfully refreshing compared to the more standard financial commentary, such as, "15% over budget due to higher than expected unit cost ... blah, blah, blah." Then a new CFO came on board. He wasn't at all keen on these monthly expense stories – was in fact embarrassed by it. The reports were quickly stopped.

A common situation in upward communication occurs when an employee has stepped out of her functional area of expertise for the first time. A junior accountant typically creates reports for a more senior accountant – they speak the same language, it is their "native" tongue, and miscommunication is rare. When that junior accountant (or lawyer, programmer, actuary, engineer, architect, buyer, etc.) gets promoted, he suddenly has to take the specialized language of his discipline and translate it into something a more general audience can *act* on. Problems are commonplace! We have seen many smart, competent people held back because they couldn't adapt their communications to a nonspecialist audience.

Knowing *how* to communicate with these groups in a way that is most effective is not straightforward. We aren't born with eloquence and oomph, but we can all learn to be more effective. When he was governor of Arkansas, former president Bill Clinton was often ridiculed by the press for his lack of presentation skills and his shy, fumbling manner. With years of practice and communication coaching he became a compelling, sought-after keynote speaker, garnering upwards of $50,000 for a 40-minute talk.

Know Your Purpose

Dashboard Communicating is about keeping leadership informed efficiently. However, underlying this is the primary purpose: to stimulate the right leadership action.

> The underlying purpose of Dashboard Communicating is to stimulate the right leadership action: what the leader should get involved in, when, and how.

This is especially critical when things are not going well, so consider your dashboard as an early warning system. For example, if you were in an update meeting with your boss, you might color code initiatives to indicate the recommended leadership action:

- Green means, "It's all good. I'm on top of it. No need to get involved."
- Yellow means, "Things are ok but I'd like to run a couple of things by you when you have a moment."
- Red means, "Help! I need your involvement and it's urgent!"

It's important to have the mindset that Dashboard Communicating is both purposeful and productive. When we forget that, it starts to feel like a burden, a waste of time, or an inconvenience instead of a core part of the job.

While the primary objective is to stimulate the right leadership action, expert Dashboard Communicating also:

✓ Enhances your credibility
✓ Makes leadership more efficient
✓ Grows in importance as your job grows

Let's have a look at each of these secondary points.

Enhancing Credibility: Your Work Does Not *Speak for Itself*

 A few years ago I had a young man on my team, Antonio, whose supervisor (my direct report) felt strongly he was management material. She recommended that we give him a chance to begin developing his people supervisory skills by reorganizing some of the work and putting junior staff under him. Although I'd heard kudos about Antonio's performance from his boss, his previous boss, and his peers, I'd had little direct contact with him.

Antonio was very quiet – never volunteering information or his perspective in meetings and responding to questions succinctly without adding context, support, or embellishment of any kind. His personality, level of engagement, and know-how was never evident to an observer. Antonio had not used the opportunities he'd been given to demonstrate his credibility and raise his profile. I gave this feedback to his supervisor who, in turn, fed it back to Antonio saying that she saw his potential, but he needed to work on raising his profile by communicating more.

I understand that Antonio was initially surprised and said he felt his work should speak for itself. Fortunately with the coaching and mentoring he received, he went on to use opportunities to demonstrate his know-how in e-mails and meetings. Six months later we created a supervisory position for Antonio. My leader, in fact, recommended it as he'd begun to notice Antonio's contributions and see him differently. Antonio has been steadily climbing the management ranks since.

There are many Antonios who undervalue communication, believing that their good work should speak for itself. It doesn't. Of course there is the flipside where people attempt to use eloquence to hide substandard work. Suffice it to say that followership communication is both an integral part of any job in an organization and an opportunity to strengthen your credibility.

Leadership Efficiency

Excellent followership communication – Dashboard Communicating – is also the best antidote to one of the least appreciated management styles: micromanagement.

Mary Anne came to us with a problem: her new boss was a micromanager constantly looking over her shoulder and asking what she was doing. Mary Anne was upset mostly because she had been working at the same job for a long time, knew how to do it with minimal supervision, and had been given good performance evaluations by her previous manager(s). The relationship was deteriorating, with Mary Anne volunteering less and less information figuring there was no point since her new boss would just come ask anyway.

This is the classic micromanaging death spiral. We've seen it a lot: an employee feels overmanaged and reacts by pulling away and communicating less. The result is more management oversight rather than less. Eventually one of the two people involved take action. Sadly, the culminating event is often a departure rather than mutual insight and agreement.

Just about the least efficient form of management is micromanagement – it's two people doing the work of one. Sometimes there is no option such as when there is a serious performance issue, training a brand-new employee, or a risk that can only be mitigated through oversight. But no one likes it. These circumstances are rare as the most common cause of micromanaging is actually insufficient communication. What we suggested to Mary Anne was to communicate more! Now this is really difficult because, when you aren't getting along with someone, the natural tendency is to distance yourself from him or her. But communication turns out to be a highly effective strategy for dealing with micromanagement. Much of the time micromanaging is due to a difference in the amount of communication a manager needs relative to what the employee prefers/thinks/wants to deliver.[27] It gets better when the gap is addressed, not ignored. How does one deliver the right amount/style/frequency of Dashboard Communicating? Ask. Try a few different formats. Engage in a discussion of your rationale for various methods. Refine it back and forth until you find the generative point where things are working well for both of you.

The best way to reduce micromanagement is to anticipate the need for relevant and timely information.

Followership communication is about helping leadership stay well informed. It reduces stress and makes leadership more efficient. Loop back on everything your boss would be interested in, he has delegated, or anything he inquired about in the past. Don't assume that because you haven't been asked about X recently, you don't need to talk to him about it. When in doubt, always err on the side of more not less, at least for breadth and for work-related items.

We all know that things come up and sometimes you need to veer off track. Keeping your boss well informed gives him an opportunity to refine priorities, get involved to eliminate roadblocks, streamline your approach, or simply gain confidence that you can be counted on to get the job done.

Expectations for Dashboard Communicating Increase as You Move Up

Consider the experience of Charlotte, a former client of ours, with a new, senior leader. Charlotte had changed companies – moving into the supplier side of her industry – nine months before a new senior vice president (SVP) was hired to oversee the Client Relationship Division. The SVP focused 100% of her time on client relationships, neglecting her team. Shortly after arriving, the SVP sent an e-mail requiring each of her direct reports to provide an update using a very specific format. The reaction was a near unanimous rebellion as most of her direct reports thought it an offensive request given their level, years of experience, and that this just "wasn't the way things worked around here."

Charlotte was the only one to comply. She prepared the report in accordance with the format and submitted it by the deadline, Monday morning at 10 a.m. She had her first one-on-one meeting booked with the SVP after lunch on Monday, knocked on her door and said, "Hi! Did you get the report I sent this morning?" The SVP looked up, smiled, and said, "Yes, thank you. It was perfect. You've just saved yourself an hour. We don't need to meet."

A year after this incident every one of Charlotte's peers had moved on, either to new opportunities within the company or outside. The SVP had, too, and Charlotte was given her job.

As with followership in general, the importance of, and expectations for, Dashboard Communicating increase as you move up the ladder. As challenges become more complex and ambiguous, you often face a wider audience with greater sophistication and increased expectations for the clarity of the communication piece. In the many interviews conducted for this book, our experience was that the more senior the person, the more likely she was to mention communicating with her boss as a big part of the job. However, it also means that when the manager changes, it is more important to adapt to the needs of the new manager. In Charlotte's case, her peers weren't able to adapt and paid a rather heavy price for it. Charlotte was more agile in her approach and thrived.

With that in mind, let's look at some ways to enhance your Dashboard Communicating.

Be the Messenger

Generally speaking, your manager wants to hear it from you, not from someone else. When you are passing along information ask yourself, "Is it complete? Is there anything in reserve? What am I holding back? What are we protecting them/ourselves from?"

Let your boss know about the things on your plate that he didn't personally assign. Perhaps he was on vacation and his boss or one of his peers asked you to look into something. Loop your boss in.

Perhaps you ran into a bigwig in the coffee line and wound up getting praised for your department's excellent customer service results. Accept thanks, defer credit to your boss and whole team, and loop your boss in.

Issues, concerns, and errors are typically hot topics and should be communicated swiftly and carefully. It's best not to bring up problems without also adding information, context, options, and possible solutions. When balancing timeliness with completeness, where to draw the line is situation specific. Some managers prefer a hot-off-the-presses e-mail. Some managers don't want to know about a problem until sufficient investigation has been done to present options, impacts, and potential solutions. Some managers prefer to be informed after the problem has been solved, solution planned thoroughly, and new controls added to ensure it never happens again. What is definite is that surprises are bad.

Be Brief: Inform, Don't Inundate

Though you can never be too good a communicator, you can communicate too much and too often. You want to inform, not inundate. Give your boss complete information that is focused on action, not exhaustive data of the FYI variety.

Whether using oral or written communication, adhering to the **4 Cs** will help you create content that is followership savvy:

1. **Confirm** purpose.
2. Be **compelling**.
3. **Condense** ruthlessly.
4. Ensure **convenience**.

Begin All Communication by Confirming the Purpose

Why are you e-mailing, calling, dropping by, or requesting a meeting? Consider their stake in what you are communicating. For example, e-mails should include the purpose in the subject line. If you are forwarding someone else's e-mail, change the subject line rather than using the default *"Fwd: Irrelevant Subject Line for You."*

Make Your Communications Compelling

Use the subject line of e-mails to provide not just the purpose but also the expected action, the sense of urgency, and the deadline. With the average office-based employee today spending between one and four hours on her daily avalanche of e-mails, compelling and straightforward e-mails are appreciated. They tend to get addressed first. An example would be *"Review and approve attached budget by 5pm tomorrow if satisfactory,"* or *"New information! Consider whether this changes how we implement project xyz."* Right up front in the e-mail be specific about how many key points you have throughout the body and, if possible, summarize them in bullet form at the beginning. Proofread all e-mails before sending to your boss (or anyone for that matter) as it affects your credibility.

Condense Ruthlessly

Reduce the volume in all your communications to focus on the key points. Every so often Marc teaches a poetry class. One of his favorite exercises is to have the participants, often fledgling poets, write a poem and then throw away the initial stanza. It's terribly distressing to them at first – "Those were my best lines!" someone invariably argues – but the condensed poem pretty much always winds up being more memorable for the deletion. It's liberating, both for the author and for the poem.

 I was invited to a status meeting for a project that my team was running. The meeting was booked for a full hour. Dianne, the meeting chair, painstakingly took us through each slide describing the progress, testing issues and resolutions, and risk mitigation tactics. Then with five minutes left in the hour she (almost) casually

mentioned that another department had decided they will discontinue supporting the project as they are now understaffed. This was like an alarm clock waking me up. Huh? Why didn't you tell me this at the beginning of the meeting? I would have wanted this brought to my attention straight away.

Avoid the punch line approach to meetings. Make sure the first 10 minutes are conducted as if your audience may get called away. Start with an overview of the agenda, highlight any issues and decisions to be made, and focus on the critical updates. If you only had 10 minutes rather than the full hour that you've booked, what would you say? It might be an issue requiring escalation; it might be a decision that you need to check in on; or it could be a decision that needs to be addressed now.

There is another perspective. A colleague of ours is a big-time introvert, and he coaches other introverts on how to thrive in an extroverted world. When it comes to communication, he tells us that introverts prefer to give background first and then the conclusion. Extroverts prefer to hear the conclusion first and then get the background. Either way is fine as long as you can get it done in 10 minutes.

> Anybody can have ideas – the difficulty is to express them without squandering a quire of paper on an idea that ought to be reduced to one glittering paragraph.
>
> – *Mark Twain*

Maybe the worst communication is the FYI (for your information). Why are you informing your boss (or the person who is taking on the leadership role)? What would you like her to do with the information? What action(s) does it provoke? If you can't answer those questions, don't do the communication.

Ensure Convenience

Ask yourself: is this really the best way to communicate your message or is it simply the most convenient for you? Better yet, ask the people you are communicating to how they would like to be kept up-to-date. Be sure to choose a method of communication suited for the purpose at hand. Dashboard Communicating should follow a systematic approach with respect to the frequency, the channel, and the method depending on the actions you are trying to stimulate and the complexity of the message.

Hot-off-the-presses issues or information bites should be communicated one issue at a time. A request for a decision should also be communicated by itself. It's irritating to get a request for two or three decisions in one e-mail or meeting as it can be easy to overlook the second item once the first has been addressed.

The primary modes of communication in organizations today are e-mail and meetings, with memos, reports, telephone conversations, and drive-bys being less frequent but all having their place. The key factors that determine the best medium are:

- The audience(s) degree of familiarity with the subject matter
- The complexity and ambiguity of the topic – the more challenging it is, the more interactive the approach
- The sense of urgency and level of importance/profile
- The status of the relationship
- Whether a formal record is required

E-mail is considered a low-context and low-touch medium, not suitable for complex or unfamiliar material. Memos are preferable if a formal record of a decision, change, or meeting is required, such as a change in operating policy or minutes for a meeting. Highly complex, unfamiliar, or important messages warrant a face-to-face discussion. When using e-mail, stick to one topic per e-mail with the exception of the update or status e-mail.

Maintaining a Living Dashboard (see Tool 12.2) provides comfort that you haven't let anything fall through the cracks. A status on each lets your boss stay in the loop and is an opportunity for her to quickly help out if needed, support your efforts, or just give praise – all appropriate leadership actions. With a Living Dashboard you never have to be asked, "What's the status of blah, blah, blah?" Add an executive or leader summary at the top as you will not have time to run through everything when you get together. This tool can really help increase understanding of roles and performance, outline with what you do for her, show how you support her, and build trust and rapport.

Tool 12.2 The Living Dashboard

Keep a master list of everything on your plate. In advance of one-on-one update meetings, add a status and executive summary and submit as an agenda. Ideally it should span the breadth of key projects, responsibilities and extra assignments; cover any issues/ decisions/ questions/ breakthroughs; highlight items completed along with the benefit derived; mention any company initiatives that you've gotten involved in; note key events in your life or your staff's; and have a placeholder for your own training, development and aspirations. It should be comprehensive, but brief and to the point.

Topics to consider in a dashboard are:

Item 1. What's hot?
  a. Accomplishments; reporting back on requests and questions
  b. Issues, opportunities, errors
Item 2. What am I working on?
  a. New work assigned, acquired or initiated
  b. How I prioritize the tasks
  c. How my time is being allocated
  d. How things are going; any roadblocks to getting the work done
Item 3. What do I need you to do?
  a. When/where/how I could use your involvement
  b. Make a decision or review a decision I've made
Item 4. What to expect and when to expect it?
Item 5. What's going on with me personally and what are my plan, hopes and dreams?
Item 6. What's going on with the team?

Another way to prepare for any update meetings is to create a list of actions you have accomplished recently with a particular emphasis on what's changed and what actions are required. For a suggested list that we have used successfully, see Tool 12.3.

!FliPtips! Tool 12. 3 Questions for the Boss

When you prepare for you next update meeting, use these questions as a guide. Think about the big stuff. Think always about purpose and impact. In other words, focus on the mini-milestones in your work life.

1. In the last two weeks where did I spend my time, what did I accomplish, and what has changed?
2. In the forthcoming two weeks where do I expect to spend my time, what will I accomplish, and what do I expect might change? This is an opportunity to confirm priorities.
3. In the forthcoming two weeks what do I need my boss to do: for example, approve something, make a decision, or give feedback on a report?

Communication Partnering Skills Summary

Leadership Skill: Cascade Communicating
In your leadership role, cascade information to team members to keep them involved, productive, and unleash the right kind of followership initiative:

✓ Share organizational priorities, results, changes, context, and rationale.
✓ Add your perspective on impact and opportunities.
✓ Give lots of opportunity for Q&A; feedback; and open, interactive discussions.

Followership Skill: Dashboard Communicating
In your followership role, provide a dashboard of information to stimulate the right leadership action AND enhance your credibility:

✓ Keep your leader in the loop and ensure NO SURPRISES.
✓ Adhere to the 4 Cs: **confirm** purpose, be **compelling**, **condense** ruthlessly, and ensure **convenience.**
✓ Suit your leader's preferred communication style.

CHAPTER 13

Performance Partnering Skills

Figure 13.1 Performance partnering skills

Honk If You Like My Driving!

Perhaps you are familiar with this story, recounted by an 88-year-old grandmother:

> Dear Granddaughter,
> The other day I went to our local bookstore and saw a 'Honk if you like my driving' bumper sticker. I bought the sticker and put it on my car. Boy, am I glad I did: what an uplifting experience followed!
>
> I was stopped at a red light at a busy intersection, lost in thought about life, when the light changed. That was when I found out that lots of people saw my sticker. As I sat there, the fellow behind me started honking like crazy. Everyone else started honking, too. I leaned out my window to wave and smile at all those loving people …

Think about how many unclear or mixed signals we live with on a daily basis. It's a wonder we get anything right! When someone honks at you on the street, you might think: "Do they want me to speed up/ slow down/move over/watch out for ducks?" When a baby cries you think, "Is she hungry/wet/in pain/want to be cuddled?" You may never know what the real intent behind the honk or cry was, and the feedback you get may reinforce exactly the wrong performance.

 This takes me back to when Marc and I were first dating. While we clicked from the get-go, we still had a few rough patches. A wonderful thing about dating in your forties is that you are a whole lot wiser: the bumps still happen but you are better equipped to smooth them out. One night coming home from a party, Marc commented that I seemed grumpy so I let 'er rip: "Do you blame me? I felt so neglected tonight. You didn't even bother to introduce me to most of the people you talked with." Marc, surprised, responded, "That wasn't my intention at all! When I neglect to introduce you, it doesn't mean that I'm not proud to be with you or that I don't want people to know that I'm with you. It actually means that I don't remember the person's name. I don't remember names well so I often avoid introductions. I see how that must have looked. I'm really sorry." We agreed we needed clearer signals. Now, when Marc can't remember a name for an introduction, he says to the person, "Have you met my wife and partner Samantha?" That's the signal for me to say, "Nice to meet you. And you are ---?"

We rarely take the time to decode unclear or mixed signals, especially in the workplace. This results in poorer performance, more frustration, disengagement, and stress. It is an issue at the heart of the research by Amabile and Kramer (2011) in their book *The Progress Principle*. The husband-and-wife team (we like that!) analyzed over 12,000 diary entries of employees in various organizations, finding that mixed signals from management were a significant source of performance issues.

Imagine all the lost productivity and opportunity from simply not being on the same page!

In the previous chapter, Communication Partnering Skills, we introduced workplace communication as fitting into one of three categories:

building relationships, developing organizational agility, and providing a framework for productivity. That chapter focused on the planned communications we do in both our leadership and followership roles to stimulate productivity. This chapter rounds out the productivity framework through Performance Partnering.

In the last four chapters we split out and summarized the leadership role and the followership role in separate sections. For this chapter on Performance Partnering, we just couldn't continue that nice, tidy format: the two are so interrelated, so interdependent, and so dynamic that it's difficult to decouple them. Because of that, we will discuss both roles together for each section throughout this chapter.

We will first continue to explore the relationship between signaling and performance. Then, we will consider how performance is a partnership agreement with two distinct aspects – the leadership role of commitment and the followership role of engagement. Finally, we'll unpack the key elements of a modern-day performance process.

Giving Clear Signals

My best-ever boss was Mike, a stellar communicator and marketing guru whose leadership never failed to impress me. You always knew where Mike stood … except for one thing: Mike was a huge ideator. He had lots of ideas, dreams, and plans. One day, about a year after I started working for him, Mike called me into his office.

"Do you know that you are the only person on my team getting the right things done? And, I've finally figured how you do it," he said to me. "You wait until I ask for something a second time and only then you do it. You're the first person to figure this out. Even I didn't know I worked this way."

That was only part of the story! Here's what else I had figured out about Mike. If he started on the work with you in his office, whatever it was, and then handed it off to you, he definitely wanted it done. By contrast, if you were in a team meeting with Mike or in his office having a one-on-one and he asked you to do something, it was quite likely just one of his (many) ideas. You could afford to wait a little. About 75% of the time he'd forget it and you'd never hear about it again. The other 25% of the time he would follow up, ask how it's going, and when he might expect it. That was his get-it-done signal.

Mike was self-aware and forever learning and developing. This revelation about the way he signaled prompted him to be more explicit with the rest of the team.

Clear signals are crucial to high-performance partnerships. How are your signals? Like Mike, we're often not as clear as we think we are. Developing greater self-awareness about signaling in your leadership role, and your interpretation and reaction to signals in your followership role, helps the partnership be more deliberate, efficient, and successful.

Our Salsa Dancing Project – Part 3 – About Performance

In salsa dancing, in addition to setting the frame, the leader's job is to plan ahead and give appropriate signals – signals about where you are going next, what direction you will move in, and what moves you will do when you get there. The followership responsibility is to be alert to the signals, properly interpret them, suggest moves, and reciprocate accordingly.

We can certainly see the potential of this concept in our dancing, but also in our work with people and organizations, AND in our business partnership and marriage. Getting the signaling right is foundational for any partnership. It is unreasonable to expect anyone could "just know" your intentions, whether it's in the workplace or personal.

Move from Your Core

The way Jeff, our salsa dancing instructor, teaches leadership signaling is to *move from your core*. He says that, as a leader, you must initiate movement by shifting the area between your hips and shoulders, not just with your feet or hands. This movement creates the fantastic hip motion that Latin dancing is known for. Moreover, it forces the leader to commit to moving. Imagine if Marc just stuck his hand up in the air and waved it in the direction he wanted Sam to go, or motioned by darting his eyes back and forth. These are all noncommittal signs. They are ambiguous because Marc could just as quickly change his mind – which he did on more than one occasion – moving his hands in one direction then deciding to go in another.

When your core hasn't shifted, it's easy to do something different and not give your partner time to react. That's why, when a cornerback in football is watching a wide receiver to anticipate where he might go next, it's the core that gives it away not the head or eyes or arms or even feet. By moving your core, shifting your own weight, it shows commitment to a course of action. When you are connected to your partner, it also gives him the opportunity to *feel* what you are doing rather than see it or guess at it. In fact, with an experienced ballroom dancing partner, you don't have to watch what he is doing at all. You can literally close your eyes, feel him shift his core, and follow.

When you move your core you don't have to force anything. The direction is crystal clear. When Mike spent an hour in his office working out an idea with a staff member, it was a sure sign he was committed to the task because he had invested in it. The old saw, "actions speak louder than words," is another way of saying that commitment is an active verb, something you do that cannot be undone easily. Correspondingly, Mike knew Marc was committed when tangible progress was being made. When the person in the followership role also moves from his core, both partners are in sync.

When both partners' signal from the core, you get the right dynamic to make the partnership look and feel great.

Moving from your core is a wonderfully kinesthetic representation of committed behavior by both partners. It allows for actions that are complementary, but not necessarily the same. It leads to generative performance partnering as long as the signals are clear and sufficient time is given to react … what is called *the And moment*.

The "And" Moment

 Working with Jeff really helped me to realize that, in my leadership role, I have to give my partner an appropriate opportunity to observe and interpret a signal. If I do that, she is much more likely to get it right.

In salsa, there is a built-in mechanism for this: a pause between the leadership action and followership response. Jeff called it *the And moment*. The basic salsa step is quick-quick-slow, quick-quick-slow, etc. Both partners use this step, and it may look like both do it at exactly the same time. But that isn't really what happens. If you watch closely, the step is actually quick-quick-slow AND quick-quick-slow AND quick-quick-slow AND. What do you think happens during the AND moment? At the beginning of the AND, the leader shifts his core, signaling where he is going on the next step. His partner waits; the direction of the shift is transmitted through the hands, which don't otherwise move; and that's how the partner knows where the next move is going. By the end of the AND, the partner has started to move in the same direction. This was a revelation! Leadership and followership are not simultaneous actions. Rather, they are a seamless flow of signals from leader to follower and back again, done so quickly you don't see the slight differences in timing unless you know what to look for.

Since finding this out, we have studied many partnerships. One graduate student of Marc's looked at how this transfer of information works in teams. He found that a mechanism for it (at least in the IT community) is muttering: the under-the-breath flow of information that gets picked up subconsciously by a teammate. In a jazz group it can happen through a slight change in the dynamic of play, or the way a phrase has been ended. On a basketball court it can be a shift of the eyes, perhaps signaling that an alley-oop play is coming. Regardless of how the signal is transmitted, it takes time and a conscious attention for giving and receiving signals to understand what message is being sent/received, as well as when and what the appropriate response is. In other words, you need to learn it as a team.

One reason some leadership training is less than effective is because signals are only taught to one of the partners, as if the signals were universal! Frankly, if the signals were so universal, they wouldn't have to be taught in the first place.

Varying, Yet Consistent Signals
Jeff also advises that a leader should use different signals for different turns. For especially complex turns, the signal should be notable, one that clearly indicates, "A Big Change Is Coming." Also, when a leader wants to change direction, he must not take steps that are too big or decide to rush because his partner needs time to make the turn, too. Finally, Jeff stresses consistency. Strong leadership enables others to relax into their followership role and confidently execute while still remaining 100% present.

One general manager we knew was infamous for being hard to pin down. His aim was to keep people on their toes and stay flexible, but he actually added even more chaos to an already chaotic, stressful environment. Staff spent countless hours trying to figure out how to build his support for their initiatives. In a most memorable situation, the CFO held a one-on-one meeting with the GM a day prior to a key senior management team meeting. At the one-on-one, the GM agreed with the CFO's plan to balance the budget by trimming new projects in the upcoming year by $2 million. At the team meeting next day, however, the head of projects introduced a number of exciting new projects. Rather than cut the project budget, the GM actually increased it on the spot!

There's a big difference between being alert and comfortable, and alert and on edge. Alert and comfortable is when you know what to expect and when expectations are reasonable. It's a lot easier to keep up so you have more energy to add creativity and value along the way.

Signals have to be clear, committed, and consistent. Leaders show commitment by moving from the core and by moving first. Two professors from Texas A&M International University found that communication works *through* action. In other words, if communication and behavior are misaligned, you get nothing.[1] On the flipside, followership shows engagement by remaining alert to core movements and using the AND moment to interpret leadership direction. This is truly complementary action!

Of course, salsa dancing isn't the same as work. In the best teams the leadership and followership roles are dynamic, switching back and forth – meaning that each person on the team has to understand your signals, and you have to know theirs. It's why a team of superstars thrown together for an event can easily lose to a less talented team who has spent a good amount of quality time with each other.[2]

How to Clearly Signal Your Intentions

Signals are often ambiguous. Always be sure to confirm your understanding unless the partnership is long standing and the subject routine. We heard a humorous story about a female project sponsor who informed her male project manager that she would be late for a meeting due to PMS problems. You can imagine the project manager's struggle over what he should do next! He tried to be helpful by rebooking the meeting for the next day although it turned out that the Purchasing

Management System (!) that was the source of the issue had only required a few minutes of her time.

!FliPtips!   Tool 13.1   Check In on Your Signals

Are the signals you give clear, committed and consistent in your role as a leader? In your role as a follower? In other relationships in your life?

Consider the answers to these questions:

1. Think about yourself in your leadership role.
   - In what ways do you give clear, committed signals? How do you know?
   - In what ways might you be giving unclear or mixed signals? Why do you suspect?
   - How might you improve?

2. Think about yourself in your followership role.
   - In what ways do you show clear commitment to those leading?
   - What are all the ways in which you could increase this visible commitment or its clarity?

3. Think about the person or people acting as your leader.
   - In what ways does she give clear, committed, consistent signals?
   - In what ways does she give unclear or mixed signals?
   - What are all the ways you might be able to help them develop stronger signals?

4. Think about the people who are following you.
   - Who gets things done that you expect and who doesn't?
   - In what ways do they give clear, committed signals to you?
   - Who comes back to you, continually seeking clarification?
   - How might you help them develop?

In your leadership role,

✓ Visibly commit to everything you want done. Don't issue a directive, then go and do something contrary. For example, if work-life balance has been an issue in your organization, you must not state your resolve to making it better while continuing to work around the clock and awarding employee of the month to the person who worked the most overtime. In your leadership role, always confirm understanding of intent, then take a committed action that is unambiguously aligned with your signal.

✓ If you do change your mind, consider the ramifications such as lost productivity, give context for your decision change and appreciate the work that has been done. If there is any way to value and reward what's already been done, do so.

In your followership role,

✓ Play back what you think you heard: For example, "Are you saying that you'd like me to take care of …?"
✓ Confirm that the actions you plan to take are what your partner anticipated. It is possible to agree on the interpretation of the signals but still not agree on the next steps. Think about how Mike (Marc's best boss ever from earlier in this chapter) didn't truly expect action until he reconfirmed later. Think about the befuddled project manager above who rushed to act when that wasn't what was required or intended.

Finally, in both roles, err on the side of transparency and positivity. We're sure every manager who says, "I'd like to see you in my office," thinks he is being efficient and neutral. On the contrary, this statement typically triggers mild to debilitating anxiety even if 80% of the time the office meetings prove to be positive. Similarly, every person who says, "It is mostly working well," or waits to discuss an issue in case it can be fixed thinks she has given assurance that everything is on plan. She hasn't.

The Commitment and Engagement Agreement

Restaurant Impossible? Not on This Show
We've been watching a Food Network TV show called *Restaurant Im-*

possible. In a typical episode, a restaurant in dire straits, **thisclose** to shutting down, is given a second chance by Robert Irvine – chef, restaurateur, and (something we hadn't expected) leadership guru! Oh yes. And he's aided in rebuilding the failing businesses by an interior decorator, a crew of carpenters, and $10,000. In just two days they make over the restaurant, retrain the staff, and update the menu along with how the food is prepared and presented.

In almost every case, the restaurant owners are desperate, woeful, and grateful in equal measures as the two-day transformation takes place. While we anticipated that the food and décor would be in need of an overhaul, it turns out that leadership is often the third pillar desperate for repair. In one show, Irvine had the owner and staff together in a team meeting and handed them each some lemons. They were to take turns giving a lemon to someone on the team they felt needed to step up in some way. A good chunk of the lemons were passed to the owner as he was asked to be more of a leader by his staff.

Later in the show, before THE BIG NIGHT when the completely redesigned space and menu get revealed, just before the restaurant gets packed with a slew of curious and hungry guests, Irvine suggested the owner give a motivational speech to his team. The owner said, "We've been given a second chance. We're all in this together. Let's go and make this work!" Irvine responded with, "That's it?! You're not here to be their friend. You're here to be their leader. Now step up!"

Okay, that sounds a bit harsh but Irvine gave accurate advice. We must embrace our leadership role, not eschew it. The people relying on us need us to do so. We certainly want them to embrace their followership role and the responsibilities that come with it. What Irvine was looking for was for the owner to visibly commit to his people, not be a coworker: for example, the owner could have said, "Thank you for giving me the feedback I needed. I will do a better job of committing to you, being a stronger leader, and taking action. In turn, I expect each of you to embrace your roles, to be totally engaged in the success of this restaurant, and to follow through on all of your responsibilities."

How Can I Make My Team More Engaged?

We regularly get asked in workshops, often by middle and senior managers, "How can I make my team more engaged?" This question remains top of mind for organizations as engagement scores plummet to new, worrisome lows. A Gallup poll of North American organizations reported 52% of people "Not Engaged" and another 19% as "Actively Disengaged." Ouch![3]

Any sensible person might wonder why it should be someone's responsibility to make another person engaged? Is it really the case that if an employee isn't engaged it's because the leader hasn't articulated a strong enough vision, made the right decision, isn't charismatic or authentic enough? There is always another reason available to explain why someone isn't engaged other than the obvious: he or she hasn't decided to be engaged. We're not saying there might not be reasons – a truly bad boss, a dysfunctional organization, an impossible situation – but more often than not it is because the employee hasn't stepped up.

Here's an easy way to diagnose a situation:

- If most people reporting into a person have the same issue, it's a leadership problem.
- If only some of the people reporting into a person have the same issue, it is likely a followership problem.

A big reason engagement scores are so poor is because of the prevailing attitude that it is something management does. Rubbish. Engagement is a personal choice, not a management action.

Leadership commitment and followership engagement are the complementary sides of a psychological contract. Whereas the other terms and conditions are typically far more explicit, this implicit agreement is arguably the most fundamental and impactful.

Leadership Commitment

We used the word "commitment" in the previous chapter in terms of signals and the work itself; now we shift to committing to *people*. For example, at Google, managers see their job as coaching, supporting, and charting the path to success for staff much more than organizing the work or assigning tasks. That's a people commitment.

Work is often a hard slog, and it doesn't always feel terribly aspirational or purposeful. Even small acts of commitment can go a long way to fuel engagement and progress. We have a small but memorable example of this from one of our training programs. First, we must say that we are big proponents of multilevel training: that is, training an entire team or organization on the same material including leadership, followership, and partnership skills. It seems bizarre to us that the majority of leadership training is rolled out one level at a time with senior, middle, or junior management being trained together but not actually practicing with the partners they need to interact with the most in the workplace or necessarily learning the same material. Can you imagine a dance teacher only training the leader to lead while leaving his partner outside twiddling her thumbs? Preposterous! Unfortunately, that's what most books, most workshops, and the majority of organizations do: they only train the (formal) leader to lead. Half the partnership is missing!

The multilevel approach to training and development is a difference maker in many regards: it gives opportunity for the more senior leaders to show their genuine commitment to their people, to progress and improvement, and to learning something new together. Funnily enough, as a by-product of these co-learning workshops, the session extends inevitably to spotting improvement opportunities in the organization.

Anyhow, this example is from an all-levels workshop aimed at improving leadership and followership communications. During a session on what makes meetings great, small groups worked with a tip sheet of best practices and discussed the impact of adhering to them in their world: how they might impact productivity, innovation, and collaboration. Some bright spark piped up, "Hey we should really do all of this stuff! We would get so much more done." A senior manager at a neighboring small group overheard and responded, "You know you are right." He nodded to the head of HR who was also participating, "Let's do this. Let's post these tips in every meeting room."

As a leader, to get engagement from your partner or team, you first need to commit. Don't say, "Well, we could do this or that ..." or, "We're all in this together." How the heck can anyone follow you? It's guaranteed your partners or team will be confused, frustrated, and unproductive. Show commitment in a tangible way. Just saying you want something or think something isn't the same as rolling up your sleeves and doing it.

We must be the change we wish to see in the world.

– Gandhi

Followership Engagement

The onus is on each of us to be engaged not on leadership to make us engaged. In fact, you can't *make* someone else engaged. As Max De Pree, the iconic, cutting-edge CEO of Herman Miller said, "It's not (the manager's) job to supervise or to motivate, but to liberate and enable." You can certainly create an environment that supports greater engagement or one that quashes it; but, at the end of the day, it comes down to the individual to choose their own attitude – what will they decide to do? That's why engagement is the primary ingredient in Peak Performing.

Do you put your best foot forward most days and give it your all? If your answer is "not so much," then what can you do to give it your all? Do you need better tools, a different environment, more sleep, to develop a skill or skills, different projects that suit you better, or a different job? Look at the elements you can influence and figure out how to change them so you can be fully engaged. Engagement is about looking at your job with a different lens, including the perspective of your leadership and the broader organization. The point is to make the best of what you have, not to worry about having the best.

Consider how Doreen and Kristen showed engagement and initiative when they decided to do a review of their department's offsite storage expenses, as they were aware of an organizational priority to reduce the operating budget. These employees of a local firm we worked with visited Iron Mountain on their lunch hour and discovered boxes and boxes of bottled water with a purchased company's former name and logo marked "store indefinitely." They discovered another meaning of the term "waste water" and saved their department $77 per month, $924 annually, just by getting rid of the bottles.

> Leadership role: I will stay committed to you and support your efforts
> Followership role: I will be engaged in my work and support your goals

The DNA of Performance

The traditional approach is for the boss to *manage* performance through an iterative process of goal setting, performance reviews, ratings, and rewards often bundled into an annual event dreaded equally by the leader and follower. Job descriptions, job families, competency dictionaries, and performance agreements are the regular tools that a leader should use to articulate the requirements of a job, or so the story goes. These tools are meant to inform a follower what is expected of him and how his performance will be evaluated. Clearly the traditional approach isn't working well! All the training programs in the world haven't made a dent in these numbers, nor have various improvements and tweaks suggested over the years.[5]

Because of this, many organizations are eschewing the standard approach along with the language that goes with it. Web-based social performance management platforms such as NetSuite, Work.com, 7geese, and Kapta Systems are presenting fresh possibilities. Like other forms of social media, these newer ways of supporting performance are integrated into daily work life, making it easier to participate, share real-time information, and collaborate. Feedback comes from anyone you relate to in the organization: your team, your peers, your leader, and even your customers. And it is just as easy to give a quick thank you for contributing to the morning's sales meeting as a more significant recognition for ongoing mentoring throughout a critical project.

Joseph Fung, Founder of TribeHR and VP of HCM Products at NetSuite describes it this way:

> We're looking at something light-years apart from paper review processes. When we talk about social performance management, we're really talking about capturing the successes, progress, and challenges that are already happening every day. We offer this power not just to managers, but also to every individual employee, giving them the ability to better steer their own performance roadmap.

Fung makes two points: first, performance is not an annual event or a cycle; it is a daily process. Second, he broadens the responsibility for performance from manager-employee to organization-employee and emphasizes the role of the employee (followership in our language).

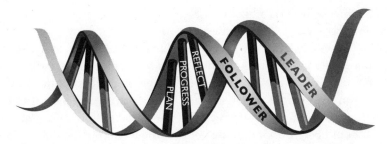

Figure 13.2 The DNA of performance – How leadership and followership are intertwined

A model for this new way of thinking about performance is as a double helix, where leadership and followership are connected strands. Together, these strands act as a tightly coupled system that produces continuous advancement, improvement, and development: in other words, performance.

The three stages of performance in this model are (1) planning, (2) making progress, and (3) reflection[6] based on real-time, multisource feedback. Rather than an annual event, each stage is short, overlapping, and builds on gains from one time to the next. A huge benefit of a shortened cycle is that individuals and teams can spot issues with performance and rapidly correct them. Similarly, opportunities can quickly be taken advantage of.

With that in mind, let's take a deeper look at each stage.

Plan

The man who starts out going nowhere generally gets there.

– Dale Carnegie

The core elements of planning include:

- What will we focus on (or focus on next)?
- Creative thinking: What are all the ways we could enable progress on each item of focus?
- Critical thinking: What shall we choose to embark on at this time? What's relevant? What's doable? What should we stop doing?

Planning feels like it is a big deal or time consuming, maybe a 50-page document covering the next five years! It needn't be anything of the sort. A plan is the name we give to agreements that break down strategy into actionable chunks. Plans should be memory-less; each time you embark on planning, where you are now is more important than where you were before. But that doesn't mean plans don't have a direction because they do, one informed by your **vision** of the future. Finally, plans should be grounded in the **goals** of the team (or leadership). We are all for taking initiative and being engaged, but engagement without grounding can be disruptive.

Let's talk more about two elements of planning: co-vision and goals.

Co-vision

The idea that permeates every leadership and management model, academic and popular, is to have a vision. A vision is what binds people together with a sense of common purpose. A vision is a way to plan without having to explicitly lay out every detail; the vision is the guide. A compelling vision positively impacts workforce engagement, motivation, performance, and teamwork.

A recent study by Kohles, Bligh, and Carsten[7] suggests that going even further – co-creating a vision, a co-vision – reaps large benefits. If everyone owns the same vision, then formal hierarchy becomes less important and generative behavior becomes more likely. Interestingly, when we look back now at the focus group results on good and great followership that we did during the early years of our work on this book, one phrase that came up in every session and was typically voted in the top five was "excellent followers are committed to THE CAUSE."

Goals: Fuzzy and Stretchy

> Part of the issue of achievement is to be able to set realistic goals, but that's one of the hardest things to do because you don't always know exactly where you're going.
>
> – *George Lucas*

Such is the nature of creative work, which, in today's knowledge and creative economy, holds the lion's share of what adds value. You don't always know where you are going, but you certainly want to be alert to opportunities and discoveries along the way.

Dr. Greg Evans of the Happiness Enhancement Group, who we met in the Partnership Principles section, says, "Perspective is not just important in interpreting objective reality but in creating reality. We get more satisfaction out of the pursuit of a goal than the realization of the goal. Pursuing goals adds to our happiness, in turn positively influencing our creativity and productivity."

His work, and that of many others, suggests that SMART goals – Specific, Measurable, Actionable, Realistic, and Time-boxed – are no longer as appropriate as once believed. While it is a useful acronym that helped generations of employees become more achievement oriented and quantitatively evaluated, it turns out not to be quite smart enough for today's work. SMART goals are useful for mechanical, routine tasks but not as useful for innovation, creativity, or cognitive work that is inherently unpredictable and opportunistic. For these types of outcomes it is more useful to have better communications and relationships,[8] and goals that are *fuzzy* and *stretchy*.

Fuzzy

A fuzzy goal recognizes that the future is unknown. It "motivates the general direction of (the) work, without blinding the team to opportunities along the journey" (Blackwell, Wilson, Street, Boulton, & Knell, 2009, p. 13).

Fuzzy goals must be directional but malleable. They must evolve and be refined often just to keep up with the flood of new information, new discoveries, and new demands. Making goals fuzzy – not too specific but not too vague – allows for greater agility while still allowing for progress. Fuzzy goals are more easily aligned to a vision, and fuzzy goals activate people's internal motivation rather than being attached to an external reward.[9]

For example, as The Beatles were evolving from their early rock 'n roll music to the more complex, boundary-breaking songs and albums of their later years, you can imagine them having a fuzzy goal such as "Express our musical vision and excellence without concern for the standard limits set by established song, album or genre boundaries." Contrast this with a SMART goal such as "After three best-selling albums in the U.K. and abroad, implement one song that has a length greater than four minutes to test acceptability." You can see how limiting the SMART version seems. At the other extreme, it is easy to be too vague and motherhood: "Be creative. Make money. Have fun."

The downside to fuzzy goals is that they are not so easy to use for evaluative purposes. The lack of clear targets to measure against can puzzle and annoy people used to having goals set for achievement, especially as many performance management systems focus on achievements. When Marc managed a product development team, for example, he set fuzzy goals for team members but it was a hard sell; the organization he was in used goals to determine bonus payments at the end of the year, and that was the focus his staff demanded.

If you find yourself in a similar situation, we suggest that you have two sets of goals: one for evaluative purposes and the other more directional or fuzzy.

Stretchy

A stretch goal can be defined this way: "[Goals] that cannot be achieved by incremental or small improvements but require extending oneself to the limit to be actualized. Expressed in the saying, you cannot cross a chasm in two steps."[10]

One of the biggest compliments I received as a people leader was that I had high expectations for my teams and genuinely believed they could accomplish more than they thought they could. My teams were regularly blown away by how much they could accomplish together and were quite proud of themselves. As was I. My teams always rocked!

Funnily enough I was later criticized for this quality, for being overly optimistic. It was initially very difficult feedback for me to deal with as it cut to the core of my leadership philosophy. I was even brought up this way: my parents had always encouraged my sister and me to stretch, try new things, and be okay with failure as long as we tried.

After much rumination (and Marc's help), I realized that it was a cultural acclimatization issue. The company I used to work for believed in stretch goals. This worked really well as long as everyone knew that goals were a stretch. The company I had moved on to had a different practice: never say you can do something that you might not be able to do, and always give a deadline you can meet.

Is there a right answer here? Was Sam's first company, which encouraged stretch goals, better at motivating performance? Actually, yes. Stretch goals *are* better, and evidence for that is unequivocal.[11] Performance improves with stretch goals.

Pygmalion Effect leadership. As mentioned before, the greater the belief placed in the skills of people, the better they do. It's easy to see that stretch goals are a consequence of Pygmalion-style leadership. We also expect Pygmalion followership – the belief that leadership is great – has reciprocal, positive benefits although no-one has researched that idea just yet![12]

Make Progress

Once you and your partners have plans – a vision of where you are heading, a sense of how each person can contribute, and goals that help you get there – you need to make progress together.

A day of progress is more valuable than a week of frustration. And progress today is much more likely to result in progress tomorrow. Like plans, progress should only be as big as it needs to be. That's why small wins are so important at the start of a project ... or the middle ... or, frankly, any time at all. If you get progress, and then more progress, it speeds up, piles up, and becomes a positive feedback loop.

In your followership role, execute the plan, stay engaged, take initiative within the frame set by the plan and by the broader context of the organization.

In your leadership role, stay committed to the people by signaling intent and by figuring out what are all the other things you can do to support progress.

Reflect

Reflection is about taking stock of what just happened. It is the learning phase that leads to greater progress in the future. It includes observations, insights, and learnings that can be stimulated by the right questions.

- How did it go?
- What worked and why?
- What didn't work and why?
- How might we change it up/do more/or act differently to keep developing?

While reflection is always useful, it is most useful for teams that are experiencing problems, as long as they are willing and able to learn from their mistakes.[13] It is also valuable when the team is in settling mode, but not so much in scouting mode.[14] Tailor the reflection to the situation.

The wrong way to use reflection is as a measuring stick. If you do so, it becomes the stick that people want to avoid or overcome in some way (as happens with most performance management systems that we've seen). When the stick is present, people excuse what just happened or explain it away as an anomaly, which introduces unintended barriers to change. You don't learn well from a stick, except how to avoid it.

Contribution and Progress

There is an alternative to fixating on variances from plan. A Contribution and Progress process replaces performance evaluations based on objectives, goals, or other fixed measures, and it can be used prospectively or retrospectively.

Questions such as the following shift the conversation from *what people have done* to *how people are contributing and progressing*. Imagine a conversation and report based on this:

1. How have you contributed to your team's goals during the period?
2. Now, what are all the ways you can contribute to the team's goals this upcoming period?
3. How have you made progress in your role?
4. Now, what are all the ways you can make progress in your role in this upcoming period?

A Contribution and Progress review or report (C&P) is put together by an employee, possibly with some assistance from coworkers and the manager, outlining the contributions that he or she has made over the year (or whatever time period seems most appropriate) to the team, the organization, the customer, and anyone else important. It also highlights progress that has been made, whether it is in personal development, new processes or system changes. This terminology and approach fosters more expansive, more creative thinking about how we can truly make a difference. It encourages initiative and reaching for new heights and stimulates dialogue of a reflective nature. It supports a more dynamic, opportunistic environment. Overall, it is far more valuable than traditional performance management.

Sheri Keffer, director of People and Culture, Perimeter Institute for Theoretical Physics (a leading center for scientific research, training, and educational outreach in foundational theoretical physics located in Waterloo, Ontario, Canada) tells us that shifting away from a traditional performance management approach and adopting the C&P report process was a game changer: "We've implemented it and it's changed everything. It alleviated the stress of feedback for a lot of people as it made it much easier to provide comments on their peers. Eliminating the ratings also made the experience more of a career progression discussion with their managers rather than being rated on their performance."

A more radical suggestion is to give the C&P report to other team members, not just the manager. Universities, for example, have been doing this for years by having professors submit reports on their contributions to the Promotions and Tenure committee. Google does the same by having peers (not managers) decide when someone is ready for promotion or other career advancement.[15]

Perhaps your organization isn't quite ready to scrap your performance management system, but focusing on contributions and progress is more beneficial than focusing on performance goals regardless of how you introduce the change.

To complement a Contribution and Progress process – or any other process you have in place – we encourage everyone to seek broader sources of feedback. A simple but powerful approach that can be implemented straight away using e-mail is the Quick 360° Feedback tool.

As with any feedback, what you get back has to be reviewed and considered carefully. Sometimes it reveals more about how you are perceived by others than any skill or performance deficiencies you might

!FliPtips! Tool 13.2   Quick and Powerful 360° Feedback

Determine who your main partners are – your boss, peers, staff, colleagues, possibly the boss's boss or key client contacts – then solicit feedback with a request such as:

I am looking for feedback on my contributions and I would appreciate your input! Please provide responses to the following questions, either directly to me or to my manager:

1. Overall, am I contributing effectively in my role?
   (Highly effective, quite effective, adequate, not effective enough)
2. What 2 or 3 things do I do which are particularly effective?
3. What 2 or 3 things could I do to increase my effectiveness?
4. What 2 or 3 things could I stop doing to increase my effectiveness?

have. The trick is to figure out what you can learn from it and how to best action it. Feedback is a gift that requires generosity and practice to give it and to receive it.

Performance Coaching: The Leadership Role

The leadership role is Performance Coaching, the core purpose of which is to optimize the team's potential and make progress by committing to the success of each and every person. What expectations have been put on your people? What challenges, opportunities, and priorities do they have? What goals and priorities still apply? What barriers can you eliminate? How can you help the team achieve?

Now that we are nearly at the end of the book, we could add a whole host of factors that contribute to a generative workplace. As a generative leader, you must understand these factors and do what you can to make them the norms. A few key ones are ensuring roles are clear and honored, stimulating engagement by visibly and fully committing yourself to the tasks and to your people, and continually improving the clarity and consistency of your signals.

Peak Performing: The Followership Role

The complementary followership role of Peak Performing is all about taking the initiative to be fully *engaged* in your work, in your ongoing development, and in the goals of your leadership.

The followership role is not about executing a series of tasks. Rather, it is about getting results, ensuring continuity, following-up, understanding the context, and taking full accountability. Work to understand and maximize contributions in each area of your work. Strive to continually improve your personal value. And think of it like you are the business: you have a mandate to outperform your previous year. Your partners expect it!

In summary, the elements of great Peak Performing include:

1. **Behave as if you are already in your dream job**. Bring engagement, positivity, and purpose to the workplace.
2. **Make commitments wisely and keep them.** Be realistic and reliable. This trust building often leads to additional opportunities.
3. **Take informed initiative.** Ensure your initiative is in line with the vision and priorities.
4. **Be purposeful.** Be sure to understand why you are doing what you've been assigned.
5. **Invest your time in what's important**. As resource allocation is your manager's job, help her invest key resources (such as yourself) wisely by tracking how your time is spent.
6. **Succession-plan yourself.** Being indispensable is not the goal. A senior manager once made this telling remark to us: "When someone is considered absolutely indispensable, it's time to get rid of him." Key skills need to be distributed across an organization. Being indispensable limits your mobility, and it limits your boss's flexibility. It is better to be appreciated than necessary.
7. **Own your own development plan.** Make sure your aspirations are known. Be clear about when you are ready for a change or a new challenge, but also come prepared with feasible ideas and plans for how your other work can get done.
8. Create your own **safe zone** in the workplace. Blow off steam in a safe direction.

Performance Partnering Skills Summary

Leadership Skill: Performance Coaching
People thrive in an environment of purpose, progress, and positivity:

- ✓ Ensure purpose with clear vision, goals, and roles.
- ✓ Facilitate progress by reducing barriers and ambiguity, and bringing in useful tools and processes.
- ✓ Foster positivity through recognition and generous coaching.

Followership Skill: Peak Performing
Make yourself a key resource that is easy to manage:

- ✓ Take the initiative to get the right job done, and the job done right.
- ✓ Invest time on the critical tasks including making commitments wisely and keeping them.
- ✓ Show accountability for engagement, on-the-job performance, and ongoing development.

CHAPTER 14

Personal, Team, and Organizational Development

The book has introduced a lot of tools, tips, and ideas along with some suggested uses and implications of each. This chapter takes the alternate perspective: instead of starting with the Generative Partnership® model (GP model), with its five principles and skills for leadership and followership, and considering how each piece can be applied separately, we start with the problem or opportunity and ask, "What are all the ways to think about and solve it using the ideas in this book?"

We have used the GP model and tools to tackle a wide variety of challenges from personal to team to organization-wide. You can use the GP model as a stand-alone, too, however it is also a great complement to other tools you may already be using – MBTI, Situational Leadership, Six Thinking Hats, 360° assessments, SWOT, decision trees, SMART goals, vision and mission statements, development plans, and more. For additional ideas and resources, check out www.leadershipishalfthe story.com.

What the GP model provides is a more expansive framework for growth. It's a strategic platform as well as a specific guide to implementation. Here are a few ways we have used it to solve personal, leadership, and organizational challenges.

Personal Development

For a specific interpersonal challenge, use the GP model as a diagnostic tool. Step through each principle and skill area and ask yourself, "In what ways can I apply this to address my challenge?"

For example, we heard from a reader who stated, "This book was a lifesaver when I wasn't getting along with my boss." She said that she gained inspiration as well as specific strategies.

- She redesigned how she was communicating upwards by building a new Dashboard in consultation with her boss.
- She constructed an operating manual for her boss by asking lots of questions, trying new things, and talking to her peers who had built better relationships with the boss.
- She performed a Deeply Shared Goals Audit to see where there were outliers and where she could make goals more deeply shared with her boss.
- She secured a mentor from another area who was instrumental in helping her understand the broader organization, which enabled her to find ways to better understand what sort of initiative would be helpful and appreciated.

For overall personal and professional development, use the assessment (tool 14.1) to find areas of strengths and opportunities. The tool is organized first by leadership actions, then by followership actions, and finally by each of the five skills. You can do the whole assessment at once, focus on either leadership or followership, or concentrate on a specific skill area.

This is a *situational* assessment, and that is quite different from most assessments you may have done before. The results reflect your current situation from your perspective, not your intrinsic capability or abilities. For instance, if you have a new staff member, you might not have had time to do relationship framing yet and that would show up in the assessment, but it doesn't mean you aren't good at it, just that it could be an important next step. Which partnership actions are your strengths at this time? Which partnership actions should you spend more time and attention on?

As your situation changes, so do the answers to these questions. Take the assessment regularly, particularly when your situation changes: a new leader, new team members, job change, or other workplace change. As you fill out the leadership skills section, think about a current leadership situation you face. As you fill out the followership skills section, think about a particular boss or group of senior people you report in to. This will ensure the results are actionable and practical.

You can also use the assessment as a 360° tool by having your team members, peers, and leader prepare it from their perspective. You can compare your perspective with theirs and monitor if your actions are seen as aligned with your intentions. Because the assessment compares items rather than using an absolute scale, it is more comfortable to prepare, share, and discuss openly.

To complete it, choose two items in each section to put into the "Top" category. These are what you are doing best right now compared to the rest of the items on the list. Then choose two items to put into the "Bottom" category. These are what you are not doing as well on right now compared to the other items on the list. That doesn't mean you aren't doing well at those items, just that you are doing other things better. And, if it is a skill you want to improve, it's a great place to start. Of course, the final two items go in the middle.

Once completed, think about how to make best use of the results. How can you share and further leverage your top abilities? What steps will you take on your bottom ones? Is it weaker because you have had less opportunity to use it? Is it a perception of others you need to correct? Or is it something you aren't as comfortable doing in this situation?

!FliPtips! Tool 14.1 Partnership Skills Assessment

Leadership Skills

Decision Framing

1. The first thing I do is consider whether I am the right person to make the decision.
2. I manage each phase of decision making to ensure everyone is onboard.
3. I engage my team and stakeholders in decisions as early as possible.
4. I allow for time to collect all the evidence and get to the root of the situation.
5. I communicate why a decision was made as soon as it is made.
6. I coach my team to be better at providing decision support.

TOP

MIDDLE

BOTTOM

Relationship Framing

1. I have a strong working relationship with each of my team members.
2. I make my work habit preferences known and understood by my team.
3. I treat everyone on the team equitably.
4. I spend time getting to know and support each of my team regularly.
5. My team talk openly and candidly with me about what's working and what's not.
6. I know each of my team member's preferred work habits and ways to be recognized and rewarded.

TOP

MIDDLE

BOTTOM

Organizational Mentoring

1. I coach and mentor my team on the behaviors that the organization favors.
2. I contribute to, and reinforce, the organizational culture.
3. My team understands the key business drivers at our organization.
4. I can articulate the important aspects of the organizational culture and how it differs across areas.
5. People come to me for mentoring.
6. I learn a lot when I mentor others.

TOP

MIDDLE

BOTTOM

Cascade Communicating

1. When I communicate with my team, I carefully consider the core purpose and what context I can add.
2. My communications stimulate my team to take initiative in the right ways at the right time.
3. I receive and act on feedback from my team about my communications.
4. I discuss rationale for organizational changes with my team.
5. I make a point of talking about the issues on everyone's mind.

TOP

MIDDLE

BOTTOM

6. When communicating organizational changes to my team, I advocate for the change.

Performance Coaching

1. I initiate talk with my peers about how we might best support each other's goals.
2. I eliminate barriers to progress for my team's work.
3. I engage my team to develop and maintain a compelling vision.
4. I make sure that the members of my team are mostly playing to their strengths.
5. I am generous with positive and constructive feedback and recognition.
6. People know where I stand: my priorities, strengths, weaknesses, and drivers.

TOP

MIDDLE

BOTTOM

Followership Skills

Decision Advocating

1. I keep my leader well informed and up-to-date about the decisions I make.
2. I build upon other people's suggestions in meetings rather than being a devil's advocate.
3. Even when a decision isn't my responsibility, I pitch in and add as much value as I can.
4. When I provide an opinion, I also share my rationale.
5. I champion decisions once they are made even when I am not sure they are right.
6. I switch my focus to implementation once a decision has been made.

TOP

MIDDLE

BOTTOM

Relationship Building

1. I take the initiative to build a strong working relationship with my leader.
2. I consciously adapt to my leader's working style and preferences.

TOP

3. I offer to do the tasks that my leader doesn't like doing.

MIDDLE

4. I give feedback to my leader about how his/her changes are being received.

BOTTOM

5. I show sincere appreciation to my leader for positive or difficult actions.
6. I offer to help out or take over some tasks when my leader is busy.

Organizational Agility

1. I seek mentoring opportunities from others.

TOP

2. When working with a new team, I first find out what's important to them.
3. People tell me that I am a good fit for my organization.

MIDDLE

4. I take advantage of networking opportunities.
5. I know how to get things done in my organization even when I don't have the formal authority to do it.

BOTTOM

6. People see me as being able to move around the organization effortlessly.

Dashboard Communicating

1. Communicating to my leader is a top priority and I allocate time to plan and do it.

TOP

2. When I communicate with my leader, I carefully consider the core purpose and what details are unnecessary.

MIDDLE

3. I summarize key points at the beginning of e-mails and meetings.

BOTTOM

4. I inquire about my leader's preferred ways of keeping up-to-date.
5. My communications to my leader get the results I expect.
6. I anticipate my leader's need for information and rarely get asked for more.

Peak Performing
1. I take initiative and accountability for my personal and professional development.
2. I know my priorities and am rarely asked to switch things around.
3. When I make commitments, I deliver what I said I would, when I said I would.
4. I am performing at my best.
5. I show enthusiasm for my job.
6. I make sure that I am useful and appreciated in my job.

TOP

MIDDLE

BOTTOM

Team Development

You can use the GP model to address pain points or gain points: you might have a specific interpersonal challenge or two that the team is struggling with right now or you might be seeking professional growth and learning within the team.

For a specific challenge, use the GP model as a diagnostic tool. Step through each principle and each skill area in the model and ask, "In what ways can we apply this to address the challenge?"

For example, perhaps you are finding that decisions are stalled, challenged, or not being implemented swiftly. Some of the possible reasons for this are the following:

- Decisions aren't framed properly.
- Team members don't understand their followership responsibilities and what the leader expects.
- Stakeholders weren't given enough opportunity to engage and contribute early and often.
- Stakeholders didn't feel they were kept connected throughout the process.
- Team members are stuck in an earlier stage in the decision lifecycle because the leader didn't signal the move to a new stage.
- Decision-making accountability isn't with the right person.

- Team members have different goals and agendas and are pulling in different directions.
- The goals are too fuzzy, or not fuzzy enough.
- The focus is on negatives and what is broken rather than on positives and improvements.
- The process used isn't considerate of the culture of the team and/or organization.

In this case, a number of tools and tips could be employed to improve the situation: the decision-making accountability rules, the decision lifecycle, the Scouting vs. Settling frame, and a Deeply Shared Goals Audit, to name a few.

Another example might be that your team is having an engagement issue. Reasons for it could include the following:

- There is a small in-group or a large out-group.
- The ratio of positive to negative reinforcement is off kilter.
- Team members are not taking accountability for their own engagement.
- Framing is incomplete and people don't understand the direction, or what they should be doing at this time.
- Dynamic leadership and followership isn't happening effectively for all team members – people are too bound up in one role.
- Communication isn't action oriented.
- There is a lack of support for organizational initiatives.

Go back to the relevant sections and review the guidance and tools recommended. Consider doing an engagement exercise with the team.

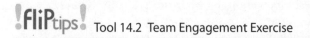 Tool 14.2 Team Engagement Exercise

1. Ask each team member to brainstorm silently and write down all the things that engage them personally in their work and workplace.
2. Have team members pair up and share their preferences.

3. Next, as a group, have everyone contribute their engagement thoughts and ideas by writing them on a big white board or flipchart.
4. Now brainstorm as a group on this question: "What are all the ways the team could create more engagement opportunities for everyone."
5. Gain agreement, support, and specific accountabilities for an action plan.

Reading this book can be a valuable team experience for professional growth and learning. Assign the book one chapter at a time. After each chapter, hold a team meeting to discuss it: consider which aspects resonated, which already work well in the team, where could the team focus more. Brainstorm together on all the ways to use the ideas to improve team collaboration and results.

Organizational Development

You can use the GP model to address pain points you are having with your organization or gain points you wish to achieve.

For example, after reading this book, you recognize that followership is not well understood at your organization, and you can see the potential for gain in productivity and collaboration. Perhaps you are finding that at your organization when people aren't leading, they are passive followers or even loose cannons taking initiative willy-nilly. Some ways to bring effective followership into your organization include:

1. Expressing desired followership competencies or capabilities. Before you dismiss this suggestion as HR mumbo jumbo, review the couple of examples below. We exploded two very common competencies – creativity and decision making – into their respective leadership and followership components. As you can see, it adds nuances and provides a powerful clarity to the competency. You can also imagine how it is possible to excel at one aspect of the skill and not the other. That's what we have found in many organiza-

!FliPtips! Tool 14.3 Competencies Expanded to Include Leadership and Followership

Creativity

Original Competency
Uses creativity to positively impact the business

Leadership Competency
Manages the creative process productively; facilitates the use of creativity tools such as brainstorming; builds an environment that fosters the creative output of others.

Followership Competency
Introduces research, facts, ideas, and other support to the creative process; provides valued input that leads to new solutions; respects and helps develop the ideas of others.

Decision Making

Original Competency
Makes good decisions based on a mixture of analysis, wisdom, experience, and judgment; most solutions are correct when judged over time; advice sought by others.

Leadership Competency
Establishes and manages a well-defined decision process; engages the right people with the right tools; deliberately avoids errors and biases; ensures clear documentation and communication

Followership Competency
Sought out by others for advice, solutions, wisdom, experience, and judgment; provides useful input and advocacy to the decision making process; supports others involved in making a decision.

tions. Rewriting the competencies to include both roles can be very helpful indeed.

2. Adding followership considerations to your performance evaluation approach. Consider a Contribution and Progress approach as outlined in Chapter 13.
3. Adding followership training to your onboarding programs, leadership development program, top talent program, executive offsites or organizational change programs, or all of the above.

Another use for organizational development is with project teams. Project teams do much of today's strategic work for organizations. People must come together, often from disparate parts of an organization, and collaborate really well without time to experiment and adjust on the partnership side. Use ideas from the book in a project team kickoff day to establish swift relationships, norms, expectations, and some useful new language and terminology. We often use the Scouting vs. Settling frame to discuss roles, expectations, and how they vary at different times in a project. We might facilitate a Lean-In activity to stimulate open discussion and agreement between new project team partners about how they will stay connected and on each other's wavelength. We would discuss communication protocols, including having four-way communications rather than one-way or two-way. And, we'd introduce useful concepts such as being a Decision Advocate (rather than a Devil's Advocate) and to "cookie-crumb your reasoning" rather than provide opinions.

Hopefully these few examples have tickled your imagination as to a bunch of way you can apply this material practically. For more ideas and resources, check out www.leadershipishalfthestory.com or contact us.

Thank you for making it all the way to the end! By now you know why leadership is half the story: it's because followership is the other half! Hopefully, too, you don't think of followership as the F-word but, rather, as a dynamic, different, yet equal complement to leadership. Both are important, and both should be appreciated.

All the best in practicing your leadership, practicing your followership, and in building great collaborations!

Notes

Preface

1 Hi-Po or hipo is slang for high potential: i.e., an employee with a lot more to offer and who is identified for a higher position in the future.
2 Kay and Shelton (2000). In particular, over half of senior managers surveyed believed that retaining talent, communication, and integrating corporate cultures were critical to the success of an acquisition.

Chapter 1

1 Hollenbeck, Beersma, and Schouten (2012).
2 Aboukhalil (2014).
3 Hipple and Sok (2013).
4 Workopolis (2014).
5 Cambridge Dictionaries Online.
6 Merriam-Webster.

Chapter 2

1 Agho (2009).
2 We are calling what Podsakoff and MacKenzie (1997) studied – followership behaviors – although strictly speaking they were researching organizational citizenship behaviors (OCBs). We recognize that equating the two – OCBs with followership – is a controversial claim, but many types of OCBs appear to be much more related to followership than leadership. For example, the three categories of OCBs that Podsakoff and MacKenzie focused on were "Helping," "Civic Virtue," and "Sportsmanship." The Civic Virtue category includes attending nonmandatory training as well

as participating in meetings, while Sportsmanship includes items such as not complaining about trivial matters, focusing on the good in his/her situation, or not finding fault with what the company is doing. These two are clearly representative of followership behaviors. Helping, however, is dissimilar to followership, which makes it intriguing to note that Helping was also the one category that was negatively associated with organizational effectiveness for insurance agents!

3 This is from Koman and Wolff (2008); and Offermann, Bailey, Vasilopoulos, Seal, and Sass (2004).

4 Rieck (2008).

5 The word "directly" is used because Rieck (2008) did show indirect effects of leadership emotional intelligence. The primary idea, however, that the emotional intelligence of the followers was the most important, is valid.

6 Examples include Schlaerth, Ensari, and Christian (2013); and Sy, Tram, and O'Hara (2006).

7 A recent review of research into emotional intelligence (Walter, Cole, & Humphrey, 2011) references many studies showing a link between leader emotional intelligence and effectiveness, but it also cautions that our current state of knowledge is preliminary. The authors conclude, however, that there is substance to the idea of emotional intelligence and its importance to leadership, if not to the extent sometimes claimed.

8 When you critically examine studies testing the relationship between emotional intelligence and leadership effectiveness, sometimes it is followership effectiveness (or personal effectiveness) that is actually being measured! For example, in a study by Rosete and Ciarrochi (2005), "leadership effectiveness" was measured by asking the boss of each leader to give an assessment of the leadership effectiveness of his direct report. In our opinion, this is more likely to be measuring followership effectiveness than leadership effectiveness.

9 Weber and Moore (2014).

10 Chaleff (1995).

11 This is from multiple sources: Ng, Eby, Sorensen, and Feldman (2005); Thompson (2006); Thacker and Wayne (1995); and Wayne and Liden (1995).

12 Gentry and Shanock (2008).

13 There is a lot of anecdotal evidence for this and at least two academic studies: Leslie and Van Velsor (1996); and Shipper and Dillard Jr. (2000).

14 Shipper and Dillard Jr. (2000).

15 As Beehr, Nair, Gudanowski, and Such (2004) note, any hidden criterion

used for evaluation that is not talked about or acknowledged puts noses out of joint, lowers morale, and destroys engagement. This occurs in the many cases where bosses and organizations value followership but don't explicitly acknowledge it. Not only are the people affected resentful of the hidden criterion, they often misascribe the reason for the evaluation (or promotion) to toxic ideas such as favoritism, foolishness (on the part of the evaluator), or boot-licking (by the person being evaluated).

16 Borman and Motowidlo (1993).

17 As in the earlier study by Podsakoff and MacKenzie (1997), the specific OCBs studied in this case by MacKenzie, Podsakoff, and Paine (1999) were Helping, Civic Virtue, and Sportsmanship.

18 Dixon and Westbrook (2003).

19 Hartung (2012, December).

20 As a follow-up to our survey, Optimum Talent, a firm that specializes in career management and transition, looked at the proportion of their clients who had recently reported to a new boss and been fired or laid off. Their number was closer to 60%. The reason for the discrepancy is probably that larger career transition consultancies deal with a lot of restructuring and downsizing, where people are losing jobs for structural rather than discretionary reasons. Our initial survey did not include data from this cause of job loss. Whichever way you look at it – 60% or 95% – the pitchfork effect has a huge role in people getting let go, and followership is a significant underlying cause.

Chapter 3

1 We are using the words "management" and "leadership" somewhat loosely. There is no best definition of either but, wherever possible, we will use management to describe being accountable for tasks such as organizing the work, determining rewards, hiring, etc. Leadership, on the other hand, is more the people side of exercising power. If we slip up and use one word when we mean the other, or use one when the situation is ambiguous and we could have used the other, we hope our meaning is clear!

2 Another finding from the study was the surprising fact that most standard leadership training programs improve at least some aspects of leadership. The single most effective training, however, was getting managers to understand just how competent and engaged their staff really was: i.e., the Pygmalion Effect. We will talk more about this effect later in the book.

3 Goasduff (2010).

4 This is from a number of sources: Aasland, Skogstad, Notelaers, Nielsen, and Einarsen (2010); Hogan and Hogan (2001); Hogan, Hogan, and Kaiser (2010); Sanborn, Malhotra, and Atchson (2010); Oswald (2010); and Doward (2010).

Chapter 4

1 Dyer, Croft, Morrell, and Krause (2009).
2 A comprehensive review of followership theory by Uhl-Bien, Riggio, Lowe, and Carsten (2014) divides leadership-followership theories into two categories: (1) leadership and followership as set roles, and (2) leadership and followership as a social construction. Most people talk as if leadership and followership are roles although fish don't behave that way and, as the authors note, you can't have leadership without followership, or the other way around. We don't believe that leadership and followership are social constructions, either: that is, just based on what people *think* leadership and followership are, or based purely on how people behave. Rather, this book takes the position that leadership and followership are a set of skills, behaviors, and influence processes that exist independently of each other but are implemented in social groups. We call this an *interactionist* approach.
3 The follow-up was done by most of the same researchers: Nakayama, Harcourt, Johnstone, and Manica (2012). In their study, personality mattered even more than we have already discussed. For example, if the bold fish went out on an excursion and the shy fish didn't follow, the bold fish was equally likely to try again. The shy fish, however, was less likely to try again if its attempt at leadership failed. Personality therefore predicted the persistence of leadership behaviors.
4 As reported by Dolgin (2009).
5 Cook and Jobs are by no means the only example. Just recently you have Zuckerberg and Sandberg at Facebook, Schmidt along with Brin and Page at Google, and many historical examples such as Noah Dietrich and Howard Hughes, or even George Marshall with Roosevelt and Churchill during WW II.
6 State of Alabama Engineering Hall of Fame (2009).
7 Retrieved from http://www.rollingstone.com/music/lists/500-greatest-albums-of-all-time-20120531/the-beatles-sgt-peppers-lonely-hearts-club-band-20120531.
8 Kouzes and Posner, B. Z. (2002, p. 25) present the results of three surveys

done over the years. We present the results of the original survey from 1987 to be consistent with Agho. In subsequent years there has been some shuffling of the order, but usually only between two adjacent items. For example, in 1995 and 2002 the priority of "competent" and "forward looking" was switched.

9 The rankings of Agho (2009) for leadership were somewhat different than those of Kouzes and Posner (1987). In the chart, we have included the top Kouzes and Posner rankings along with the top followership rankings from Agho. We have conducted similar surveys over the last eight years but using a 7-point Likert scale rather than rankings. Our results suggest that the differences between leadership and followership are smaller than the chart suggests.

10 Surveys of the sort done by Kouzes and Posner (1987), or Agho (2009), tap into what is called *Implicit Theories*. An implicit theory of leadership (ILT) is important because it represents what people think an ideal leader should do and behave like. Anyone violating these implicit beliefs is less likely to become a leader, and may have less success as a leader. In that regard, implicit beliefs are important. However, just because someone fits the popular conception of a leader doesn't mean he or she is effective or that the behaviors promote a positive workplace. For example, there are cultures where totalitarian leadership is accepted as the norm; in another culture, it might be the brash, hard-driving leader with little regard for the opinions of his or her followers. We would be hard pressed to suggest either as admirable or productive leadership traits! There are numerous examples where the traits associated with leadership in a particular culture have led to disaster. So, while ILTs matter, that isn't sufficient for deciding what leadership (or followership) ought to be.

11 This is from Weisbert, Keil, Goodstein, Rawson, and Gray (2008); and McCabe, and Castel, A. D. (2008).

12 Gilboa, Shirom, Fried, and Cooper (2008).

Chapter 5

1 Mintzberg (2009) considers the primary roles of a manager to be framing, scheduling, controlling, and communicating all around. His definition of framing is similarly expansive, though slightly – not materially – different: "Managers frame their work by making particular decisions, focusing on particular issues, developing particular strategies, and so forth, to establish the context for everyone else working in the unit."

Chapter 6

1 Bryant (2011).

Chapter 7

1 Regression to the mean is the idea that extreme events are usually followed by more average outcomes simply because the average is more
likely. So, after rolling a "1," the next roll of the die is likely to be higher. In
fact, the odds of rolling higher than a one are 5:1.
2 Avey, Reichard, Luthans, and Mhatre (2011).
3 Burris (2012).
4 Mills, Fleck, and Kozikowski (2013).
5 Chang, Lin, and Chen (2012).
6 O'Boyle and Harter (2013).
7 Ibid.
8 Tim Hortons is the Canadian coffee and donut shop. For example, when
Canada was assisting in the military action in Afghanistan, their main base
at Kandahar had a Tim Hortons restaurant.
9 Dr. Evans reported this particular ratio to us. While we do know that having more positive feedback than negative is crucial, how much is enough,
and how much is too much is too little, is still a topic of hot debate (Fredrickson, 2013). We suspect that the optimal ratio of positive to negative
feedback also varies by person.
10 Taylor (2013).
11 Gray, Brown, and Macanufo (2010).
12 One of the major issues with goal setting is that people fail to plan for
roadblocks. When a roadblock occurs, as often happens, it disrupts the
plan and the goal gets discarded. This is not planning what to do if something fails; it is planning how to make sure the inevitable challenges that
come along don't stop people achieving the goals.

Chapter 8

1 Sequential interdependence is like the example we just gave: B can't do his
work until A is finished; C can't do her work until B is finished; etc. Each
person in the sequence depends on the previous person to get their work
done first.
2 Locke and Latham (2002).

Chapter 9

1 Dijksterhuis, Bos, van der Leij, and van Baaren (2009).
2 The initial estimate of how much information we can hold in mind at one time is actually seven, plus or minus two, based on an article by George Miller (1956). The article was the motivation for standardizing telephone numbers at seven digits. Subsequent research suggests seven may be high and, depending on what is being measured, it could be anything from one to six, with four or five being the most common estimates.
3 Early languages were written without vowels. Hebrew and Arabic, for example, can still be written that way.
4 This is known as somatic marker theory, or embodied cognition (Reimann et al., 2012).
5 Bechara, Damasio, Tranel, and Damasio (1997) investigated how people with lesions in the ventromedial prefrontal cortex would do at a simple gambling task compared to a neurologically normal group. The patients could recognize which choices were most advantageous in a gambling situation but, unlike normal participants, did not change behavior accordingly. A number of similar experiments have been conducted since that suggests people with brain lesions related to emotional functioning commit errors in decision making that neurologically normal people don't.
6 The optimal technique is to start with conscious thought and then follow it up with unconscious thought (Nordgren, Bos, & Dijksterhuis, 2011).
7 The target goal, however, can still be defined in a fuzzy way as long as a good frame it set.
8 This is a riff on the Tony Robbins quote: "Stay committed to your decisions, but stay flexible in your approach."
9 There is a fascinating body of literature on this based on the work of Dr. Arnold Mindell known as *deep democracy*. Deep democracy is a way of facilitating conflict through giving voice to everyone: the majority, the minority, and even individuals.
10 Much more has been written about the evidence-decision link than the criteria-decision link. For example, Tingling and Brydon (2010) argue that the role of evidence depends on whether it is used to make a decision, inform a decision, or support a decision. Sometimes it can be appropriate to find evidence for a decision after making it. We agree. In fact, the role of intuition and unconscious processing supports their conclusion. But we also believe that decision-making *criteria* should be specified in advance.
11 Bos, Dijksterhuis, and van Baaren (2008).

12 This advice is aligned with the earlier discussion on having a frame that is
    fuzzy (Chapter 5) and a later discussion on fuzzy goals (Chapter 13). Clar-
    ity, here, means articulating the goals well, not in making them more spe-
    cific. It goes back to the idea that the best frames are neither too restrictive
    nor too loose.
13 Strick et al. (2011).
14 There is a counterargument that more choices, even irrelevant ones, can
    prevent optimal decisions from being made. For example, Louie and Glim-
    cher (2012) found that increasing the number of choices actually made it
    harder to pick the best option. It implies there is a balance to be struck be-
    tween having enough choices but not too many. Alternatively, you could
    eliminate obvious, bad options before making a choice (that's what we
    would recommend).
15 Tim Hurson (2008) explains these tools in greater detail in one of our
    favorite books on creativity, *Think Better*. If you haven't read it, you are
    missing an engaging and engrossing read. It lays out a methodology for in-
    creasing creativity – Productive Thinking – along with a host of useful tools.
16 The term *devil's advocate* is from the canonization process in the Roman
    Catholic religion. As part of the process, a canon lawyer argues against the
    person being granted sainthood – the devil's advocate role – presumably
    to ensure that recognition isn't given without due consideration of all the
    facts. Devil's advocate is an important role, but three circumstances make
    it unique to this type of setting: (1) both the devil's advocate and the god's
    advocate (that's the person who argues in favor of canonization) are law-
    yers trained to be dispassionate in their arguments, (2) it is a formal setting
    with codified rules and a level playing field, and (3) the facts are known
    ahead of time. None of these conditions hold in most of the meetings we
    have attended.

Chapter 10

1 Lasker (1951).
2 Woolley, Chabris, Pentland, Hashimi, and Malone (2010).
3 It has been widely reported that the relationship with the manager is the
   main reason people leave their jobs (Holtom, Mitchell, Lee, & Eberly, 2008;
   O'Boyle & Harter, 2013). The CEO of Gallup, for example, says that, "How
   employees feel about their job starts and ends with their direct supervisor." Evidence doesn't bear out such an extreme claim – people leave
   for all sorts of reasons such as the nature of the job, having a better offer
   somewhere else, coworkers, workplace environment, not having had a

realistic job preview, changes in life circumstance, stress and more – however, the manager is a major influence in as many as 75% of the situations for people leaving.

4 In the Scandura and Graen (1984) study, employees didn't score higher than controls or the high LMX group on the quantity of output produced, but quality improved leading to the estimated gains.

5 Kouzes and Posner (2002) note, "At the heart of collaboration is trust. It's *the* central issue in human relationship within and outside organizations" (p. 244).

6 McKnight, Cummings, and Chervany (1998).

7 Cook and Wall (1980).

8 As Snyder and Stukas (1999) pithily state, "For many expectations, particularly those that concern morality, negative actions are taken by perceivers as more diagnostic (e.g., one theft makes you dishonest) than positive actions ..." (p. 291).

9 For example, if something goes wrong with a recent purchase and the seller makes the situation better through great service, your satisfaction is likely to be higher than if you never had a problem in the first place. This is an example where a competence-based violation – didn't make the product well – followed by a quick remediation can create trust! You walk away thinking, "Even if something does happen to go wrong, they will fix it quickly." Of course, if this happens repeatedly you will lose trust, realizing that they just aren't competent at all.

10 Taken from Kim, Ferrin, Cooper, and Dirks (2004); and Kim, Dirks, and Cooper (2009).

11 This brings us back to Polarity Thinking – www.polaritypartnerships. com. As the founder, Barry Johnson, is wont to say, "Sometimes you have a problem to fix, sometimes you have a polarity to leverage." If it is a polarity you can't fix it. Instead you have to acknowledge that there are two mutually exclusive alternatives both of which have value (i.e., a polarity) and learn to incorporate both. In this case, the polarity is balancing giving individual consideration with building a team.

12 The Conger and Fishel (2007) article is from 2007 so we don't know if Bank of America is still using the same onboarding program. Given how successful it has proven to be, we hope the answer is yes!

13 Watkins (2003).

14 Gentry and Shanock (2008).

15 See "The Style Conversation" (pp. 117–120) of Watkins (2003) or leaf through almost anywhere in the book, *The 360° Leader* (Maxwell, 2005), to see examples of solid followership advice being called something else.

16 In fact, Watkins (2003) suggests it is 100% your responsibility as a follower to make the relationship work.

Chapter 11

1 Jermyn (2010) is quoting Leslie Brans-Baker, Mars Canada communications manager.
2 The poll (Santoli, 2011) was conducted on 270 chief financial officers: 54% said they were most rewarded by the satisfaction of mentoring while 18% said it helped them stay current. Only 3% did not find mentoring to be a rewarding experience.
3 Eby, Allen, Evans, Ng, and DuBois (2008).
4 It is the responsibility of the mentee to set the agenda. Without ownership of the agenda the mentee becomes a passive (and often unresponsive) learner.
5 Earley and Ang (2003).

Chapter 12

1 A provost at most universities is the chief operating officer of the educational institution, reporting to the vice-chancellor or president.
2 Jablin (1979) refers to his dissertation work in which he compared different types of responses: positive content responses, positive relational responses, negative content responses, negative relational responses, and irrelevant responses. The irrelevant responses were never appropriate while all other types had some utility depending on the circumstance.
3 Goleman (2006).
4 Lee and Jablin (1995) found avoidance to be the most common communication "strategy" in many different situations.
5 Collectively these three categories are known as Motivation Language Theory (Mayfield, 2009; Sullivan, 1998), which was developed after extensive reviews of organizational communications at many companies over a number of years. The first and third categories could also be thought of as concern for the person and task focus, the two primary dimensions of leadership responsibility identified in the 1950s in the rather famous Ohio State studies. After many years of testing, research, and practice (including being the basis for Situational Leadership), these two dimensions are still widely regarded as the basis of leadership capability. The second category, developing organizational agility, is called meaning-making or locutionary acts in Motivational Language theory.

6 There are a couple of caveats. First off, Sharbrough, Simmons, and Cantrill (2006) only studied the impact of supervisor communication on staff so you would be right to wonder what the impact of effective followership communication would be? Motivational language theory is based purely on leadership communication; there could also be different categories for followership communication. Our (untested) belief is that the same categories would apply to followership with similar results, except that the task focused category takes on a slightly different meaning.

7 We rather hoped this was a unique analogy when we first came up with it. Since then we have read a first-rate article by one of the thought leaders in organization communication, Dennis Tourish, in which he used the same one-way elevator analogy. Sigh. All credit to Tourish for coming up with it; we're just borrowing it if that's okay?

8 Kay and Christophel (1995).

9 Jablin (1979).

10 Notice, too, that the blame for this communication failure has been shifted from management to employee, suggesting that it is incompetence or belligerence mucking up the communication process. This is called *blame reassignment*, and unfortunately it's all too common. It is also counterproductive.

11 Mintzberg (2009) has the 40% estimate. Jablin (1979) suggests the proportion of time managers spend communicating is more like 33%–66% while Luthans and Larsen (1986) suggest between 60%–80% depending on the study. Regardless of the exact percentage, a lot of management time is spent communicating.

12 Detert, Burris, Harrison, and Martin (2013).

13 Kay and Christophel (1995).

14 Browne and Neitzel (1952).

15 Reacting to negative feedback more than positive feedback is called the *automatic vigilance effect*. Using the salience of the negative feedback in overestimating its frequency is an *availability error* due to the fact that negative feedback is more memorable, probably because it evokes a greater emotional reaction.

16 The original model that suggested 6:1 was flawed and the results no longer accepted. However, it is widely accepted that there is an optimal ratio. As an intriguing example of how this idea has been used in practice, Gottman and Levenson (2000) were able to predict with 93% accuracy (!) whether a couple would get divorced during the first 14 years of marriage just by analyzing three 15-minutes conversations. What characterized couples headed toward the divorce courts was the ratio of negative-to-

positive affect moments. Couples that divorced early made many more negative comments and fewer positive comments than those having lasting marriages.

17 Luthans and Larsen (1986).

18 The question is worded to solicit multiple responses. If you ask a question such as, "How can this be made better?" or "What would you do to make it better?," you often get only one response.

19 As Tourish (2005) finds, in his article on upward communication, that senior managers often believe their staff are better informed than the employees would say, and that communication channels were more open and robust.

20 Ibid. More specifically, managers believe they treat all subordinates alike (Graen & Scandura, 1987). How managers actually communicate depends on the interpersonal relationship with each employee (Lee & Jablin, 1995).

21 You can already tell bad stuff is coming. A town hall meeting should never have more than about 150 people. The minute we heard it was 1,000 people we knew the format was wrong. Not to say you can't deliver a presentation to that many people, but you can't do an effective town hall that includes meaningful two-way or, better yet, four-way communication.

22 The introduction of brain science to make a point has become the latest justification of all sorts of stupid stuff. It does nothing except make Marc angry at the misapplication of neuroscience! Bah.

23 The Followership and Leadership section of this book explode the idea of heroic leadership. What's new here is that one of the outcomes of this mindset has been poor communications. Even many of the leadership models we admire and teach – Servant-Leadership, Ethical Leadership, Transformational Leadership, and Authentic Leadership – retain a Parent-to-Child flavor.

24 Johnson (2006).

25 Tourish (2005).

26 Tengblad (2000).

27 This is what we have observed time and again. However, when we talk with people, they usually ascribe micromanagement to the person rather than the situation, that is, "My boss micromanages because that's her style …" It is an example of the fundamental attribution error that leads to a fight-or-flight reaction by the employee. But it needn't be that way. Better communication and leaning in usually resolves all but the few cases where micromanaging is actually a style issue.

Chapter 13

1 Mayfield and Mayfield (2009).
2 The classic example of this was the shocking loss of the USA men's basketball team to Argentina in 2004. When you look at the team rosters, Argentina had one future NBA All Star player, Manu Ginobili. The USA, by contrast, had some of the greats of all time including LeBron James; Dwayne Wade; and Ginobili's teammate on the San Antonio Spurs, Tim Duncan.
3 Blacksmith and Harter, J. (2011).
4 Ashford (2013).
5 Nevertheless, goal setting can be extremely important. Latham and Locke have been researching the value of goals on performance for many years. There is plenty of evidence that the right types of goals do improve performance. What we are suggesting, then, is not the abolition of goal setting, but the abolition of the way goals are embedded in the performance management cycle.
6 This is similar to but not the same as the Deming cycle: Plan-Do-Check-Act or PDCA model. The similarities include the fact that both have the goal of continuous improvement, and both start with planning following by progress. The difference is that the Check-Act stages are control-based, that is, asking questions such as, "What is the variance from plan and how do we get back on plan or Adjust (a recent change, replacing Act)?" Reflection, in our model, is about considering where we are now and where we want to go from here. It doesn't look backwards, it looks forward. And it takes each new step as a fresh start rather than as a (potential) variance from an earlier place. As such, it encourages agility and is a natural complement to fuzzy goals.
7 Kohles, Bligh, and Carsten (2012) discuss the importance of strong bidirectional communication in assisting followers (their term, not ours) to integrate the vision. We take it a step further. If you eliminate the idea of followers or leaders, then vision becomes a shared activity of which bidirectional communication is one piece.
8 Pulakos and O'Leary's (2011) arguments both for and against SMART goals as well as other standard performance management techniques are persuasive, that is, that the existing methods aren't terribly effective in today's workplace.
9 The value of internal vs. external motivation is a hot area of research. It would be lovely to say that one is necessarily better than the other, that is, money is the best motivator (external) or people only get motivated by

what they deeply believe in (internal). So far, evidence suggests that both have a place.

10 www.businessdictionary.com.

11 Locke and Latham (2002).

12 As of the writing of this book, the ratio of research on leadership to that on followership is around 1000:1. If you are a budding researcher, you could build a solid career out of seeing what "leadership" effects are actually due to followership, or in replicating leadership studies using a follower-ship lens.

13 Schippers, Homan, and van Knippenberg (2013).

14 Gevers, van Eerde, and Rutte (2001) don't discuss reflection in terms scouting and settling, but the sentiment is much the same.

15 This isn't surprising. The founders of Google were both graduate students when they started the company and purposefully wanted to maintain the "campus" ideal of free-flowing ideas.

References

Aasland, M.S., Skogstad, A., Notelaers, G., Nielsen, M.B., & Einarsen, S. (2010). The prevalence of destructive leadership behaviour. *British Journal of Management, 21,* 438–452.

Aboukhalil, R. (2014). The rising trend in authorship. *The Winnower.* Retrieved from https://thewinnower.com/papers/the-rising-trend-in-authorship

Agho, A.O. (2009). Perspectives of senior-level executives on effective followership and leadership. *Journal of Organizational Studies, 16*(2), 159–166.

Amabile, T., & Kramer, T. (2011). *The progress principle: Using small wins to ignite joy, engagement, and creativity at work.* Boston, MA: Harvard Business Review Press.

Ashford, O. (2013). Mercer's 2013 global performance management survey report: Executive summary. Mercer. Retrieved from http://www.mercer.ca/content/dam/mercer/attachments/north-america/canada/Mercer_2013_Global_PM_Survey_ExecSummary_SEC.pdf

Avey, J.B., Reichard, R.J., Luthans, F., & Mhatre, K.H. (2011). Meta-analysis of the impact of positive psychological capital on employee attitudes, behaviors, and performance. *Human Resource Development Quarterly, 22*(2), 127–152.

Avolio, B.J., Reichard, R R., Hannah, S.T., Walumbwa F.O., & Chan A. (2009). A meta-analytic review of leadership impact research: Experimental and quasi-experimental studies. *Leadership Quarterly, 20,* 764–784.

Bechara, A., Damasio , H., Tranel , D., & Damasio , A. R. (1997). Deciding advantageously before knowing the advantageous strategy. *Science, 275,* 1293–1295.

Beehr, T.A., Nair, V. N., Gudanowski, D.M., & Such, M. (2004). Perceptions of reasons for promotion of self and others. *Human Relations, 57*(4), 431–438.

Blacksmith, N., & Harter, J. (2011, October). Majority of American workers not engaged in their jobs. *Gallup Well-Being.* Retrieved from Oct. 28, 2011 gallup.com/poll/150383/majority-american-workers-not-engaged-jobs.aspx

Blackwell, A.F., Wilson, L., Street, A., Boulton, C., & Knell, J. (2009, November). Radical innovation: Crossing knowledge boundaries with interdisciplinary teams. *Technical report 760, University of Cambridge Computer Laboratory*. Retrieved from http://www.cl.cam.ac.uk/techreports/UCAM-CL-TR-760.pdf?utm_source=twitterfeed&utm_medium=twitter

Borman, W.C., & Motowidlo, S. J. (1993). Expanding the criterion domain to include elements of contextual performance. In N. Schmitt, & W.C. Borman (Eds.), *Personnel Selection in Organizations* (pp. 71–98). San Francisco, CA: Jossey-Bass.

Bos, M.W., Dijksterhuis, A., & van Baaren, R.B. (2008). On the goal-dependency of unconscious thought. *Journal of Experimental Social Psychology, 44*(4), 1114–1120.

Bossidy, L. (2007). What your leader expects of you. *Harvard Business Review, 85*(4), 58–65.

Browne, G.G., & Neitzel, B.J. (1952). Communication, supervision and morale. *Journal of Applied Psychology, 36*(2), 86–91.

Bryant, A. (2011, March). Google's quest to build a better boss. *The New York Times*. Retrieved from http://www.nytimes.com/2011/03/13/business/13hire.html?pagewanted=all&_r=0

Burris, E. R. (2012). The risks and rewards of speaking up: Managerial responses to employee voice. *Academy of Management Journal, 55*(4), 851–875.

Campeau, M. (2011, September). Using your inside voice: An effective internal communications strategy is no longer a luxury. *HR Professional, 18*–26.

Chaleff, I. (1995). *The courageous follower: Standing up to and for our leaders*. San Francisco, CA: Berrett-Koehler Publishers.

Chang, Y-P., Lin, Y-C., & Chen, L. H. (2012). Pay it forward: Gratitude in social networks. *Journal of Happiness Studies, 13*(5), 761–781.

Collins, J. (2001). *Good to great: Why some companies make the leap ... and others don't*. New York, NY: Collins.

Conger, J.A., & Fishel, B. (2007). Accelerating leadership performance at the top: Lessons from the Bank of America's executive on-boarding process. *Human Resource Management Review, 17*(4), 442–454.

Cook, J., & Wall, T. (1980). New work attitude measures of trust, organizational commitment and personal need non-fulfillment. *Journal of Occupational Psychology, 53*, 39–52.

Coyne, K.P., & Coyne Sr., E.J. (2007). Surviving your new CEO. *Harvard Business Review, 85*(5), 62–69.

Detert, J. R., Burris, E.R., Harrison, D.A., & Martin, S.R. (2013). Voice flows to and around leaders: Understanding when units are helped or hurt by employee voice. *Administrative Science Quarterly, 58*(4), 624–668.

Dijksterhuis, A., Bos, M. W., van der Leij, A., & van Baaren, R.B. (2009). Predicting soccer matches after unconscious and conscious thought as a function of expertise. *Psychological Science, 20*(11), 1381–1467.

Dixon, G., & Westbrook, J. (2003). Followers revealed. *Engineering Management Journal, 15,* 19–25.

Dolgin, E. (2009, January). Follow the fish leader. *The Scientist.* Retrieved from at http://www.the-scientist.com/?articles.view/articleNo/27107/title/Follow-the-fish-leader/

Doward, J. (2010, July). Happy people really do work harder. *The Observer.* Retrieved from http://www.theguardian.com/science/2010/jul/11/happy-workers-are-more-productive

Dyer, R.G., Croft, D.P., Morrell, L.J., & Krause, J. (2009). Shoal composition determines foraging success in the guppy. *Behavioral Ecology, 20*(1), 165–171.

Earley, P. C., & Ang, S. (2003). *Cultural intelligence: Individual interactions across cultures.* Stanford, CA: Stanford University Press.

Eby, L.T., Allen, T.D., Evans, S.C., Ng, T., & DuBois, D. (2008). Does mentoring matter? A multidisciplinary meta-analysis comparing mentored and non-mentored individuals. *Journal of Vocational Behavior, 72*(2), 254–267.

Ferrin, D.L., Bligh, M.C., and & Kohles, J. C. (2008). It takes two to tango: An interdependence analysis of the spiraling of perceived trustworthiness and cooperation in interpersonal and intergroup relationships. *Organizational Behavior and Human Decision Processes, 107*(2), 161–178.

Fredrickson, B L. (2013). Updated thinking on positivity ratios. *American Psychologist, 68*(9), 814–822.

Gentry, W.A., & Shanock, L.R. (2008). View of managerial derailment from above and below: The importance of a good relationship with upper management and putting people at ease. *Journal of Applied Social Psychology, 38,* 2469–2494.

Gevers, J.M.P., van Eerde, W., & Rutte, C.G. (2001). Time pressure, potency, and progress in project groups. *European Journal of Work and Organizational Psychology, 10*(12), 205–221.

Gilboa, S., Shirom, A., Fried, Y., & Cooper, C. (2008). A meta-analysis of work demands stressors and job performance: Examining main and moderating effects. *Personnel Psychology, 61*(2), 227–271.

Gladwell, M. (2008). *Outliers: The story of success.* New York, NY: Little, Brown and Company.

Goasduff, L. (2010, August). Gartner says the world of work will witness 10 changes during the next 10 years. *Gartner Newsroom.* Retrieved from http://www.gartner.com/newsroom/id/1416513

Goldsmith, M. (2003, December). All of us are stuck on suck-ups. *Fast Compa-*

ny. Retrieved from http://www.fastcompany.com/47569/all-us-are-stuck-suck-ups

Goldstein, D. G., & Gigerenzer, G. (2002). Models of ecological rationality: The recognition heuristic. *Psychological Review, 109*(1), 75–90.

Goleman, D. (2006). *Social intelligence: The new science of human relationships.* New York, NY: Bantam Dell.

Gottman, J.M., & Levenson, R.W. (2000). The timing of divorce: Predicting when a couple will divorce over a 14-year period. *Journal of Marriage and the Family, 62*, 737–745.

Graen, G.B., & Scandura, T. (1987). Toward a psychology of dyadic organizing. In B.M. Staw, L.L. Cummings, & R.I. Sutton (Eds.), *Research in organizational behavior* (Vol. 9, pp. 175–208). Greenwich, CT: JAI Press.

Gray, D., Brown, S., & Macanufo, J. (2010). Gamestorming: A playbook for innovators, rulebreakers, and changemakers. Sebastopol, CA: O'Reilly Media Inc.

Harcourt, J.L., Ang, T.Z., Sweetman, G., Johnstone, R.A., & Manica, A. (2009). Social feedback and the emergence of leaders and followers. *Current Biology, 19*, 248–252.

Hartung, A. (2012, December). Oops! Five CEOs who should have already been fired (Cisco, GE, WalMart, Sears, Microsoft). *Forbes Online*. Retrieved from http://www.forbes.com/sites/adamhartung/2012/05/12/oops-5-ceos-that-should-have-already-been-fired-cisco-ge-walmart-sears-microsoft/

Hipple, S.F., & Sok, E. (2013). Tenure of American workers. U.S. Bureau of Labor Statistics. Retrieved from http://www.bls.gov/spotlight/2013/tenure/home.htm

Hogan, J., Hogan, R., & Kaiser, R.B. (2010). Management derailment. In S. Zedeck (Ed.), *American Psychological Association Handbook of Industrial and Organizational Psychology, Vol. 3* (pp. 555–575). Washington, DC: American Psychological Association.

Hogan, R., & Hogan, J. (2001). Assessing leadership: A view of the dark side. *International Journal of Selection and Assessment, 9*(1/2), 40–51.

Hollenbeck, J.R., Beersma, B., & Schouten, M.E. (2012). Beyond team types and taxonomies: A dimensional scaling conceptualization for team description. *Academy of Management Review, 37*(1), 82–106.

Holtom, B.C., Mitchell, T.R., Lee, T.W., & Eberly, M.B. (2008). Turnover and retention research: A glance at the past, a closer review of the present, and a venture into the future. *The Academy of Management Annals, 2*(1), 231–274.

Hurson, T. (2008). *Think better*. New York, NY: McGraw-Hill.

IBM CEO Study (2012). *Leading through connections: Insights from the global chief executive officer study.* IBM CEO C-suite Studies.

Jablin, F. M. (1979). Superior-subordinate communication: The state of the art. *Psychological Bulletin, 86*(6), 1201–1222.

Javidan, M., Dorfman, P.W., Sully de Luque, M., & House, R.J. (2006). In the eye of the beholder: Cross cultural lessons in leadership from Project GLOBE. *Academy of Management Perspectives, 20*(1), 67–90.

Jermyn, D. (2010, November 21). How candy makers sweeten the job. *The Globe and Mail.* Retrieved from http://www.theglobeandmail.com/news/toronto/how-candy-makers-sweeten-the-job/article1315228/

Johnson, B. (1996). *Polarity management: Identifying and managing unsolvable problems.* Amherst, MA: HRD Press.

Johnson, C. (2006, September 17). Cutting through advertising clutter. *CBS News Sunday Morning* (online). Retrieved from http://www.cbsnews.com/news/cutting-through-advertising-clutter/

Kay, B., & Christophel, D.M. (1995). The relationships among manager communication openness, nonverbal immediacy, and subordinate motivation. *Communication Research Reports, 12*(2), 200–205.

Kay, I.T., & Shelton, M. (2000). The people problems in mergers. *The McKinsey Quarterly, 4,* 29–37.

Kelley, R.E. (1992). *The power of followership.* New York, NY: Doubleday Currency.

Kelley, R.E. (1998). *How to be a star at work: 9 breakthrough strategies you need to succeed.* New York, NY: Three Rivers Press.

Kim, B., & Rudin, C. (2014). Learning about meetings. *Data Mining and Knowledge Discovery.* doi: 10.1007/s10618-014-0348-z

Kim, P. H., Dirks, K.T., & Cooper, C.D. (2009). The repair of trust: A dynamic bilateral perspective and multilevel conceptualization. *Academy of Management Review, 34*(3), 401–422.

Kim, P.H., Ferrin, D.L., Cooper, C.D., & Dirks, K.T. (2004). Removing the shadow of suspicion: The effects of apology vs. denial for repairing competence- vs. integrity-based trust violations. *Journal of Applied Psychology, 89*(1), 104–118.

Kohles, J.C., Bligh, M.C., & Carsten, M.K. (2012). A follower-centric approach to the vision integration process. *The Leadership Quarterly, 23*(3), 476–487.

Koman, E.S., & Wolff, S.B. (2008). Emotional intelligence competencies in the team and team leader: A multi-level examination of emotional intelligence on team performance. *Journal of Management Development, 27*(1), 55–75.

Kouzes, J.M., & Posner, B.Z. (2002). *The leadership challenge* (3rd ed.). San Francisco, CA: Jossey-Bass.

Lasker, E. (1951). *Chess secrets I learned from the master.* Mineola, NY: Dover Publications, Inc.

Lee, J., & Jablin, F.M. (1995). Maintenance communication in superior-subordinate work relationships. *Human Communication Research, 22*(2), 220–257.

Leslie, J.B., & Van Velsor, E. (1996). *A look at derailment today: North America and Europe.* Greensboro, NC: Center for Creative Leadership.

Locke, E.A., & Latham, G.P. (2002). Building a practically useful theory of goal setting and task motivation: A 35-year odyssey. *American Psychologist, 57*(9), 705–717.

Louie, K., & Glimcher, P.W. (2012). Set-size effects and the neural representation of value. In R.J. Dolan & T. Sharot (Eds.), *Neuroscience of preference and choice: Cognitive and neural mechanisms.* London: Academic Press.

Luthans, F., & Larsen, J.K. (1986). How managers really communicate. *Human Relations, 39*(2), 161–178.

MacKenzie, S.B., Podsakoff, P.M., & Paine, J.B. (1999). Do citizenship behaviors matter more for managers than for salespeople? *Journal of the Academy of Marketing Science, 27*(4), 396–410.

Maxwell, J.C. (2005). *The 360 leader: Developing your influence from anywhere in the organization.* Nashville, TN: Nelson Business.

Mayfield, J. (2009). Motivating language: A meaningful guide for leader communications. *Development and Learning in Organizations, 23*(1), 9–11.

Mayfield, M., & Mayfield, J. (2009). The role of leader-follower relationships in leader communication: A test using the LMX and Motivating Language models. *The Journal of Business Inquiry, 8*(1), 6–85.

McCabe, D.P. & Castel, A.D. (2008). Seeing is believing: The effect of brain images on judgments of scientific reasoning. *Cognition, 107*(1), 343–352.

McKnight, D.H., Cummings, L.L., & Chervany, N.L. (1998). Initial trust formation in new organizational relationships. *Academy of Management Review, 23*(3), 473–490.

Meilinger, P.S. (2001). The ten rules of good followership. In R.I. Lester & A.G. Morton (Eds.), *AU-24 Concepts for Air Force Leadership.* Maxwell AFB, AL: Air University Press.

Miller, G.A. (1956). The magical number seven, plus or minus two: Some limits on our capacity for processing information. *Psychological Review, 63*(2), 81–97.

Mills, M.J., Fleck, C.R., & Kozikowski, A. (2013). Positive psychology at work: A conceptual review, state-of-practice assessment, and a look ahead. *The Journal of Positive Psychology, 8*(2), 153–164.

Mintzberg, H. (2009). *Managing.* San Francisco, CA: Berrett-Koehler Publishers, Inc.

Nakayama, S., Harcourt, J.L., Johnstone, R.A., & Manica, A. (2012). Initiative, personality and leadership in pairs of foraging fish. *PLoS ONE 7(5), e36606.* doi 10.1371/journal.pone.0036606

Ng, T.W.H., Eby, L.T., Sorensen, K.L., & Feldman, D.C. (2005). Predictors of objective and subjective career success: A meta-analysis. *Personnel Psychology, 58,* 367–408.

Nordgren, L.F., Bos, M.W., & Dijksterhuis, A. (2011). The best of both worlds: Integrating conscious and unconscious thought best supports complex decisions. *Journal of Experimental Social Psychology, 47(2),* 509–511.

O'Boyle, E. & Harter, J. (2013). *State of the global workplace: Employee engagement insights for business leaders worldwide.* Gallup, Inc. Retrieved from http://www.gallup.com/strategicconsulting/164735/state-global-workplace.aspx

Offermann, L.R., Bailey, J.R., Vasilopoulos, N.L., Seal, C. & Sass, M. (2004). The relative contribution of emotional competence and cognitive ability to individual and team performance. *Human Performance, 17(2),* 219–243.

Oswald, A.J. (2010). Emotional prosperity and the Stiglitz Commission. *British Journal of Industrial Relations, 48(4),* 651–669.

Podsakoff, P.M., & MacKenzie, S.B. (1997). Impact of organizational citizenship behavior on organizational performance: A review and suggestions for future research. *Human Performance, 10(2),* 133–151.

Pulakos, E.D., & O'Leary, R.S. (2011). Why is performance management broken? *Industrial and Organizational Psychology, 4(2),* 146–164.

Reimann, M., Feye, W., Malter, A.J., Ackerman, J.M., Castano, R., Nitika, G., ..., Zhong, C-B. (2012). Embodiment in judgment and choice. *Journal of Neuroscience, Psychology, and Economics, 5(2),* 104–123.

Rieck, T. (2008). *Emotional intelligence and team task performance: Does EI make a difference?* Unpublished master's thesis, University of Guelph, Guelph, Ontario, Canada.

Robinson, J. (2008). Turning around employee turnover. Gallup Business Journal (online).

Rolling Stone Music. The Beatles, "Sgt. Pepper's Lonely Hearts Club Band." *500 Greatest Albums of All Time.* Retrieved from http://www.rollingstone.com/music/lists/500-greatest-albums-of-all-time-20120531/the-beatles-sgt-peppers-lonely-hearts-club-band-20120531

Rosenthal, R., & Jacobson, L. (1968). *Pygmalion in the classroom.* New York, NY: Holt, Rinehart & Winston.

Rosete, D., & Ciarrochi, J. (2005). Emotional intelligence and its relationship to workplace performance outcomes of leadership effectiveness. *Leadership & Organization Development Journal, 26(5),* 388–399.

Sanborn, P., Malhotra, R., & Atchson, A. (2010). *Trends in global employee engagement.* Aon Consulting.

Santoli, N. (2011). The gift that gives back – Robert Half Management resources survey: Personal satisfaction greatest benefit of mentoring. *CNW.* Retrieved from http://www.newswire.ca/en/story/769831/the-gift-that-gives-back-robert-half-management-resources-survey-personal-satisfaction-greatest-benefit-of-mentoring

Scandura, T.A., & Graen, G.B. (1984). Moderating effects of initial leader-member exchange status on the effects of a leadership intervention. *Journal of Applied Psychology, 69*(3), 428–436.

Schippers, M.C., Homan, A.C., & van Knippenberg, D. (2013). To reflect or not reflect: Prior team performance as a boundary condition on the effects of reflexivity on learning and final team performance. *Journal of Organizational Behavior, 34*(1), 6–23.

Schlaerth, A., Ensari, N., & Christian, J. (2013). A meta-analytical review of the relationship between emotional intelligence and leaders' constructive conflict management. *Group Processes & Intergroup Relations, 16*(1), 126–136.

Schmidt, L.M. (2009). *Executive women's perceptions of their career derailment.* Unpublished doctoral thesis, Fielding Graduate University, Santa Barbara, California, USA.

Senge, P.M. (2006). *The fifth discipline: The art and practice of the learning organization* (2nd Ed.). New York, NY: Doubleday.

Sharbrough, W.C., Simmons, S.A., & Cantrill, D.A. (2006). Motivating language in industry: Its impact on job satisfaction and perceived supervisor effectiveness. *The Journal of Business Communication, 43*(4), 322–343.

Shipper, F., & Dillard Jr., J.E. (2000). A study of impending derailment and recovery of middle managers across career stages. *Human Resource Management, 39*, 331–334.

Snyder, M., & Stukas Jr., A.A. (1999). Interpersonal processes: The interplay of cognitive, motivational, and behavioral activities in social interaction. *Annual Reviews of Psychology, 50*, 273–303.

State of Alabama Engineering Hall of Fame. (2009). *Timothy D. Cook: The story behind the story.* Alabama, USA. Retrieved from http://aehof.eng.ua.edu/members/timothy-d-cook/

Strick, M., Dijksterhuis, A., Bos, M.W., Sjoerdsma, A., & van Baaren, R.B. (2011). A meta-analysis on unconscious thought effects. *Social Cognition, 29*(6), 738–762.

Sullivan, J.J. (1988). Three roles of language in motivation theory. *Academy of Management Review, 13*(1), 104–115.

Sy, T., Tram, S., & O'Hara, L.A. (2006). Relation of employee and manager emotional intelligence to job satisfaction and performance. *Journal of Vocational Behavior, 68*, 461–682.

Taylor, L.C. (2013, June). How to be effective at meetings? Say "yeah." *The To-*

ronto Star. Retrieved from http://www.thestar.com/business/2013/06/28/ how_to_be_effective_at_meetings_say_yeah.html

Tengblad, S. (2000). *Continuity and Change in Managerial Work*. GUPEA, GRI Report, 2000:3. Göteborg University, Göteborg, Sweden.

Thacker, R.A., & Wayne, S.J. (1995). An examination of the relationship between upward influence tactics and assessments of promotability. *Journal of Management, 21*(2), 739–759.

Thompson, J.A. (2006). Proactive personality and job performance: A social capital perspective. *Journal of Applied Psychology, 90*, 1011–1017.

Tingling, P.M., & Brydon, M.J. (2010, Summer). Is decision-based evidence making necessarily bad? MIT Sloan Management Review. Retrieved from http://sloanreview.mit.edu/article/is-decision-based-evidence-making-necessarily-bad/

Tourish, D. (2005). Critical upward communication: Ten commandments for improving strategy and decision making. *Long Range Planning, 38*(5), 485–503.

Uhl-Bien, M., Riggio, R.E., Lowe, K.B., & Carsten, M.K. (2014). Followership theory: A review and research agenda. *The Leadership Quarterly, 25*, 83–104.

Walter, F., Cole, M.S., & Humphrey, R.H. (2011). Emotional intelligence: Sine qua non of leadership or folderol? *Academy of Management Perspectives, 25*(1), 45–59.

Watkins, M. (2003). *The first 90 days*. Boston, MA: Harvard Business School Publishing.

Wayne, S.J., & Liden, R.C. (1995). Effects of impression management on performance ratings: A longitudinal study. *Academy of Management Journal, 38*, 232–260.

Weber, J.M., & Moore, C. (2014). Squires: Key followers and the social facilitation of charismatic leadership. *Organizational Psychology Review, 4*(3), 199227.

Weisbert, D.S., Keil, F.C., Goodstein, J., Rawson, E., & Gray, J.R. (2008). The seductive allure of neuroscience explanations. *Journal of Cognitive Neuroscience, 20*(3), 470–477.

Woolley, A.W., Chabris, C.F., Pentland, A., Hashimi, N., & Malone, T.W. (2010). Evidence for a collective intelligence factor in the performance of human groups. *Science, 330*(6004), 686–688.

Workopolis (2014). "Time" to work. Retrieved from http://www.workopolis .com/solutions/en/thinkopolis/thinkopolis-time-to-work

Index